GUILT

GUILT

LETTING GO

Lucy Freeman
Herbert S. Strean

JOHN WILEY & SONS

New York · Chichester · Brisbane · Toronto · Singapore

Library of Congress Cataloging in Publication Data:

Freeman, Lucy.
  Guilt: letting go.

  I. Guilt.   I. Strean, Herbert S.   II. Title.

  BF575.G8F73   1986   152.4   86-15873
  ISBN 0-471-83636-2

Printed in the United States of America

10 9 8 7 6 5 4 3 2

PREFACE

Guilt is the emotion Shakespeare described as making "cowards of us all." Or, as was said nineteen centuries earlier by an unknown Arabian court scholar, "Guilty consciences always make people cowards."

But guilt does not have to make cowards of us all. We can become courageous if we know how to free ourselves from the irrational guilt that torments us. We can then use the vital energy that has served to guard against the escape of our guilt feelings for more effective love and work.

This book will describe how to face and ease our guilt. It will explore the causes of guilt and discuss how guilt can be vanquished. Both the realistic causes of guilt and the unrealistic causes that stem from our fantasies and secret wishes will be explained. The book will discuss why guilt causes needless unhappiness. It will describe the destructive outlets for guilt: physical illness, alcoholism, drug addiction, accident proneness, overeating, not eating enough, overwork, inability to be productive, gambling, frigidity, impotence, depression, masochism and sadism. Guilt over sexual desires will be discussed, as well as the differences between the guilt of men and women. The guilt that follows a loss, ranging from the death of a loved one to a wallet, will be explained.

Then there are the ways guilt is manipulated by those who wish to influence us in our political decisions or in our purchases of commercial products. And how others try to make us feel guilty to relieve their own guilt or how we try to relieve our guilt by manipulating others. The book will also explain why we feel guilty over success. Why guilt may drive some to commit crimes—from the less serious such as theft, to the extreme crime of murder, illustrated by two specific murder cases. We will also discuss the psychopath in everyday life.

There are no rational reasons why we feel guilty much of the time. The unreal reasons for most of our guilt will be described at length—they are the heart of the book—in the hope readers will grasp the underlying causes of their guilt and understand how they can lessen guilt significantly.

Guilt does not have to haunt us if we can expose its roots to the light of reason. The easing of guilt will give new freedom as we shed the senseless shames that have caused us unnecessary terror, anxiety and rage.

LUCY FREEMAN
HERBERT S. STREAN

New York, New York
October 1986

ACKNOWLEDGMENTS

We wish to thank, first of all, Herb Reich, an exceptionally sensitive and knowledgeable editor, for his help in initiating, planning and bringing this book to realization. He possesses an unusual understanding of the human mind and a number of the ideas in this book were contributed by him.

We also wish to thank Judith Overton, of John Wiley & Sons, who made the experience of writing the book more enjoyable and who gave helpful ideas. She also suggested the title for this book.

Our thanks to Marcia Strean, wife of Dr. Herbert Strean, for going over the manuscript, and to Richard and Billy Strean for their contributions. We thank our colleagues at the New York Center for Psychoanalytic Training for their support, some of whom are quoted in the book. Ellen Gilbert, Director of the

ACKNOWLEDGMENTS

Brill Library of the New York Psychoanalytic Institute, and Jeanette Taylor, of the library staff, made research material available.

We also wish to express our gratitude to each other because, as a result of the hour-by-hour discussions of guilt, we found ourselves feeling less guilty about many areas of life.

L.F.
H.S.S.

CONTENTS

Part II
LETTING GO OF GUILT

GUILT

PART
I

UNDERSTANDING
YOUR GUILT

1

WHY WE FEEL GUILTY

THE PREVALENCE OF GUILT

No one is exempt from guilt. As with every emotion we possess, guilt serves a purpose. It is part of our psychic survival.

A certain amount of guilt guarantees our control over wild, primitive feelings that might be destructive to ourselves and others. We need guilt to form a conscience that allows us to become civilized. To cope with society's demands and taboos, to live peaceably in this difficult, complex and often dangerous world.

Many of us feel guilty only occasionally. But there are those who feel guilty much of the time. And some who feel guilty at almost everything they do, believing anything that goes wrong is their fault. They live in a maze of apologies. "Forgive me, forgive me," goes their guilty cry.

We may burden ourselves with too much guilt, punish ourselves without real cause, if we possess too tyrannical a conscience. Unfortunately many of us live as though prisoners in a continuous courtroom drama waiting to hear the verdict: "Guilty or not guilty?" These are among the most dreaded words in our language, both for an actual accused prisoner and those of us who fantasize we are prisoners and judge ourselves many times a day. Perhaps many times an hour.

This courtroom scene is dramatic portrayal of the inner script of our lives. We play all the roles: prisoner, defense attorney, prosecutor, judge and jury. As prosecutor, we seek the guilty verdict. As defense attorney, we plead innocent.

Guilt in one sense could be called our "number One killer." It far surpasses cancer and heart failure, accidents, addictions, suicides and murders, for guilt is a major contributor to all these. Guilt may drive us to suffer physical illness, to commit an accident, to become an addict, to be driven to suicide or murder. If we could rid ourselves of the irrational guilt that is the source of most of our terror and distress, many of us would live longer, spare ourselves much of the pain of our lives.

Some feel so guilty they are never able to marry. Or guilt drives them to marry many times, unable to cope with the intimacy of a lasting sexual partner. Others feel so guilty with a spouse they engage in promiscuous affairs or hide a second but unofficial sexual relationship. Then there are those whose guilt forces them to stay with a marital partner they dislike, seeking punishment for their hate.

Guilt may cause us to live unfulfilled, warped or terrorized lives. Or to work too compulsively or to be unable to work, asking others to support us. Guilt may stifle our creativity, restrict our natural imaginative spirits. Because of our guilt we punish ourselves in ways that lead only to grief and sorrow.

THE SEEDS OF GUILT

Our seeds of guilt are sown in the cradle. We know the feel of rage from the moment we open our mouths as babies to scream because we are hungry, cold or wet and feel pain. We slowly learn the feel of the guilt that always follows anger.

By the end of the first year of life we are tacitly instructed not to indulge in certain acts such as screaming in temper tantrums and as we repress our rage we feel frustrated, angry, then guilty. As children we are taught to observe many rules that restrict our activities. We learn to control our feelings of greed, envy, sexual desire, hate and jealousy. We may no longer call the world our oyster and demand all the pearls. This was our privilege only as helpless infants.

For most of us the flowering of current guilt is seeded by past threats of punishment. Or actual punishment that caused us to fear our parents might withdraw their love. Even if we committed no crime, the threats produced guilt.

How our conscience formed determined the severity of our guilt. Not enough guilt or too much guilt—either extreme—created destructive wishes toward the self or others, as we learned what was "right" and what was "wrong" from our parents. We heard further of the "goods" and "bads" from sisters and brothers, grandparents, aunts and uncles, teachers, friends and religious leaders.

Voices instructed: Thou shalt not steal. Thou shalt not tell lies. Thou shalt not talk back to thy mother or father. Thou shall love thy neighbor as thyself. Thou shalt not strike another child. Thou shalt get high marks in first grade and all through school. Thou shalt not use obscene words.

We soon learned to observe society's regulations and thus qualify as civilized, but within we often seethed as we yearned to defy some of the rules. We found we could not always "do unto others" as we wished them to do unto us. Our tempers sometimes exploded if we were driven emotionally beyond a certain point. We then felt guilty, knowing we had broken a rule and were "bad." We may have rebuked ourselves, slapping our own hands and repeating our mother's words, "bad boy" or "bad girl." At times we may have prevented ourselves from doing damage by pointing to a forbidden vase or dish, cautioning, "See, don't touch," or "Look at, don't break," as our mother advised.

Our guilt arose, in large part, out of our desperate need to be loved. Every child wishes to be loved, *needs* to be loved, to

5

survive emotionally. Parents know this and use the child's need for love to help him acquire a conscience. When a child feels loved by parents he is far freer to accept their "do's" and "dont's." (The word "he" throughout this book, used in a generic sense, refers to either he or she unless otherwise specified.) A child whose vulnerabilities and conflicts are understood by parents accepts frustrations with far greater ease than the child who feels unloved.

All of us, loved or unloved, face the conflict of wishing to please our parents by accepting their mandates and, at the same time, wanting all our wishes gratified. As children, we punish ourselves through guilt if we break one of society's many "ethical imperatives." To be human—imperfect and vulnerable—means we all break rules at one time or another. We can expect punishment, ranging from a verbal lashing to imprisonment if the crime is severe. No society exists that does not inflict penalties on lawbreakers. Even some animals punish their rebels by death or a measure of taming.

At the very start of life, our guilt feelings are closely bound to those we love. We never feel much guilt toward someone who means little or nothing. The more attached we are, the guiltier we feel if we hurt another person in any way. In childhood particularly, guilt may heighten emotional difficulties. Child guidance clinics are crowded with troubled children. Many a child wishes consciously to obey his parents but inwardly opposes them with such defiance the result is either a paralyzing guilt or, in opposite behavior, compulsive display of violent feelings.

Some parents make demands beyond all reason. They ask a child to be an overachiever or want him to be "perfect" in behavior and appearance. Our society is an ambitious culture and parents often ask a child to achieve too much too quickly. Our small children sometimes suffer large conflicts. They are caught between the wish to carry out a parent's command and the feeling they do not possess the intellectual or emotional strength to do so.

6

A two-and-a-half year old boy may be pressured by his mother to learn to read and though he wants to please her he finds this beyond his capacity. He feels angry at her for imposing such a difficult task, then guilty. Another little boy that age might wish to follow his mother's orders and learn to defecate in the toilet but also wish to keep the freedom of the past when there was no such restriction. He tries to control himself and produce on the toilet but finds he cannot. As soon as he leaves the bathroom however he defecates in his pants, then feels guilty. He fears his mother will punish him. If she understands his inner battle, she will be patient and in a short time he will be toilet trained.

Many children feel a conflict between the wish to masturbate and the order given by a parent that they must refrain from touching their bodies in places that give pleasure. They are also conflicted when forced to start school and give up the freedom of everlasting play. And when they are told not to hit a child who has seized a toy from them.

The main fear of a child is that his parents will abandon him, which means death to the child, who believes he will not survive without them. The screams of a very young child who fears his mother is leaving him forever, though she is absent only a few minutes, tell of his fear of dying. He also expects death if a parent rejects him or displays violent hatred. He has the additional fear death will be meted out to him for his anger at the violent, rejecting or abandoning parent.

It is no accident most adult murders occur when a loved one threatens to leave. The one who kills cannot bear the thought of being abandoned. It revives his devastating childhood terror that his mother has deserted him, left him to die. Suicide is murder turned on the self. The suicidal man, woman or adolescent attacks himself instead of murdering someone who has abandoned him. He prefers death to desertion, so acute the fear in his infant life when he felt agonizing rage, then guilt, at parents who left him alone at times he needed them. Or they may have threatened to abandon him if he did not behave.

EVERY CHILD'S GUILT

No love is pure, it is always tinged with some hate, for no one is perfect. The ambivalence we all face for those on whom we depend during our early existence creates our guilt. Where there is love there is guilt and where there is hate there is guilt. This does not mean guilt always follows the feeling of hate. We may hate someone and not feel guilty, such as an Adolf Hitler or an adult who sexually abuses a child. But the flash of hate we feel for someone we need, love or value—a mother, father, brother, sister, husband, wife, son, daughter or friend—usually will be followed by the feeling of guilt.

Because as children we so acutely need a parent's love and repress our rage to get it, as adults we feel guilty at times because of our intense repressed rage when it becomes activated by a current provocation. A parent may be dead or living thousands of miles away but we still seek childhood love and approval. Those early "voices" of reproof haunt us forever if we do not make peace with them.

Most children of rejecting parents are angry, wishing the death of their parents. And every child who wishes this fate for a parent lives with the expectation of retaliation and severe punishment—an eye for an eye. A child who has death wishes for a parent, and most children do when in the grip of rage, feels like the accused man in court. Many of us, starting in childhood, imprison ourselves in psychological jails because we cannot tolerate our guilt over death wishes for parents.

Most adults do not recognize the fact that children are ridden with guilt. The extreme vulnerability of childhood creates deep guilt because a child is so dependent on the love of his mother and father he dares not express his rage. Parents are ambivalent too but if a parent primarily loves a child, the child will primarily love both himself and the parent. Whereas if a parent primarily hates a child, the child primarily hates himself and the parent. A child absorbs psychologically the evaluation the parent places on him, accepts it as his own. A child also accepts as his own the parent's way of life.

8

Many a child blames himself, feels he is "bad," to keep the love of his parent even though he may believe the parent wrong. This conflict is also seen in the employee who prefers to think he is inadequate rather than argue with an unjust employer and jeopardize his security. Or in the wife or husband who will submit to outrageous demands from the partner rather than face abandonment.

One reason we accept guilt so easily is because we are taught early in life anger is not an acceptable emotion, that we must "turn the other cheek." Sometimes when enraged, we hurl a pillow, slam a door or strike an inanimate object, rather than hit a person who has angered us, but there is guilt because of the very wish to hurt someone. Often the recipient of our rage does not feel as hurt as we imagine but we remain convinced we should be punished. Guilt is nothing more and nothing less than the belief we should atone for something we have done to hurt someone for whom we care. Or for having gone against a principle in which we believe.

It is sad but very true that children, and adults, sometimes punish themselves more severely than their parents did. A child magnifies the threat and the punishment—and the guilt—because of his fear of losing the parent's love. The child who hits his head ferociously against the wall may only have been slapped lightly by a parent for misbehaving.

One father knew he and his wife had brought up their son with love and understanding and when the son, a junior at Princeton, wrote he wanted to drop a course in sociology but was afraid his father might not approve, the father answered, "By all means drop the course. Go out and have fun on dates." He wanted his son, a serious student, to have a social life.

The son replied, "My conscience is more powerful than your permission, dad. I'm staying with the course." In spite of his father's approval he felt he had to finish what he started. The conscience of children is severe because they think of their parents as all-powerful and fear their wrath. Parents, to a child, are gods who possess the right over the life and death of the child. A simple declarative statement to a child becomes a mandate. And, as adults, we transfer this fantasied possession of power to those we marry, to our employers and to our friends. We see others as omnipotent tyrants to whom we must subjugate ourselves.

A fourteen-year old boy, catcher on the school baseball team, was ordered by his father, "Be first in everything you do. In your studies and on the baseball field. Hit home runs. Don't drop a pitch." The implicit threat was that as long as the son was always the "first" his father would love him, but if he failed his father would be ashamed of him, contemptuous and angry. The boy wanted his father's love not for his prowess on the diamond but just for "being."

As an adult, we bring to love the many memories and fantasies that have aroused our mixed emotions of love and hate throughout childhood and adolescence. This means a certain amount of guilt will haunt us. We are apt however to bury the hate that is etched in guilt, deny the guilt and believe we escape both.

THE MIXED MESSAGE

It is not guilt per se, for we need a certain amount of guilt to conform to society's demands, but the overkill in guilt that causes most of us to feel we are to blame for crimes never committed. One thing that makes guilt excessive and such a universal occurrence is the mixed messages parents give a child.

The child is told to "look before you leap" but also "he who hesitates is lost." The child is confused, he wants to comply with edicts from his parents but wonders how he can look before he leaps and at the same time not hesitate and become "lost."

When children are told to cooperate but be aggressive, to enjoy themselves but work hard, to be assertive yet compliant, they are bewildered. Then they feel angry at these orders to perform the impossible. Children know they cannot carry out conflicting orders yet because they want to gratify their parents' wishes they try to make sense out of parental non-sense.

A child feels guilty at mixed messages for two reasons. Because of his anger at his parents for asking him to do the impossible, an anger that produces guilt. And the belief he deserves punishment because he is guilty of failing to do what his parents ordered—that in some magical way he is expected to surmount the insurmountable. Mixed messages tax the child's immature mind as he tries to figure out how he can justify anger at parents he believes can never be wrong.

Consider a thirty-five-year old woman who had been the victim of mixed messages as she grew up. Her mother encouraged her to be both compliant—"Never antagonize a man you love"—and aggressive—"Don't let any man stand in the way of achieving what you want." Her mother also told her to dress sexy and flirt with the boys but never let them touch her. Her mother and father quarreled constantly as to the way she should be raised and she often felt when she pleased her father she was displeasing her mother and vice versa.

These mixed messages had an effect on her later life: she told a friend she suffered guilt from the moment she opened her eyes in the morning until she fell into bed at night. She explained, "I get up feeling guilty about what I have dreamed. Then I feel guilty because I don't take time to serve my husband a decent breakfast before both of us rush to work.

"After dressing, I race to catch a taxi to my office, feel guilty at spending the money but the bus is too slow. If I'm two minutes late to work, I feel guilty. And then because I haven't had time to prepare for the big ad campaign, I sit silent through the meeting. When my boss says sarcastically, 'Cat got your tongue?' I say sweetly, 'I need time to mull this over,' but think, 'You bastard, I don't have to take this from you,' and feel more guilt. It's an endless cycle of guilt."

This woman was the victim of childhood mixed messages that produced confusion, terror, anger and guilt. She was always trying to be the "good little girl." Each time she dared assert herself she felt she was destroying someone and would lose the love of those on whom she depended for emotional and economic sustenance. She could not feel independent and sure of herself but helplessly kept punishing herself because of her guilt.

A father who had been a star athlete in his youth kept telling his thirteen-year old son, "I want you to be the star of the football team. Let them know you're there." Whereas the boy's mother insisted he be quiet around the house, keep his room neat, urging, "Be like your sister, kind and considerate."

He received the messages that his mother would love him if he acted submissively, caused no trouble in the house, whereas his father would love him if he were aggressive, competing on the football team. He could conclude only that if he did not make the team and plough into his opponents his father would not love him but if he did not act in opposite fashion, be quiet and considerate, his mother would not love him.

To some extent this happens to every child, for most parents convey mixed messages at times. One father insisted his daughter attend a "liberal, progressive" college so she would learn new ideas, be stimulated to think for herself. But when she came home for Thanksgiving vacation, he flew into a fury when she dared question whether communism might have some merits, which her professor of political science had asked the students to consider.

Parents sometimes give mixed messages about their sexual feelings toward children. A parent will kiss and hug and ask to be kissed and hugged by a young child but when the child starts developing physically and the parent finds himself somewhat stimulated by the child's affectionate touch, he will abruptly cease all physical contact. The child, puzzled, wonders what he has done wrong to cause the parent to stop loving him. He feels rejected, then angry, then guilty. This is a common mixed message from parents who subtly seduce a younger child then covertly reject him as he grows older. The child does not know how to regain the parent's love, a loss for which he feels he is to blame.

Most adolescents are extremely ambivalent to begin with.

Outwardly they want independence but secretly yearn for the familiar dependency. They wish to act on their burgeoning sexual impulses but also seek controls. Some parents convey to their adolescent or child, "Live by what I say, not by what I do." This confuses the adolescent who has been ordered not to touch liquor or drugs but watches his mother and father drink night after night or smoke marijuana. If teenagers witness inconsistency between a parent's behavior and words they become confused. When parents say one thing and do another, they compound the teenager's ambivalence, make adolescence more turbulent than it normally is.

Children whose parents act inconsistently often emerge as inhibited adults, afraid to assert themselves. They fear, as they did when children, that parents will punish them for any wrongdoing. They turn their spouse, employer or colleague into the punishing parent, expect rebuke or abandonment, and feel guilty. Childhood guilt rules their lives, a guilt not derived from present reality but nonetheless powerful.

SHAME OR GUILT?

There is a difference between shame and guilt, though they are closely related in our feelings. In the past not much attention was given the emotion of shame but recently there has been growing interest. A paper entitled "Shame and the Development of Autonomy" was presented at the New York meeting in 1985 of the American Psychoanalytic Association. The authors, Dr. Sally K. Severino, Dr. Edith R. McNutt and Dr. Samuel L. Feder, offered the theory that shame is connected to feelings "of inadequacies" while guilt is the result of aggressive acts, wishes and thoughts.

They also concluded shame is experienced only when a "defective sense of self is exposed," usually to someone else. They pointed out Freud stated our ego was "first and foremost a body ego." Thus an implied or fantasied inadequacy in the body brings shameful feelings. Our first shame occurs in relation to

---

13

early idealized images of ourselves and our bodies, what therapists call our "idealized self image."

Shame appears at about eighteen months of age as we start to separate emotionally from our mothers. As we grow, shame becomes closely related to our anxiety about the loss of our mother's love. Shame may be associated with the experience of ourselves as greedy, dependent, in need of a mother. Or the self as not in control or unable to perform as expected. Or the self as humiliated and mortified by the Oedipal defeats. Or the self as "bad" in relation to the expectations of our conscience, as Severino, who read the paper, maintained.

Because of our expectations there is a connection between shame and guilt. Psychiatrist Dr. Willard Gaylin pointed out that men and women often complain of feeling guilty and ashamed at the same time. For instance, we may, at the age of four feel shame if a parent criticizes us for wetting the bed when we are supposed to have learned control of our urinary functions. But we will feel anger at the parent because he censures rather than loves us, then feel guilty.

Erik Erikson linked shame with toilet training, a time, he said, when the child's task was to develop a sense of autonomy without being overwhelmed by feelings of shame or self-doubt. Erikson held that, given a sense of trust, the child achieves this autonomy, does not feel shame because he believes he has exposed himself in a derogatory way. But without the trust, he suffers an inner sense of badness, resulting in shame, at the "exposure" of some inner inadequacy. The exposure may be due to a parent's unreal expectations of the child but the child has no way of knowing this.

Freud at first believed shame a feminine characteristic but later analysts found men, as well as women, suffered shame. Severino stated it was important for an adult to recognize his sources of early shame, for the managing of the emotion of shame is "intimately connected to the regulation of self-esteem." If we cannot accept past feelings of shame, we may experience each current failure as "confirmation of ourselves as defective." We are unable to tolerate shame, become overwhelmed by it. We fail to realize our shame is based on childhood experiences and fantasies and there is no real need to hate the self for the feelings of shame in the past.

Parents can increase a child's sense of shame as they try to set standards of behavior. "Shame on you!" is the cry often aimed at us in childhood. We may hear all too often the accusation of those who appear shocked at something "unspeakable" we have done, said or shown (the latter, principally the naked, sexual part of our bodies).

A little girl stole five fudge cookies after her mother ordered her not to touch them. When her mother accused her of eating the forbidden cookies, the little girl at first denied the charge, then broke down crying, explained she had been hungry. The mother said, "You should be ashamed of yourself not only for disobeying me but for telling a lie. I won't punish you this time but don't do it again. If you are hungry ask if you may have a cookie." When a child possesses an understanding parent, rather than one who screams incessantly or punishes severely, he is apt to stop stealing, lying or committing other acts of which his parents do not approve.

One college student did not want her mother to know she was living with a young man because she was ashamed of indulging in behavior her mother had warned her against. She felt guilty at living a lie, the guilt following her shame. A sixty-five year old woman was caught without makeup by a male friend who arrived half an hour early for a date. She was ashamed at the lines in her face which, she thought, added years to her life but felt no guilt, just sadness, at the idea of growing old. A man suddenly realized his fly was open as he walked down the street and saw a pretty teenager stare at him. He felt shame at being thus exposed—literally speaking—then guilt about a sexual fantasy involving the teenager.

A woman who had an appointment to see her internist for a yearly check-up arrived at ten in the morning. His nurse was ill and had taken the day off. He thought the woman had an eleven o'clock appointment, telling her, "You're an hour early." She was sure she had appeared at the designated time but did not want to contradict him.

He looked up the hour in his appointment book, then apologized, admitting he had made the mistake. She had felt ashamed to suggest he might have been wrong. In her mind, the "man" never made a mistake—as a girl she had believed her father always right. She had never heard him confess he was wrong even though at times she knew he was in error. She had preferred to accept the blame so he would love her, not hate her for correcting him. All her adult life she wanted men to like her, think her the charming woman, the "good" (compliant) child.

At the internist's office there had been no reason for her to feel guilty but she still felt irrational shame. She was ashamed of correcting anyone in authority because if she had done this to her father, if he were wrong he would have rebuked her, ordered her not to pass judgment on him and she would have felt rejected and hated.

After the experience with the internist she admitted to herself a deeper shame. The shame of not being able to stand up for herself when a man was involved, which, she knew, meant she, as a woman, felt inferior to the more powerful man. She decided the next time she had a difference of opinion with a man she would quietly stand up for her own rights—even the right to be wrong. A right her father had never allowed himself or her.

We all experience shame, anger and guilt at various times in our lives. As children, we are asked each day to give up pleasures, a cause for anger, then guilt. The baby, in the first months of life, feels angry when he cannot have his mother carry out his every wish, then feels guilty. When she weans him or asks him to give up the bottle, he is angry, then guilty. The two-year old child is furious for the many "no's" imposed on him.

All these frustrations may cause a child to feel powerless, angry and guilty. The child carries into adulthood these feelings of frustration and anger, still reacting to them, though not aware he does. While the frustration, anger and guilt were all real to his childhood, they become irrational if he is possessed by such feelings as an adult.

2

THE FORBIDDEN WISH

PLEASURE VERSUS REALITY

As we sit in daily judgment of ourselves, what is the crime of which we are accused? In essence, we charge ourselves with wanting to gratify our deepest wishes, ones that originate in the part of our minds Freud named the "id."

At birth, we are virtually all id, before we develop our ability to use reason. The id is the source of our primitive, instinctual wishes. The desire to have sex with anyone we wish. To steal whatever strikes our fancy. To kill at once anyone who threatens our self-esteem. Our id is totally without morals, it is ruthless, aims only at fulfilling the pleasure of the moment.

One of the prime contributions to unhappiness and the development of guilt is our failure to accept what Freud called "the reality principle" as distinguished from "the pleasure principle." He believed these two principles rule our lives.

The reality principle refers to that part of our reasonable self that learns to accept life as it is, people as they are and fate as it exists. The reality principle involves knowing the limitations of the self and others, recognizes that instant gratification is not always possible and that no one can achieve everything.

In contrast, the pleasure principle refers to that part of us which constantly seeks gratification of our sensual and violent wishes. The pleasure principle insists on instant fulfillment, calls out in pleading tone, "I must have it now." The reality principle asks for acceptance of frustration, replying, "I must wait a while." When we seek only or chiefly the pleasure principle at the expense of ignoring the reality principle, we are, like the child, pleasure bound and will suffer. Reality exacts a price if we are not aware of its demands.

With the help of parents, we slowly realize there are "correct" and "incorrect" ways to handle life's inevitable conflicts. Our parents give us rules about the "right" and "wrong" ways to deal with our feelings, to gratify or withhold our wishes. Even in the first few months of our lives we become aware our mothers and fathers will not love us if we scream—they far prefer the smile.

Slowly we develop what psychoanalysts call our "superego." This is the conscience that warns "thou shalt not" when we are tempted by forbidden pleasures. It also holds what Freud named the "ego ideal" which "answers in every way to what is expected of the higher nature of man. It contains the germ from which all religions have evolved." In other words, the "thou shalts."

Freud stated that "the tension between the demands of conscience and the actual attainments of the ego is experienced as a sense of guilt." He declared that "the sense of guilt" is "the most important problem in the evolution of culture," which is built on the attempt to turn murderous fantasies into peaceful uses. Murderous fantasies thus form an undercurrent in every life.

The third and final part of our mind is the "ego." It makes all our decisions, acts as mediator between the id and superego. Shall we gratify a passionate impulse as we listen to the id? Or shall we say "no," as the superego advises? We could compare the mind to a car. The id is the engine that powers us, the ego is our driver or decision maker, and the superego is our back-seat driver. Guilt is always a function of the super-ego. Psychoanalysts call guilt "superego punishment."

The three parts of the mind are often in conflict. Even such an innocent, habitual act as waking to the ring of the alarm at seven A.M. may produce psychic war among id, ego and superego. Our id argues, "Sleep on, enjoy another half hour of rest, you work hard all day." Our superego counterorders, "Stop being so lazy, get out of bed and hustle on your way." The ego wrestles with this dilemma, asks, "Shall I get up, like a good soldier, and be on time for work? Or snatch a few precious minutes of extra sleep?"

If we allow ourselves to gratify our wish to sleep another half hour, when we wake we will feel guilty, as though we have stolen something from family or employer. We have transgressed against the powerful demands of our superego. The courtroom scene is played out as we await decision of judge and jury, "Guilty or not guilty?" We fear the ever-present threat of punishment for daring to break one of the rigid rules of society: "Thou must report on time for work." The world depends on this strict adherence to the clock, whether we are clerk in a store or president of a large corporation.

The defense argues, "It was legitimate for him to sleep, he did nothing criminal and deserved that extra half hour." The prosecutor snaps, "He is bad, bad, bad, to want to indulge himself when he knows he must report to work at nine A.M." And so it goes, for weeks, months and years, as we suspend ourselves in time awaiting the verdict.

No one escapes the id—ego—superego clash of demands in the natural war between our instincts and our reason. Even after we make decisions we are not free of guilt. A man may decide not to engage in sexual intimacy with his beautiful secretary but remain faithful to his wife yet still feel guilty because of his wish to be unfaithful.

THE POWER OF A WISH

The sad truth about guilt comes from the fact that most of the guilt we suffer arises not from what we do but from the wishes we believe dangerous and forbidden. Wishes we may never carry into action but only dream of. Because of the way in which our minds work, we feel as guilty at the *wish* to break a sacrosanct rule as we do in committing the foulest of deeds.

We feel guilty because in the primitive, unconscious part of our mind, which does not know rationale or reason, the wish is the same as the deed. As Freud put it, "In the beginning was the deed." He meant that before man started to use his mind to think rationally, he acted impulsively. To wish was to do. If an angry wish rose to mind, he promptly killed the one who angered him. If he felt sexual desire, he seized any woman on the scene. A child believes he has only to wish and the deed is done. In some primitive tribes, when a native sticks a pin into a doll fashioned to resemble an enemy, he believes his murderous wish kills the enemy.

The child who wishes his mother would "drop dead" because she refuses his request to stay up late and watch a special television show feels as guilty as though he had shot her. The unconscious part of his mind does not know the difference between the wish and the act. Only as his conscious mind develops, as he learns more about reality, can he tell the difference between the wish and the act. Adults who do not accept enough of reality may live too much in fantasy and continue to feel guilty about their wishes, consider them the same as the forbidden deeds.

Our dreams at night contain our deepest wishes. Dreams are a safety valve for our guilt and the partial release of deep feelings we have repressed, kept out of awareness. In a dream each of the characters stands for a part of ourselves. If we dream of someone committing an act we consider forbidden—lying, stealing and engaging in illicit sex—that "other person" is our secret self showing what we really wish, forbidden though it is. Dreams do not tell us directly of our forbidden wishes. But if we can decipher a dream by following our thoughts about each scene, each person, each spoken word, we will discover the underlying wish. This discovery will lessen our guilt as we accept that the wish is from childhood.

We rarely can talk of guilt without relating it to the forbidden wish. We are usually conscious of the feeling of guilt but not of the forbidden wish that has caused it. A woman may feel guilty at the wish to be sexually intimate with a stranger she has just met at a party but she is not aware the guilt arises because of a forbidden wish. The handsome stranger resembles in facial features, in tone of voice and manner, her father whom she adored as she grew up. Her wish is thus an incestuous one and causes guilt.

Our mind works on command of the wish. It is the wish that fuels our acts. We first *wish* to get up in the morning, then our body obeys the wish to rise. We first wish to eat, then we feed ourselves. We first wish to dress, then we select and put on what we wear. We first wish to go to work, then we walk out of the house. These wishes most of us accept, wishes we need to function in reality.

But we also have wishes society does not so heartily approve. These are our forbidden wishes, held secretly within our hearts. Wishes to love someone who is taboo, to do away with someone we hate, to steal an object we covet, to demean those who do not love us, to possess more power.

Each forbidden wish makes us guilty, the very word "forbidden" forecasts guilt. The forbidden wish provokes a punishment of the self, either by the self or by others we provoke into punishing us to ease our guilt. Since we all possess strong ids most of us suffer guilt because of the forbidden wishes that arise from our intense natural instincts.

THE ROLE OF THE UNCONSCIOUS

There are two main kinds of guilt: the guilt of which we are aware and the guilt of which we are unaware. If we steal something we will consciously feel guilt at taking someone's possessions. If we are sexually unfaithful, we will feel guilty about hurting someone toward whom we have loving feelings. "What one has rather clumsily to call the unconscious sense of guilt can be extremely severe and impose great suffering. The ego defends itself against such suffering, using for that purpose its most powerful weapon—repression." These are the words of Dr. Ernest Jones, the renowned psychoanalyst.

Most of us are unaware of the power of the unconscious part of our minds. It is dedicated to our wish to survive—physically and psychologically. We all experience degrees of hostility, a reaction to fear. We may be slightly annoyed, moderately enraged or frantic with fury when a situation arises that threatens our self-esteem. But no matter how slight the flash of anger, in the unconscious part of our minds we equate our rage with a need for immediate revenge and murder. The slightest insult to our bodies or minds and we prepare, in the unconscious, to defend ourselves—a universal reaction to danger. There is no such thing as a "slight wish to murder." The unconscious always responds to hate with immediate desire for vengeance.

If a stranger attacks us in the street and demands our money, we react with fear. We can, as Dr. Walter B. Cannon showed, engage in "fight or flight." If we believe we can defeat the thief, we decide to fight. If we think we cannot stand up to him, we may decide either to run away or to hand over the money.

Cannon found, through physiological experiments, that

> Our conscious feeling about an emotion results in the interaction between the processes of our thalamus, the seat of our primitive feelings, and our cortex, the thinking part of our mind. Though not too much as yet is known about it, there exists what scientists call the limbic system. It is a sort of message center that facilitates the exchange between the thalamus and the cerebral cortex.

Cannon was the first to prove Freud's theories of the power of unconscious thought. Cannon linked "fear" to the way our mind responds to it—both conscious and unconscious reactions. He showed the close connection between what he called "the seat of our primitive feelings," the thalamus, and the cortex, the part of our mind that thinks. The latter is the "gray matter," the outermost part of our brain.

Most mental activity goes on outside of our awareness in the part of our mind Freud called the "unconscious." Often our sexual and aggressive desires, our two most powerful drives, are unconscious. Our superego is largely unconscious and thus we are not aware of the commands of our conscience that influence us much of the time with "do's" and "don'ts."

The ego, as it mediates between id wishes and superego edicts, is partially conscious, when we reason and think. But when we defend ourselves through denial, projection and rationalization, these processes are almost always unconscious. We are unaware we protect ourselves from a danger when we avow a fear does not exist in us but in others. Or when we attribute an unpleasant characteristic about ourselves such as incessant complaining to someone else, as though to shed our shortcomings.

The unconscious thinking we engage in almost every minute of the day and night (at night evident in our dreams) contributes to our creativity, our productivity, our ability to love, but also to our wishes to destroy, to hate, to reap revenge. Consciously we may know we hate but we are frequently unaware that the wish to destroy those we hate propels and sustains our guilt. "Off with his head!" is not only the Red Queen's constant command but the constant command inside all of us.

THE FORBIDDEN WISH AND GUILT

Some of us are able to tolerate guilt more easily than others but no one escapes the guilt of the forbidden wish. Because our natural reaction to guilt is to punish ourselves for the crime we believe we have committed, we seek that punishment. The Bible says, "The wicked flee when no man pursueth." A wicked thought is enough to make us flee as though it were the crime, because of our guilt. We take the will for the deed and are filled with anxiety. Hesiod, a Greek who lived 800 years before Christ, declared, "The evil wish is most evil to the wisher." Because of our guilt over the wish.

We may set out for a quiet walk along a tree-shaded street but return home with a headache, unconsciously punishing ourselves for some forbidden wish—to steal a luxurious Cadillac, to sleep with a neighbor's spouse, to strike someone who gets in our way as we cross the street. These forbidden wishes lead to anxiety, depression, the feeling we are unlovable and, most of all, to pervasive guilt.

Guilt over a forbidden wish starts in childhood. It is natural for instance to wish, from the day of birth, to be special, admired. This wish never completely disappears. If anyone interferes with the gratification of this wish, we unconsciously want to destroy him. As we grow up and our sexual wishes become intense, we feel hate when sexually frustrated, or anger when conflicts ensue.

A boy of six is smitten with the nine-year old sister of his playmate. He wants to be with her constantly, feels like hugging and kissing her but fears losing his playmate for preferring his sister. Unconsciously she reminds the boy of his own pretty sister, the same age, toward whom he is secretly attracted. When he tries to speak gently to his playmate's sister, his lips quiver, his breathing quickens and he cannot get out the tender words. Instead, he finds himself saying in a nasty tone, "You're just a girl, you shouldn't be playing with the boys. Go home to your dolls." She looks stunned, tosses her head and walks away, feeling rejected. His heart sinks but he also feels relieved. His guilt lifts, his incestuous feelings are no longer a danger. He is also free to play with his friend without fear of losing him.

26

The "Catch 22" in sex is that adults unconsciously expect their sexual partner to be the idealized parent of childhood. A husband thinks, "I want my wife to be my all-giving mother." Most men possess this wish to some degree and, if not too intense, it will not affect their marriage. But if the wish is powerful, the husband may feel guilty because he is breaking the taboo against sex with a mother. He may then provoke his wife to punish him for his wish. Perhaps she will leave him if he angers her enough, or he will leave her, to ease his guilt.

The wish of a husband to be mothered by a wife, or a wife to consider her husband as a parent, is rarely acceptable to an adult's conscious mind. Childish behavior in an adult is consciously repugnant though unconsciously it may represent his most fervent wish.

The reason many marriages fail is that husbands and wives feel guilty about loving or being loved passionately and consistently. This may seem a surprise, for is not passionate love the romantic ideal for marriage? But marriages fail because the love is accompanied by fantasies in which the partner is unconsciously making the spouse into a mother or father. Thus passion feels like incest and the guilt is unbearable.

The play, *Who's Afraid of Virginia Wolff?*, is dramatic example of a husband and wife physically and emotionally attracted to each other but who feel guilty each time they love or have sex. They attack each other verbally as punishment because each, in fantasy, has become a forbidden parental figure. By loving, then hating and punishing, they ease their anxiety over carrying out forbidden, incestuous wishes and expiate their guilt. The vicious cycle goes on between this tragic twosome for years.

Frequently when we act in anger we cover up guilty feelings about forbidden wishes. It is easier for a husband who has a drink with his boss and arrives home late to attack his wife for an unappetizing meal than to admit his guilty feelings. Or for a student, who flunks a term examination for which he did not study, to condemn the teacher as inadequate.

The little boy mentioned previously, in provoking the anger of his playmate's sister, felt stirrings of sexuality toward her that related to his first loves—his mother and his sister—over which he felt the real guilt. Our first loves are always the members of our family, as are our first hates. Who else is ever so close? And for so long. The need for love may precede the reaction of hate. A baby comes into the world wanting to be fed, embraced and kept warm. When his mother fails to provide the warmth of love, he feels hate as a protective response. Even in a physical sense anger stirs warmth into the blood. We say "my blood rose" when we feel furious.

Western civilization is more of a hate culture than a love culture, according to Dr. Reuben Fine in *The Meaning of Love in Human Experience*. Our personal relationships are marked more by competition than cooperation, more by derision and anger than tenderness and understanding. Fine attributes the reason for the hate to the fact that children in our culture are inadequately loved by their parents and therefore cannot feel or express much love as adults. They use hate as a protective device, as their parents did with them, to cope with the anxiety the lack of love activates.

Writers of and philosophers about human relationships over the ages have not been aware, for the most part, that anger and hate are defenses to protect against the anxiety lack of love stirs. If we could allow ourselves to love more freely, depend more on others, cooperate with others and be more tolerant of all our forbidden wishes, we would not have to hate as much or suffer so much guilt.

It is natural to have sexual fantasies about members of the same sex—a daughter has loved her mother since birth and a son his father. Where there is love, there follows sexual fantasies, often swiftly denied and banished by psychic messengers to the underground of our unconscious. There to seethe until released in some distorted way. Sometimes through dreams. Sometimes in physical symptoms. Sometimes in destructive acts to the self or others.

It is natural for parents to have sexual feelings for their children though this is difficult for most parents to admit. One father was overconcerned about his fifteen-year old daughter, worried about the hour she came home from dates and whether she was allowing boys to make sexual advances. He watched the clock every night she was out, scolded her if she entered the door ten minutes late.

Her anger mounted and one night, when she walked in half an hour late and he reprimanded her, she asked why he could not trust her. He ordered her to obey him without further question. Her patience at an end, she asked sarcastically if he was afraid she was "making out" every night in the back seat of the car or a motel room. He slapped her viciously, unable to control his anger. She burst into tears, ran to her room.

He sank into a chair, consumed with guilt at losing his temper. Her accusation made him face the truth, he did not trust her to make her own decisions. His jealousy had eroded his ability to reason. He realized he thought of her as his possession, wanted her to remain a virgin, sexually faithful to him. He knew he had to allow her to start making her own decisions about sexual behavior and all else. To show true concern about her meant allowing her these freedoms.

Parents need to accept they will have sexual feelings for the child of the opposite sex, even the same sex, for love is never free of some sexual threads. *Especially* in the family where sexual development starts and where a child's sexual desires are first felt for his mother, father, brothers and sisters. It is a fact of life that a parent will feel sexual stirrings for his child and it is wiser for him to be aware of this than to deny it, as the father cited previously did, for the happiness of both child and parent. The way to control an incestuous feeling is to recognize it and accept the prohibition as part of reality. If our incestuous wishes were not so powerful, there would be no taboo against acting them out.

Every boy, when he is little, yearns to be cuddled by his father or older brother, and every girl by her mother or older sister. But we are taught these wishes are forbidden. We fear they might lead to incest, the crime of crimes, or to homosexuality. Though psychologists have established without doubt that all of us are to some extent bisexual, many sectors of our society condemn the expression of affection toward members of the same sex. Schools, colleges and other institutions such as the military condemn any such overt expression of love. Often the guilt over sexual fantasies toward the same sex is profound, yet rarely acknowledged is this universal expression of love.

Sometimes a man, if he experiences a desire to be emotionally or physically intimate with another man, unconsciously provokes a fight. This wards off any possible expression of love and gives his forbidden wish at least partial expression in that there is some bodily contact, even though violent. If the one who provokes the fight hurts the other man, he feels anguished, walks off consumed with guilt. If he is the one hurt, he feels punished for his forbidden wish for intimacy.

Psychologists who have studied young men who have killed or wounded a president of the United States, a governor or other high official, conclude that the assassins, in addition to feeling violent, also felt attracted to the man they tried to destroy. What most observers of the behavior of assassins fail to understand is that the assassins feel so guilty about their homosexual attraction they try to dissipate it and deny it by killing the one who attracts them. This is related to the childhood fantasy that if you destroy the one who in any way arouses you, you eliminate your forbidden desire.

THE PURPOSE OF FANTASY

Each one of our forbidden wishes contains one or more fantasies. In understanding why guilt occurs it is necessary to give fantasy its due. What do we mean by fantasy and what is its purpose? When is it useful and when is it destructive?

Fantasy is an imaginary idea or notion. It may be conscious, as in our daydreams, or it may be unconscious, appearing in our dreams, buried from full awareness. Unconscious fantasy drives us to commit many acts even though we are unaware of the fantasy. Never underestimate the power of a fantasy. Some fantasies can be as destructive, though in far slower fashion, as a bullet.

Fantasy is the reaction of our mind to a bodily sensation. The moment an emotion seizes us, a fantasy lights up our mind. If a physical sensation arouses us, it will be accompanied by a fantasy. When we feel sexually aroused, we have the fantasy of indulging in the sexual act.

The validity of fantasies was substantiated by a Canadian neurologist, Dr. Wilder Penfield, and his associates at the Montreal Neurological Institute. In experiments Penfield proved what Freud held to be true seventy years before—somewhere in the brain existed a storehouse of our memories and fantasies. Penfield "stumbled," he said, on his discovery by accident. In *Speech and Brain-Mechanisms*, written with Dr. Lamar Roberts, Penfield explained he was trying to throw new light on the speech mechanisms of the brain as he "listened to the humming of the mind's machinery, and where words came from." He performed 190 craniotomies under local anesthesia, which prevented pain yet left the brain normally active so the patient could talk and be fully conscious as his brain was exposed.

Penfield used electrodes to mildly stimulate parts of the brain and, unexpectedly, patients started to talk freely about their pasts. This, Penfield discovered, happened only when the electrodes were applied to spots on the cortex just above the two temporal lobes. These sections of the brain lie under the temple on each side of the head—the location of our thought processes and memory, according to Penfield.

The electrical stimulation caused a "stream of consciousness" to flow in which patients described and emotionally relived their past experiences. Penfield reported that since no psychical responses resulted from stimulation of other lobes in the brain, it seemed fair to conclude these particular areas of the cortex "have a particular relationship to the *record of experience* and the reactivation of that record." He compared that part of the brain where memory is stored to a continuous film strip with a sound track. He described how one man at first heard a piano playing and, when stimulated again, remembered the song was "Oh Marie, Oh Marie!" and recalled a voice singing it. Another man said, " a familiar sight danced into my mind and away again." A woman relived an episode from early childhood and the fear she felt at the time. Another described her feelings while giving birth.

Penfield called each of these instances an "experiential memory." Sometimes, he said, there would be a false sense of familiarity, everything seemed "strange and absurd, as in a dream," the patient felt "far away" from himself and the world (perhaps how the unconscious seems). Some called this experiential memory a dream, others referred to it as a flashback. All agreed it was more vivid than anything they were able to recall voluntarily. One woman heard her small son talking in the yard outside the kitchen years before and spoke of "neighborhood sounds" as well. Ten days after her cranial operation, when asked about the sounds, she could not recollect a one though she had spoken previously of the honking of car horns, the barking of dogs and the shrill cries of other children.

Penfield declared that the discovery of this type of response argued for the existence of a permanent neuronal recording of the stream of consciousness. He maintained the record of that stream was preserved in the brain in a specialized mechanism, otherwise the experiential responses to the electrode applied locally would have been impossible. It seemed likely, he added, current situations which required judgment were influenced by memories, and fantasies woven around those memories, that distorted the truth. Present judgments of the past are not always the truest.

Penfield noted the patients did not look on their recollections as a "remembering" but rather as a "hearing-again and seeing-again—a living through moments of past time." In living through previous experiences, each patient felt a double consciousness, which Penfield described: "He [the patient] enters the stream of the past and it is the same as it was in the past, but when he looks at the banks of the stream, he is aware of the present as well." He concluded that everyone forms a neuronal record of his own stream of consciousness. In Penfield's eloquent words:

> Consciousness, "forever flowing" past us, makes no record of itself, and yet the recordings of its counterpart within the brain is astonishingly complete . . . . The thread of time remains with us in the form of a succession of "abiding" facilitations . . . . It runs through the waking hours of each man, from childhood to the grave.

Some memories were accurate but some, as patients later reported, were false, distortions of what had really happened. Some patients also spoke of a threat when there was no real danger, just a fantasized one, as they later confirmed.

As these fantasies came into the awareness of the patient they lost the power of being the threat that, as Penfield said, held "no real danger." The fantasies originally had caused repressed anxiety, anger and guilt. When the fantasies became conscious, the reasoning part of the mind could then accept them as harmless. The anxiety and guilt disappeared.

Penfield's work holds important implications for the study of guilt. It proves that fantasies connected to guilty feelings lie buried in the "storehouse" of our minds. These fantasies over the years have caused much of our unhappiness because we are not aware of them and cannot use our reason to realize that, while they frightened us as children, currently they hold no realistic fear.

Fantasies have many functions, some constructive, some destructive. Fantasies inspire our creative work—art, composing music, writing and designing homes, buildings and cities. Or we may use fantasies for destructive purposes—planning to harm someone who has rejected us, taking to alcoholism or drugs in the belief we will be happier. We fantasize in the name of love and we fantasize in the name of hate.

Fantasies occur during the many stages of our physical and

33

emotional development. Therapists refer to "constellations of fantasies," the many fantasies that cluster around a particular emotion or wish. Some defend against their fantasies and the terrifying feelings they produce by deadening all emotion. The catatonic patient in a mental hospital is an example of this defense against tormenting fantasies.

Sexual fantasies are used to reduce fear over incestuous wishes. If a man during intercourse pictures his wife as Joan Collins he will suffer less guilt than if in fantasy she is the forbidden mother of childhood. If a wife imagines her husband as Robert Redford, her guilt is less than if she thinks of him as her father.

Our fantasies may cause us to stumble and fall as we race down a crowded street or the stairs of our homes. We may ascribe our clumsiness to carelessness or preoccupation but if we suffer the same accident repetitively most likely we hide an unconscious wish to punish ourselves, feeling guilty about some forbidden wish. Accidents rarely happen by chance, even the accidental pregnancy. Studies show such pregnancy is rarely an accident but wished for by the young mother as fulfillment of her oedipal fantasy.

One woman was hurrying along an icy street late for an appointment. The heel of her shoe caught in the frozen ice of a grate topping the subway. She pitched forward and fell to the ground. She hurt her left arm as she landed on it to cushion the fall. As she lifted herself painfully from the ground, she thought, "Why wasn't I more careful?"

At the moment her shoe caught in the grate she had been thinking how angry her boss would be if she were late to the appointment—it meant money if she got approval of a project. She felt anger at her employer for sending her out in such dangerous weather—he was throwing her, she thought, "to the wolves" (as she threw herself, by accident, to the icy ground). She also thought of her fear of the woman she was meeting, who had the power to accept or reject the project. She realized she was angry for several reasons and had unconsciously caused her fall by hurrying. She also knew, from her reading

---

34

of books on psychology, that the "boss" and the "woman with power" stood for the mother and father of her childhood, who had been controlling and often aroused her anger.

Fantasies, as we explore them, lead to the buried truths of our lives, tell us much about our furies, dreams and desires. They tell us too about our fears, our suffering and our losses. We can never escape fantasy. It is always with us, the moment we move a muscle, blink an eyelash or, as this young woman did, race down the street.

Our excessively hostile fantasies are our defenses against the killing blows of early life. As children, we have no way of fighting back except in fantasies, when parents are cruel or harsh. Luckily, most of us escape the vicious parent who stirs intense hatred and desire for vengeance. But because there is always some hate, even in the best of child-parent relationships, there will be some fantasies of revenge on the part of the child and therefore some guilt.

When we are adult, a sexual or aggressive fantasy should not make us feel guilt, though many of us do, perhaps the majority. Descartes philosophized, "I think, therefore I am," and modern man adds, "I have sexual fantasies, therefore I am a pervert," or "I feel angry enough to kill, therefore I am a murderer," then feels guilty.

When guilt persists, we may be sure a fantasy chains us to some pain of the past. A pain we need not suffer if we trace it to the forbidden wish that terrified us in childhood but need hold no horror for our adult mind, which possesses our greatest weapon—reason.

But the ability to use reason depends on how much we have freed ourselves from haunting fantasies and are able to use our capacity to think and judge, unimpeded by fear, hate and guilt.

3

THE TERRIFYING TRIO

ANXIETY, ANGER AND ANGUISH

Guilt does not evolve in a mental vacuum. It is the result of three emotions that precede it: anxiety, anger and anguish.

First we feel anxiety because of a forbidden wish, usually to indulge in a sexual act or to commit violence. Then we feel anger and hate for those who frustrate our wish. This is followed by anguish, then guilt because we have broken or are thinking of breaking one of our parent's or society's sacred rules.

A guest at a party smashed "by accident" an expensive hand-blown glass vase in the home of her hostess. The woman knew she hated the hostess, with whom her husband confessed he had an affair before marriage. After two martinis the woman had flung out her arm and "accidently" demolished the vase. She showed her anger by unconsciously destroying a valuable possession of her hostess, of whom she felt excessively jealous. Her jealousy had created anxiety, she then felt anger, anguish and guilt.

She also provoked punishment for her hostile act, rebukes

37

from her husband and payment of $500 for the broken vase. But via an "accident" to the vase she had committed an act far less dangerous than seizing it and hitting her rival on the head. She did not risk injuring, perhaps killing, because of her fantasies of hate.

The displacement of anger and guilt onto an inanimate object was also shown by another wife whose husband had just left her, after describing their marriage as intolerable. She raced out of the house into her car, feeling abandoned and furious, to seek solace at the home of a friend. On the way she grazed another car, dented the right fender.

The friend, knowing from the husband of his intention to leave home, realized the wife wanted to "put a dent" in him, hit and demolish him. The wife could talk only of the car, insisting it could be "fixed" (expressing the wish her broken marriage could be fixed). Though she did not speak directly about her vanished husband, she was indirectly telling her friend of her anguish and fury.

How we drive a car, incidentally, tells much about our feelings of hate and guilt. The driver who speeds furiously, then slams on the brakes to keep from smashing into the car ahead, inflicts his hostile feelings on the car and nervous passengers, as well as risking a serious accident that may hurt others. The driver who curses other drivers tells how he feels about those close to him he dare not curse. The person who will not drive at all frequently fears his aggression and guilt, does not trust himself to drive safely.

To escape the anger and disapproval of those we love or depend on, occasionally we lie. On a summer morning a young man wished to play golf with a friend who had the day off, who had invited him to an exclusive country club. The young man wanted fervently to enjoy this rare pleasure and debated whether to lie to his wife, who would disapprove, and to his boss, who would certainly deny him the day off unless he were ill.

He decided to join his friend and called his office, leaving the message he was in bed with a severe sore throat but would

38

report the following day. He told his wife he was going to work and set out to meet his friend at the golf club. Did he enjoy this unexpected pleasure? Not one single shot down the fairway or subsequent putt. He was beset by anxiety, wondered if his boss would call him at home to ask if he felt better and his wife would say, in shocked tone, he had gone to work. Then both she and his boss would know he had told a lie and despise him.

He felt so angry at himself for jeopardizing his job and for lying to his wife because of a forbidden pleasure that had turned into a torment, that he played erratic golf. He could not wait for the game to end, raced home to make sure his boss had not phoned. He was consumed with anguish—he had taken the chance of risking his professional reputation, possibly his weekly income, and his wife's opinion of him as an honest man.

He thought of the time he was fourteen and had disobeyed his parents by playing hookey from school to go fishing with friends. On that day he had also felt anxious, then angry at himself for being a dishonest son and lying to school authorities about an imaginary stomach ache. Anguished at his perfidy, he suffered so much guilt he did not enjoy that day either. He remembered too a twinge of pleasure at defying the authorities in his life—his parents, the teacher and principal— when he went fishing, just as he now enjoyed defying his wife and employer.

This man had acted out a forbidden wish, in both instances. He had broken a law of society by not attending school and, later, by neglecting his job. He had also told a lie, one of the strong parental and societal "thou shalt nots." His guilt, in both cases, was his way of punishing himself not only for his perfidious act but also for his strong rebellious and murderous fantasies toward his boss and toward his wife. He experienced both as the controlling parents at whom he felt vengeful.

Particularly in our society, men feel anxious when at times they yearn to be little boys and fear losing their virile, macho image. Any wish that brings a loss of self-esteem such as displaced hatred, illicit sexual desire or the wish to be dependent on someone will cause us to feel anxiety—a forerunner to guilt. Forbidden pleasures for the moment may hold the taste of honey but the aftertaste is apt to be sour because of the guilt.

One way to cope with anxiety brought on by a forbidden wish is to verbally or physically attack the one who causes the anxiety. If it is someone else's fault, we can then deny the anxiety-causing wish. If a man yearns to be hugged by a male friend, he may feel anxious, for men are not supposed to want to be hugged by other men. He may criticize his friend, thinking, "Who needs him?" The harassed mother who would like to take a day off and shop with a woman friend, feels anxiety at the wish to neglect her children so she attacks her friend, thinking, "Who needs her?" The adolescent who secretly craves his parents' approval but feels anxiety because the need for their approval interferes with his burgeoning wish to be independent, may have the vengeful thought, "I don't love you, I hate you." Anguish follows as he thinks, "How can I feel hate for someone I love?" He is learning of the ambivalence he will one day need to accept if he wants to avoid excessive guilt.

We cannot escape some effect on our lives of this terrifying trio but we can lessen the terror if we understand how they operate in collusion and how we can prevent anxiety, anger, anguish and the guilt that follows, by looking squarely at our forbidden wishes.

THE NATURE OF ANXIETY

There is no guilt without first feeling an amorphous, anxious sensation in our bodies. Anxiety is the signal of danger, telling us a forbidden wish threatens. Anxiety starts with the emergence of the wish in our minds, then spreads to our flesh and blood in symptoms of nervousness, loss of breath, heart palpitations, trembling, stuttering, headaches. Both body and mind try to ease the discomfort we feel at the powerful wish we know we should not carry out. The physical discomfort may range from minor to acute and may last a few minutes, several days or for years.

Anxiety differs from the emotion of fear. Fear is a natural, adaptive response to a realistic danger. If you walk across a busy street as the light turns green and suddenly realize a speeding car has disobeyed the red light and is heading directly at you, you feel fear. You think, "That crazy driver wants to kill me, I'd better jump out of his way." Your fear has saved your life, which has actually been in jeopardy. You have avoided what might have been death or severe crippling by taking action to survive. If you had felt no fear, believed yourself immortal, you might be dead.

But most of our guilt is a result not of fear but anxiety. Anxiety is the response to an unrealistic danger, or the response to our own unique interpretation of a situation. Nobody menaces your life when you feel anxious. There is only ephemeral danger, one that does not exist in the real world but in your fantasy. You have created the danger within—you are both victim and villain.

It is realistic to feel fear when walking down a deserted street at midnight in Chicago or New York. But if you roam the peaceful countryside of Topeka, Kansas at ten A.M. on a sunny day and feel afraid, this is anxiety. Your frightened feelings relate not to any actual danger but a danger within, carried from the past. Perhaps your mother warned you as a child about walking alone in deserted fields where you might meet a menacing stranger—though you never met one, your mother's warning remains strong.

The response to an unreal danger occurs far more often in our lives than the response to a real danger. Many of us go through life without ever being challenged by real danger. We have never faced starving to death, threat of death by a stranger or loved one or by a speeding automobile in the hands of a drunken driver.

Freud described four main causes of anxiety: fear of the loss of a loved one (abandonment), fear of loss of love, fear of physical hurt and fear of social ostracism. We feel anxiety when we fear that someone we need and love will leave us, never return. We feel anxiety when we fear someone's love will turn to hate. We feel anxiety when we risk being physically hurt, as the battered wife does. Finally we feel anxiety at the fear of becoming a social outcast, left without a friend, if we break one of society's rules.

It is difficult to acknowledge the feeling of anxiety, always frightening and distasteful. To avoid it, we may attack, provoke or run. When we commit any of these acts, we usually have some hostile fantasy. We may dream of long-sought vengeance or of a sexual affair with someone taboo. The fantasy creates anxiety as we anticipate punishment, then guilt.

Anxiety originates in childhood, it may start the moment we are born. An infant feels something akin to anxiety, he does not as yet know when fear is real. He is dependent on another person, a stranger to him at first, for his survival. If this person does not feed him when he is hungry, he will die. If this person disappears when he is cold and fails to return to make him warm, he fears imminent death. As he develops, slowly he becomes aware he is able to survive without his mother's presence. He starts to test his abilities to take care of himself as he learns to speak, to stand up, to walk and to run.

If as children we learn a fair amount of trust in our parents, which means eventually in ourselves, we will not suffer much anxiety or guilt as we grow up. But if our parents are selfish and uncaring, too involved in their own anxiety, if their voices are seldom soft and gentle but often raised in anger, we will be anxious. We will carry the anxiety we felt as a child into current situations, which easily turn into crises. To an anxious child or an anxious adult, there are many crises and few moments of calm.

The crises are often related to the feeling of being abandoned by someone we love for what we consider an unreasonable length of time. If someone to whom we are close is late we may feel anxious, then furious. We hide our anger, then feel like a guilty child.

THE NATURE OF ANXIETY

A woman on her way to lunch with a friend stood in the snow one day trying to catch a taxi in the busy streets of New York. She suddenly thought of a wintry day when she was eight and her mother failed to pick her up at school for lunch. She stood in the snow waiting almost an hour. Finally a teacher walked by, took her inside the school, called the girl's mother. The mother said she had phoned the school in the morning to report she was unable to get the car out of the garage and asked that her daughter eat lunch at school.

Standing in the snow of city streets thirty years later, this woman, through her earlier memory realized it had not been her mother's fault she had felt abandoned. For years she had held it against her mother for leaving her alone in the cold, starving to death. She had felt like a terrified child, beset by the fear her mother was abandoning her, unable to accept the truth—the school was responsible for her plight by forgetting to relay her mother's call.

The hurt child has a hard time forgiving a parent when the child believes the parent has deserted him. The child is incapable of being on his own, does not know where to turn. Sometimes this feeling is carried into adult life. One woman, when she felt depressed, would cry out to an empty room, "Mother, mother, where *are* you?" though her mother had been dead eight years.

When someone we believe loves us fails to pay enough attention, we may feel the anxiety of abandonment. A young woman went to a party with her fiancé and though he was attentive at first, he started to flirt with other women. She tried not to notice as she downed several drinks and talked with strange men, occasionally looking wistfully in her fiancé's direction. Finally consumed with jealousy, she quietly slipped out the door, deciding to leave the party rather than make a scene.

Her fiancé saw her leave, ran after her, asked what was wrong. She said she felt tired, was heading home. He became angry because he felt deserted. She accused him of flirting

---

43

with every woman in the room and neglecting her all evening. He assured her he loved her, he was only being sociable. She tried to persuade him to return to the party, saying she had too much to drink and would go home alone. He accompanied her to the apartment they shared but it was never the same. Her need to have him pay excessive attention, as though he belonged solely to her, made him realize the torment he would endure if they married. And she became aware of his need to seduce in a superficial sense all the women he met. They broke the engagement.

This young woman had suffered many small abandonments in her early life, expected men to inflict them on her. Her mother had frequently been ill and unavailable and her father, a traveling sales representative, was absent much of the time. She felt acute anxiety when she got close to a man. Sometimes, without any explanation, she would abruptly walk out on a man with whom she had an affair. To abandon—the active act—usually provokes less anxiety than being abandoned—the passive act.

Dr. Karen Horney, one of the first to write extensively about female psychology, described what she called "basic anxiety." Whenever we feel anxious, she said, we feel "lonely in a hostile world." Her father was captain of ocean-going vessels, occasionally took her on voyages but more often left her home feeling deserted and lonely. Like any child in such circumstances, she felt angry, had fantasies he would drown at sea. Her destructive thoughts led to guilt and made it difficult for her in later life to cultivate lasting relationships with men, both personally and professionally.

Anxiety causes many guilt-ridden men and women to feel like angry orphans. They attack their parents and later parental figures for both real and imagined separations they endured as children, then suffer unconscionable guilt.

Without anxiety, we can feel sorry minus any guilt, says Theodor Reik in *The Need to Be Loved*. "Feeling guilty is as useless as crying over spilled milk," he maintains. "One may regret having done something wrong without being emotionally crushed by it . . . A clear understanding of the significance of our misdeeds or wrongdoings is emotionally healthier than hopeless misery afterward. 'I have done this; it was wrong; it is done with,' is perhaps the better attitude." Though sometimes the far more difficult to achieve.

THE INEVITABLE ANGER

Little guilt occurs without anger—its driving force. Not even the most understanding, empathic person in the world can give us the paradise we seek. The Garden of Eden we expected as a child and also planned to dwell in the rest of our lives. We are all doomed to be somewhat angry at those who fail to provide this glorious existence. Then we deny and repress our anger, believing if the ones we love knew of it they would leave us at once. But because of our repressed anger, we feel constant guilt and provoke punishment from others or ourselves to temporarily ease the guilt.

As adults we are apt to forget how vulnerable we were as children to any rejection of ourselves or our wishes, which caused us at once to feel hatred and a desire for revenge. This is the nature of the beast in man—the beast some psychologists call the "savage self." The self that is driven to survive, sometimes against high emotional odds. The self that knows life must one day end, with all its torments and joys. The self that tries to get the most pleasure possible out of a daily existence that may often be grim, unrewarding or simply boring.

The more powerful our anxiety, the more we are inclined to feel sadistic wishes, murderous thoughts and destructive fantasies. And the more we feel these forms of hatred, the more we seek punishment. Many of us are driven almost to explosive rage at the frustration of our wish to be gratified *at once*. The still persistent, childhood wish within to be fed the moment we feel hunger makes us furious when we have to wait for food. It is not unusual to see a man or woman complain angrily to a restaurant waiter at delay in service. Sometimes a drink will quiet anxiety, unless we drink too much and then may feel even more impatient and angry.

For every pleasure denied we will feel anger, and then guilt. Since we are frequently angry about what we do not get and then dislike ourselves for our childish rage, we are apt to feel guilt much of the time. Especially when a childhood wish springs to mind and is then frustrated.

A wife became extremely upset one night when her husband was an hour late for dinner. At first she felt desolate, thought he did not care very much about her if he were this inconsiderate. After waiting twenty more minutes she was livid with rage. She wanted to kill him for causing her so much emotional pain. Suddenly she felt anguish, thinking he might have had an accident, then guilt over her former anger. When she heard his car drive onto the gravel road, she was overcome with relief, rushed out to greet him. He apologized, explained he had no chance to call. He had been in bumper-to-bumper traffic after one of his colleagues had asked for a lift home, taking him twenty miles out of the way.

This story poignantly explains how much of our guilt arises. The wife had turned her husband into a parent who, she believed, should never disappoint her or keep her waiting. Thus, at those times she did not have her husband in her physical grasp, she felt what psychoanalysts call "separation anxiety," much like the child Horney describes as "alone in a hostile world." This wife felt acute anger because her husband was not there when she expected him to be and had failed to call to explain his absence. She also had the fantasy he was enjoying a drink with his pretty, young blonde secretary, whom he was always praising for her efficiency. The wife imagined his destruction not only for keeping her waiting but for cheating on her with another woman. Then anguished because of her death wishes, she felt guilty.

If we feel dominated or obsessed by childhood wishes, we will feel anxiety, anger, anguish and guilt. In all successful marital relationships, wives provide a certain degree of mothering, as do husbands to wives. Often when men and women are inhibited in their relationships they unconsciously punish themselves for turning an adult relationship into a forbidden child-parent relationship. This is unnecessary guilt unless the demand for mothering is excessive.

A businessman in his forties started to date a woman his age. He was strongly attracted to her as she was to him. He wished she would hold him close, kiss him gently, caress him tenderly. Then he thought, "No self-respecting man my age wants to be mothered, I'll be reduced to a baby if I get involved with her." He became inhibited, could not allow himself to court her. But as he thought of his objections, he realized he believed that to be mothered would make him an infant and for this suffered guilt.

He called the woman, made a date, and over the ensuing weeks enjoyed her company, her kisses, her caresses, as she seemed to enjoy his. He could accept his pleasure in being with her only after he faced the fact that childish wishes exist in all of us and we are not reduced to children if, to some degree, we fulfill them.

Expecting an employer to act like a parent is also the result of a childhood wish. Almost every employee wishes to receive more money and higher status and thus tries to please his employer. But this submissiveness makes the employee angry, awakens memories of trying to please a parent who could never be pleased. The employee then feels guilty at his anger, knowing he must continue to please the employer or face the loss of his income.

The wish to please in order to gain or maintain love occurs in many human relationships to some degree. The submission inherent in the wish causes us anger, then guilt. The trouble with such anger is that while a momentary easing of anxiety ensues, it occurs at the cost of the forbidden wish kept out of awareness. We do not face and accept the specific wish from childhood over which we, as adults, need feel no guilt.

If we live in cities, we are apt to be driven many times a day

47

into high anger as we stand in line waiting—in the supermar: ket, the department store, the post office and to board a train, bus or subway—as others are served first. By the time we reach the head of the line, unclenching our teeth, we manage a smile, a "How are you today?" and control our anger, not wanting to be thought one of the "crazies" who stand in the street angrily cursing their parents or others who have hurt them, curse also those who now ignore them.

A woman rushed into her mid-Manhattan post office, usually deserted at ten A.M., to discover such a long line she was practically out on the street again as she stood at the end of it. Suddenly she heard what she thought an obscene sound. The young man directly in front of her was crunching away on a cone filled with chocolate ice cream. She tried to control her rage as the crunches grew louder. She felt like hitting the young man in the mouth. Finally she left the line, fearing she would erupt in fury at the creature who dared bring food into the post office, a place for feeding letters into the proper slots or carts, not food into the mouth. She had become more and more enraged standing in the slow-moving line, the last straw was the sight and sound of the young man in front of her.

This woman, poised in most situations, felt anxiety, anger, remorse, then guilt for fleeing what all the others in line seemed to consider a normal scene. She knew it was inappropriate to feel so impatient, to have such murderous fantasies about the young man. Her forbidden wish to be served immediately by a postal clerk, she realized, related to her demand as a child to have every wish gratified immediately. The young man's noisy crunching had hit a sensitive nerve in her constellation of memories about early feeding. When she was only a year and nine months, she had to watch a rival brother receive first place in her mother's love and regime of feeding. The older child could wait, the baby now came first. She had felt jealousy and rage at the new baby as it "crunched" away while she waited to be fed. This jealousy had been aroused in memory by the young man in front of her at the post office.

THE ONSET OF ANGUISH

First we feel the anxiety, then the rage, then the anguish. Accompanying anguish goes the dread of being made helpless, weakened and rejected. These threatening feelings occur almost simultaneously—anxiety over an imminent danger, anger because a forbidden wish is frustrated, and the feeling of helplessness that prevents us from taking action to rescue ourselves from this loss of self-esteem.

We all know the anguish that occurs when we feel in danger of losing love or being scorned. At this moment we hate ourselves, as well as the one inflicting the pain. We feel reduced to the level of a child who does not know where to turn, who is without resources. Frequently we feel like crying, long to be comforted and rescued.

A writer of short stories applied as an editor at a woman's magazine. He was nervous about the interview with the managing editor. When he arrived at the latter's office, the secretary informed him the managing editor was busy, asked him to be seated. After ten minutes of waiting, the writer was in a cold sweat. He thought he was not going to get the job and should leave. But he decided to leaf through a magazine, though he could not focus on the words. After twenty more minutes he stood up, determined to leave, insulted at being kept waiting half an hour. At that moment the secretary signalled him to go into the managing editor's office.

The interview went smoothly and he was offered the job. As he left the office, he thought of how his anger and anguish had almost prevented him from seeing the managing editor— a warm, gracious man who admired the writer's qualifications and gave him a chance to return to editorial work he had done effectively years before. The writer realized that in his anxiety he had regressed to a little boy who wanted his father to take care of him *at once*. He had been unable to empathize with the busy editor. Feeling powerless and deprived, his anguish intensified into almost utter helplessness.

49

If we are in possession of ourselves, rather than wishing to possess others so they will gratify all our wishes, we will feel little anguish. If someone keeps us waiting, we will take advantage of the chance to catch up on work or chores. Or we will relax by reading or watching television if we are at home. We allow the other person to be late, knowing emergencies arise in every life. We do not worry unduly because we do not fantasize the other person is deliberately late to insult us or does not love us.

The mature adult is not beset by constant anxiety. Therefore he does not indulge in murderous fantasies in relation to imaginary enemies. One of the main reasons we feel so guilty so often is because we nourish distortions about the people in our lives. The husband who does not arrive promptly is not the parent the wife needed when a girl. The employer who fails to consistently pat his employees on the back is not the good mother who must praise their every movement. Too often many of us unconsciously feel like a child who needs the love, protection and emotional support of parents.

When we feel like anguished children, we will become angry, want to attack, are struck by remorse, then guilt. It is the wish to attack, sometimes at a violent pitch, followed by remorse, that leads to guilt. A reduction in rage always leads to a reduction in guilt.

4

OUR UNREAL EXPECTATIONS

THE MYTH OF PERFECTION

Our guilt could be greatly reduced if we understood one of the hardest lessons of all: life cannot be perfect, we cannot be perfect. We can never be the god we were as a baby, most of us not even a Don Larsen, who pitched the only "perfect" game in a World Series in 1956. Or an Elizabeth Taylor, who has the "perfect" face and career.

One reason for our excessive guilt is the unreal expectations we possess about ourselves and others. Because no one can possibly meet such expectations, we cause ourselves much guilt when we fail. We are apt to remain in an almost constant rage because we refuse to accept limitations on our excessive desires and, when these desires are not gratified, feel frustrated, furious, then guilty.

Perhaps once for a short while our lives appeared perfect. When we were born and for a few months thereafter all our wishes may have been fulfilled. If we were hungry, we were fed, if we desired comfort from pain, warm arms encircled us. All this without our saying a word or conveying a thought. A wise parent intuitively knows an infant needs constant watching, care and love. Food stokes the body but love is the most vital emotional nutrient. Without love, babies die, literally.

Dr. John Bowlby, the British child psychiatrist, showed through extensive studies that when a baby is left unattended by a depressed or absent mother, his first reaction is to protest by cries and screams. If the protest does not bring a response, the baby falls into a state of despair. If despair does not attract attention, he becomes detached, as though he no longer cares about living. If detachment does not work, he gives up all hope, lies as if dead and may die. Infants who are victims of maternal neglect thus go through the emotional stages of protest, despair, detachment, vegetation and death as they feel a lack of love in the air.

The fate of the unloved infant was further described in the work of Dr. René Spitz, who studied children deserted by their mothers. The infants spent the first months of life in hospitals or other institutions. With no one to embrace them, treat them as special, look at them tenderly, smile at them, many died. The complete absence of mothering made their losses too devastating. It equalled "emotional starvation," in Spitz's words, led to "a progressive deterioration engulfing the child's whole person."

The "protest" of the infant shows his desperate need for personal care, including the loving touch. The protest is a cry for love. The protest of an adult against an unmet need or a rejection is usually far less of a crisis. To reach adulthood signifies there has been some love during infancy and childhood, at least in most instances. But there are exceptions, particularly the early lives of murderers, where the lack of love and care is clearly apparent, and appalling.

An infant does not as yet know the meaning of love but he is aware of a familiar face and body that appear when he is hungry or when he cries because he is cold or in pain. It seems to him his wishes are promptly and magically granted in this perfect world. But as he grows he learns he must wait at times and some wishes will always remain unfulfilled. He slowly starts to accept postponement of wishes, gives up entirely the gratification of a few.

No child accepts denial of wishes without some feeling of anger and resentment, even though he may not show his emotions. Who copes easily with the acute pangs of hunger? Who gets pleasure out of crying to an empty house? We continue throughout life to try to gratify wishes, accepting with lesser or greater rage the knowledge we will not always get our way. But unrealistically we also keep seeking a perfect world which, we hope, will bring fulfillment of our wishes as our mother once did.

The wish to be perfect, a mythical state, dies hard because it arises so early in life and is so intense. It is related at first to our emotional life and death—or possibly also a child's physical death, as Bowlby showed, if no loving figure is there to embrace him. As adults we know intellectually there is no such thing as a perfect mother, for either baby or adult. But we keep wishing for one, especially when we are unhappy. When no perfect mother appears, we become angry, believing no one loves us, especially not those in whom we placed our highest hopes. The anger brings guilt as we feel like a "bad" child for hating the one we have chosen to love us and to whom we have pledged our love.

A woman married a man who seemed loving and charming until, during the fourth month of marriage, he suddenly started to berate her, sometimes in front of company. He accused her of neglecting him and the house which, he said, resembled a pigpen. He told her they should have known each other better before marrying. He also now refused to have sex. She felt it was beyond all human possibility to fulfill his gargantuan needs. She tended their home, cooked the meals, held a full-time job, showed him as much love as she was capable of giving and he still was not satisfied.

She realized she had married a man who desperately needed a mother, not a wife. The warm, loving mother he never had, for he spoke of his mother angrily as a cruel, uncaring woman who had shown no tenderness. The wife felt it impossible to cope with a husband who so often appeared like a demanding baby and she gave up on the marriage. She thought if she remained with him she would only add to his and her own suffering and guilt.

Most of us, perhaps all of us, wish at times to regress to infancy and be taken care of, partially or completely. Probably hundreds of thousands of men and women suffering from ulcers or migraine headaches could ease their pain if they acknowledged the wish to be taken care of more tenderly. It is not accidental that milk eases an ulcer attack. We recognize that a drink akin to mothers' milk can do away with stress and tension. Nor is it a coincidence that ice cream is so popular in its soothing effect on child and adult.

Many parents believe if they were perfect no catastrophe would befall their child. Often a child becomes ill or feels depressed and though the parent had nothing to do with it he feels guilty because he fails to prevent the illness or depression. The child's momentary mood or sickness wounds the parent's feeling he should be omnipotent. The wish to be omnipotent is interwoven with the wish to be perfect for perfection implies omnipotence—the belief we will always get our own way, everyone must accede to our demands.

The wish to be omnipotent and the wish to be perfect go hand-in-hand in their effect on guilt. The wish to be perfect feeds the omnipotent feelings of the child as parents cater to his whims. Many a child calls a parent "mean" even when the parent refuses to grant a request that might harm the child. Such as refusing to let him stay overnight at a friend's house when the child should be studying for the next day's examination.

The compulsive need to be neat is part of the desire to be perfect. We are told on the one hand, "Don't cry over spilt milk," but spend hours crying over the way we believe we have messed up our lives. Many a "Craig's wife" keeps an immaculate house but at the cost of losing her husband's love. For his reasons, he has chosen a rigid, obsessive wife but then may forsake her for a less controlling woman, as did the husband in the movie, *Craig's Wife.*

A seventy-year old widower, married for twenty-six years to his first wife, fell in love with a woman his age, also widowed, and they married. She was wealthy and he moved into her spacious house after she assured him, "My home is your home." Then he discovered her need for mastery: "John, don't sit on my best satin chair, it's only for company." "John, close all the windows at once so the flies won't come in." "John, turn off that terrible television and come to bed." He found it increasingly difficult to deal with her constant wish to be in control. One day he packed a suitcase and left. She had wanted her home and her life to be in perfect order and was unable to consider that her husband might have different tastes and wishes.

To be human is to recognize we do not have unlimited control over our lives, much less the lives of others. The spouse who insists on control over every decision, from where to vacation to choosing a painting for the living room wall, is like the child who says, "Submit to me, let me be the boss, otherwise I'll make your life miserable." The dominating person does not cope easily with the reality that many things cannot be controlled or predicted. He goes into a fury when the "fates" go against him, then feels guilty for acting like a spoiled child. The philosophy of "rolling with the punch" has never occurred to him.

The need to be perfect may also be a way we retain in memory our close ties of love and hate to the absent parents with whom we spent so many years and who taught us to be "clean" and wanted us to be perfect. To be "dirty" was to be imperfect and intolerable, sloppiness was a crime and disorganization a crisis. Cleanliness was next to godliness, perhaps above it, and dirt on us, around us or on others, made us feel sacriligious. As adults we feel guilty if we play "dirty tricks" or listen to or tell "dirty jokes."

The less perfect we have to be, the less anger and guilt we

will feel, the more self-esteem we will have and the more we can laugh at ourselves. Only a mature person is able to laugh at himself, according to Robert Waelder, a well-known psychoanalyst. The mature person recognizes he cannot be perfect and the world can never be a perfect place no matter how loud his cries of protest.

The laugh that responds to the telling of a joke frees guilt both in the one who tells the joke and the one who listens, according to Dr. Martin Grotjahn in *Beyond Laughter.* He points out:

> Increasing demands for repression through the ages have changed aggression from assault into wit. Where we would have struck a person in earlier times, we now restrict our hostility and often repress it entirely. Aggressive wit gives us a new way of admitting dangerous aggression to our consciousness—but it has to be done in cleverly disguised form.

He explains that the one who tells the joke verbally attacks a second person, the butt of the joke. The wish to attack someone important to him is temporarily repressed, pushed into the unconscious where "it is disguised by the wit work." To test whether the disguising of the aggressive wish is successful, the one who tells the joke depends on the reaction of a third person, who judges only the disguise of the underlying aggression. If he reacts with laughter, the teller may join him in the laughter with relief—the disguise has succeeded.

"Hostile jokes lift repressions and open up otherwise inaccessible sources of pleasure," Grotjahn says. He cites as example the Emperor Augustus who, on noticing a remarkable resemblance between himself and a stranger in the crowd, asks, "Was your mother ever in my house?" The stranger replies, "No, but my father was," reversing the implication of bastardy from himself to the Emperor. The laughs at this joke release hostility against the father, the employer or anyone in command.

Grotjahn points out that the obscene joke offers reassurance in a different form. He illustrates this in the story of a girl who fell asleep in the green grass of a peaceful meadow. When she suddenly awoke she saw the young, handsome face of her movie idol smiling down on her and saying, "I am Prince Charming and I grant you three wishes." She answered, "I have only one wish but I wish it three times." Grotjahn explains this shows how an aggressive tendency may be successfully disguised through a sexual wish. The girl is being told by hostile men, "We know you—you are not any better than dirty little boys in their fantasies."

Along with the wish for perfection goes the wish to retain that "specialness" we felt as a child. Psychologists have found this a universal wish. A child is always special to his parents no matter how old he grows. We suffer from wishing to be special only when our need to be loved and praised becomes so strong it is totally unrealistic in that we expect excessive attention from everyone. This wish to be special becomes a problem if we wish to destroy all who prevent us from attaining the specialness only a child rightfully deserves.

For many who cannot accept imperfections in themselves and others, giving to someone means loss. Cooperation means submission. Sacrifice means being a slave. The child within has no concept of sharing, of bestowing love, tenderness and respect. He still screams, "Me first!" When we want to be first all of the time in all ways we will feel guilty.

THE PROJECTION OF PERFECTION AND OMNIPOTENCE

All of us, whether or not we are aware of it, would rather make others feel guilty than admit our own guilt. So we project our image of perfection on others, demanding they be perfect. We do not allow for a difference of opinion and criticize or condemn them for differing in any way from us.

Often one adult will accuse another, to whom he is close, of some "disgraceful" trait. The mature person knows every accusation hurled against him is not necessarily true. Enough people have enough malice so they will exaggerate or concoct lies to hurt others. But when "bad luck" befalls us this does not mean others are evil, rather, we often play a part in bringing about our own bad luck.

Gamblers will report a "bad day" at the races when they lose money, failing to take into account they selected each horse, placed each bet. No one forced them to take a chance with odds against them. Sometimes "lady luck" plays a part, as in the million-dollar lotteries. But for the one winner there are hundreds of thousands who lose and lose and lose. The odds are so high against winning that most people who steadily play the numbers game are living out a fantasy that costs them dearly.

In our projection of perfection, we even demand umpires of baseball games be perfect. When an umpire calls a strike on a ball we clearly see on the television screen was outside the strike zone, we feel outraged and scream, "Kill the bum!" The umpire cannot always be expected to be right. After all, baseball is a matter of inches, as Casey Stengel aptly put it. Perhaps even quarter inches, though it may not seem fair when a game is won or lost on one wrong call by an umpire. We cannot expect doctors to be right every time in their diagnosis or treatment, or judges in their decisions on a case. The expert in any area is fallible, as proven over and over.

Children view parents as giants who know all, possess all, can make anything possible with their magical qualities and power. This belief in the omnipotence of the parent exists among many adults. It accounts for the popularity of astrologists (as parental images) who predict the future and serve as hallowed guides for so many lives. The astrologist announces, "I have the power to tell you how long you will live, if you will marry, when you will marry and whether you should be careful on the ides of March or in mid-November." Almost every newspaper runs a daily column by an astrologer. Fortune-tellers are also supposed to be omniscient, ascribed the power of the parent who controls the "fortunes" of the child.

The tragedy of Jonestown, Guyana, shocked the world. It

never would have occurred if unknowing, gullible, emotionally dependent men and women had not sought out and placed their unhappy lives in the hands of an irresponsible, sadistic, immoral man they believed a "Reverend" who would lead them to paradise. Their need for somebody to tell them what to do cost them their lives and the lives of their children when they meekly obeyed his final order to give poisoned drinks to their children, and then kill themselves.

This is the highest price to pay for not being able to give up attachment to an omnipotent figure believed to hold all the answers on how to achieve a perfect life. These unfortunate people, who had failed to gain much emotional independence from their parents, blindly projected their wish for omnipotence onto Jim Jones without considering whether he was a criminal, a man without morals, which he proved to be. His downfall came when he ordered the slaughter of several visitors from America, including a Congressman, who had gone to Guyana to investigate his questionable new settlement.

When we believe omnipotence available to us by projection, we court psychological disaster. We are bound to be frustrated and enraged, sometimes to the point of violence, then strong guilt overcomes us.

A stalwart member of a church fell into deep depression when he learned his minister could not answer all his prayers. He became furious when the minister could not arrange with God to make him a millionaire. He eventually accepted that even a servant of God has limitations, made peace with his anger and guilt.

A woman thought her psychoanalyst was God, that he would bring salvation, all her conflicts would disappear if she stayed in analysis long enough. After six years she realized a psychoanalyst was human too and could not change her childhood or be a "good" mother or father. Analysis can only help us understand what caused our suffering so we may gain the strength to be more independent, make wiser choices in love and work and stop projecting our wish for perfection and omnipotence on others.

If we believe others should be sensitive to all our vulnerabilities, love us without qualification, intuitively know what makes us happy, they will inevitably disappoint us. It is an unhappy but necessary task to accept that everyone else is as narcissistic as we are. It is too much to expect others will never neglect us, never insult us, never fail to cherish us, have no sour moods, bad tempers or desperate days. Yet many of us become indignant and angry if loved ones overlook us for one moment, slight us or reject us. We think, "How dare he do this to *me*, he should think of *my* feelings, cater to *my* needs." The mighty, in such a fantasy, have nowhere to go but to guilt.

THE WISH TO BE NUMBER ONE

Most parents want their child to achieve, to get marks that will place him at the head of his class, as well as to be the best-behaved pupil in school, the greatest athlete, the finest debater. There is nothing wrong with wishing to be or being at the top of the heap. Most of us wish to excel, try to excel in whatever we do. But many of us feel guilty if we do not become number One. Every setback makes us feel inferior and guilty. This guilt is a residue of our childhood feelings that to be loved by our parents we must aim for the top. Thus we live trying to fulfill another unreal expectation.

Many a housewife feels depressed because she never became the ballet dancer or opera star her mother wished her to be. Many a frustrated actor feels guilty because he is not starring in a Broadway hit as his parents often voiced the desire he do. Underestimated in the cause of such guilt is the fantasy that being at the top, becoming the king or queen, the prince or princess, will bring that ephemeral "happiness."

The late Marilyn Monroe is a tragic example of the fantasy that to be at the top will end all suffering, all feelings of inferiority, all self-hate. Though admired and lusted after by the majority of American men, highly successful in her career as a film actress, financially secure as a result of her own abilities, she remained deeply unhappy and suffered such intense guilt that she eventually committed suicide.

From what we know of her past, she was the illegitimate daughter of an extremely depressed, emotionally disturbed mother who placed her in a foster home. She yearned for the realization of a fantasy that could never be gratified—the wish to make the world her good mother, a mother who would never abandon her, who would rock her, nurse her, love her. No man, not Arthur Miller nor Joe DiMaggio, two of her three husbands, could give her the bliss she felt essential for happiness.

In many ways her successes must have felt like teasers. Applause for her films from millions of viewers made her believe some day she would find that perfect mother. In his perceptive play, *After the Fall*, Miller portrays the dependence on him she felt sexually and emotionally, a dependence he eventually could not bear. When she finally went to a prominent Los Angeles psychoanalyst, she found an empathic man who invited her to his home for meals, introduced her to his wife and children, but was unable to offer her the permanent home she had sought all her life. Part of the desperation that caused her suicide may have been the thwarting of her wish to belong to a family as she had never belonged when a child.

In his recent book, *Legend: The Life and Death of Marilyn Monroe*, Fred Lawrence Guiles tells of the abortion she went through a few months before she took her life. The father of the child she was bearing could have been President John Kennedy, with whom she had an affair, or his brother Robert, then attorney general, with whom she was involved just before she killed herself, or other men, according to Guiles.

The abortion had to awaken in her a deep rage, stirring memories of her abandonment as a little girl as she, in essence, did what was done unto her and abandoned her baby—not even giving it a chance to survive. Frequently when a woman feels guilty about a wish to have an abortion, or has an abortion, she identifies with the infant abandoned before birth.

She feels as much remorse and guilt as if she were the wicked mother of her past on whom she projects her rage and guilt.

The unhappy person who does not feel driven to the extreme of wiping himself off the face of the earth also yearns for the impossible but fights to live. In Marilyn's case, the fantasy mother she sought was so out of reach, as her own mother had been, that Marilyn was furious most of the time. She wished to kill the deserting mother, whose emotional illness had caused her to place her beautiful little daughter in a foster home—caused her in the first place to conceive that daughter out of wedlock, so she was deprived of a father. At the height of Marilyn's success she sought out the man she believed her father but he refused to see her.

Unconsciously, as she committed suicide, Marilyn tried to make her parents feel guilty about their abandonment of her as a child. She had expected far too much of herself and of others. She remained possessed by an inner fury because her unrealistic wishes could not come true. The fury brought a guilt that drove her to death by her own hand as she consumed a lethal combination of pills and alcohol.

The usual suicide note to the living is accusation: "You have made me feel like a worthless, despicable person. You have not loved me enough, admired me sufficiently, supported me adequately. I will die and you will suffer." The suicide is an expert at laying guilt on his survivors but is rarely aware he does so. If he recognized his rages and guilts he would not wish to make others suffer nor need to kill himself.

When we constantly strive to be at the top, we may feel a steady fury and guilt because we chase an unrealizable fantasy: the wish to return to the state of the baby who sees the world as his—an impossible dream for an adult.

The husband who orders his wife, "Bring me my slippers," is like the baby crying, "Bring me the bottle." Many a wife wishes to rebel but dares not, at constant orders from a husband. If a tired wife finally protests, "Get your own slippers," the husband may lash out at her like the protesting baby screams. He usually then feels guilt for his attack. If the wife responds with tears, he feels even guiltier. The more unrealistic his wants, the angrier he becomes. The angrier he feels, the more guilt.

Sometimes tears do not work. One husband, a hospital administrator, carried into the home his need to keep a large institution well organized. One day his wife burst into tears after he found dust under the sofa and berated her for not keeping the living room immaculate. Staring at the tears flowing down her cheeks, he snarled, "Don't bother putting on a show of crying. Your tears don't move me one bit."

She knew he meant this, he was a cold, aloof man who hated any show of emotion. She wondered if he were repeating the suffering of his early life when his tears had failed to move a cold, aloof mother. He had told his wife several times that his mother was an extremely depressed woman who could barely take care of herself, let alone her only son. His father had left them both behind as he walked out of the house when his son was eight, obviously not caring what happened to the boy.

Frequently overlooked is the psychological fact that the one who attacks desperately needs the one he is attacking. This is why he feels remorse and guilt. He is guilty not only because of the current relationship but also for the imagined crimes of infancy—those perpetrated against him for which he seeks vengeance and those he wished to commit but did not dare.

The husband previously described could never, as an only child, attack his sad, depressed mother but in later life he could choose a woman similar to his mother and voice the complaints he had held back for years. As though to say to the world, "See what cruelty was inflicted on me as a child, cruelty I could not fight, and now my wife is repeating the pattern and I cannot take it. Pity me. Someone, please take care of me!"

Those at the top because of their wealth, like a Rockefeller, or through a position of power, like a policeman, may equate this power with control over "lesser" beings. One policeman, with fantasies of omnipotence (becoming a policeman allows one to officially act out the very fantasy of omnipotence), who even looked like Napoleon (short and slightly bald), arrested driver after driver for minor infractions of the law such as speeding three miles over the limit or driving in the wrong lane for a few seconds.

He brutalized, as if he were emperor of the highways, essentially innocent men and women. He commanded his victims, to stand or sit. He enjoyed placing their wrists in handcuffs, usually behind their backs, a position that caused acute aches in their shoulders. He made them feel like criminals who had committed murder. But no sooner were his victims powerless than he showed remorse and guilt. He would say, "I'm sorry I had to do this. It hurts me more than it hurts you." Yet he kept repeating the sadistic ritual day after day. He arrested some for "disorderly conduct" if they even faintly protested his sadism, though he was the one to act "disorderly."

This policeman was undoubtedly doing to his victims what had been done to him as a child. He was making those over whom he had power, feel helpless and weak as he had felt with his dictatorial parents who wanted him to obey their every law. He knew his bullying manner was not warranted by such minor infractions of the law and he punished himself by apologizing and feeling guilty.

The police stand near the top of authority in our society. If we disobey their commands, we are hauled off to jail, there to await decision on "guilty or not guilty?" In this instance the decision lies not within ourselves but is handed down by an outsider. The accusation is real, not fantasy.

Those who are driven to exert control over others lack the only control that matters—control over their own threatening, destructive feelings. They have remained largely the helpless child who has a need to control the world by temper tantrums and edicts. Even as children play at being Superman or Wonder Woman, they know it is fantasy. If parents do not encourage a child to live too much in the world of imagination, if they teach a child enough of reality, the child will learn the difference between fantasy and reality and use fantasy constructively, rather than to hurt himself and others.

One of the most important causes of guilt is our need to achieve and possess in the vain hope we will love ourselves more and others will love us to a greater degree. When these wishes are frustrated, we are furious and want to lash out. We then feel guilty for our extreme fury. If we need to be a millionaire to feel self-esteem, we are unrealistic. Much guilt arises if we try to be supermen, superwomen or some other kind of nonhuman. We would feel less guilty if we wanted less.

THE NEED TO ACCEPT FRUSTRATION

The guilt-ridden person usually wants too much and is angry because he cannot achieve the impossible, then feels anguish and guilt. He dreams of the perfect marriage, fantasizes the perfect affair, wishes to raise the perfect child, build the perfect home with the perfect car in the garage. He wants it all.

If desires are insatiable, if we cannot accept the inevitable disappointments and limitations of life but instead yearn for too much, we will feel guilty if we do not achieve all we desire. We may, as a result of our inability to accept frustration, dislike our spouse, resent our peers, despise the community and society in which we live. We feel depressed, believe something is wrong with us because we have failed to reach the top. We think of ourselves as powerless, without resources.

Life is full of frustrations that have to be accepted philosophically, with perhaps grudging grace, not angry rebellion. When we attack a marital partner for failing us, we accuse him wrongfully of depriving us of happiness. When we blame a spouse, we will frequently feel guilty because of our unwarranted attack.

Maturity means we have to curb our appetites, tame our wishes, take "no" for an answer at times. These are hard lessons, especially if we have not been taught them in early childhood. Many a child who has difficulty learning to read and write, or who later becomes a college drop-out or unemployed, is saying to the world, "I want it my way, and if I can't have it my way I'll quit trying."

Every personal relationship induces frustrating experiences. Euphoria occurs only momentarily yet, in a sense, man demands a perpetual erection and orgasm and, from the playpen stage of his life, perfection. We fall in love, idealize the loved one, believe we have found the perfect mate, though how we can expect, on what usually is short acquaintance, to know the other person well enough to wish to spend the rest of our lives with him, is sheer fantasy in itself. The mate also idealizes us as we both look forward to eternal bliss. What wishful words these are—"eternal" and "bliss."

Then, for many of us all too soon doubts steal in. Romeo referred to romantic love as "a choking gall" and "bittersweet." He may have sensed not only the enemy families of the Capulets and Montagues would halt the love affair but that young Juliet, beautiful though she was, could never satisfy all his demands, nor he, hers (Shakespeare seemed to know the truth about the deeper emotions). As statistics show, more than half of all marriages self-destruct because the concept of eternal bliss is sheer illusion. It cannot exist between mortals, no mortal is perfect and thus cannot provide that desperately wished-for euphoria to himself or someone else.

Our society encourages the fantasy that all desires can be gratified overnight. Advertisements would have us believe that with the purchase of a certain perfume comes eternal love. Or that a young man who uses after-shave can seduce any woman he wishes. We buy the highly touted products and feel deprived, angry and guilty when they do not lead to instant romance.

Many of us do not fully accept the realistic problems in life: the earning of money to feed and shelter ourselves, the bringing up of children, the ability to live compatibly with a member of the opposite sex, to enjoy friends and be creative in work and artistic pursuits. These activities should produce satisfaction, not conflicts, if we can accept frustration of our childish wishes to be perfect and omnipotent.

66

Often we try to deny the vulnerable child within and his feelings of grief, sorrow, anger, remorse and guilt when his wishes are frustrated. Any time a child is deprived he feels rejected and abandoned. If he is too angry, if there is a strong need in him for revenge on parents who were unloving and unprotective, the fury of the child may take over adulthood. Recent movies showing creatures from the occult or outer space invading the home and causing destruction and death are but the child, in fantasy, getting even with his terrorizing parents. One reason for the immense popularity of *E.T.* was that the invader from another world proved a gentle, humane, sympathetic creature (as we wish our parents had been).

SIBLING RIVALRY

A great cause of frustration in early life is the existence of siblings. Sibling rivalry—the wish to be the one and only—may lead to intense frustration on the part of a child. It may cause him to act in hostile ways, burden him with guilt if he does not accept his siblings as friends as well as enemies.

The Bible tells of sibling horrors—Cain and Abel, Joseph and his eleven brothers—as does one of our most popular fairy tales, "Cinderella," whose wicked stepsisters hated her. Every child feels sibling rivalry, even the child without a brother or sister lives in fear he may someday have a rival.

Men and women of this age of women's liberation view each other unconsciously as siblings. A man may believe that if a woman achieves success and becomes prestigious, he is a deprived sibling. Or a successful woman may feel guilty at times, believing she is depriving a man (in fantasy, a brother) of his acclaim and love. The battle of the sexes often seems like a war of siblings where the success of one sex means the doom of the other.

Achievements in careers may also be thought of as guilty triumphs over siblings. One man promoted from associate professor to full professor at a Midwestern college at first felt elated. After a period of time he became depressed, guilty and remorseful. As he examined his thoughts he realized he had idealized full professors, making them Goliaths, and this promotion for him involved the fantasy of killing his colleagues with a slingshot. He also felt the rival professors over whom he had triumphed were his two brothers whom, in fantasy, he was destroying. After facing the truth, he started to enjoy his promotion, now aware he had always been in battle with his two brothers and his father, quarreling violently at times with them.

Facing his murderous thoughts about the brothers he wished had never been born was a helpful step for this man. He was able to separate his fights with them from the reality of his current success (this separation follows automatically when the tie to the past has been accepted). He thought, "Though I may have wished to destroy my rivals as a child, I have never killed anyone, and if I keep living in a childhood fantasy battle, it's a no-win situation."

A woman violinist struggling for ten years to make a living was finally hired by a large symphony orchestra. She was excited for a week, then felt depressed and guilty. She kept thinking of her friends in the music field who were still unemployed. One violinist told her he thought he deserved the opening, that her selection was due to the orchestra leader's wish for the praise of the women's movement. Until she could admit her guilt was due not so much to the feeling she had triumphed over this man or her other musical companions but her brothers in childhood, she could not enjoy her success.

A thirty-year old man carried guilt from the age of eight when he had spilled ink on his mother's satin bedspread. Terrified at losing her love and fearing punishment, he blurted out, "My sister did it." His younger sister, intimidated by both her mother and brother, took the blame. But he felt so guilty, a few weeks later he confessed he was the one to spill the ink. The guilt, however, remained throughout the years because he had blamed an innocent victim for his crime.

The more we wish to outdo siblings the more jealous we are

apt to become as adults of those outside the family who are more successful than we are. We become jealous when we think someone else is more perfect, more loved or achieves something we desperately wish to achieve.

THE ILLUSION OF HAPPINESS

Our failure to recognize we chase an unrealistic rainbow leads to much of our unhappiness, as well as guilt. We do not settle as a measure of happiness for the small but solid achievements. The quiet love of a spouse, a child, a friend, a colleague. The ability to earn a fair living and take joy in our work. If these fail to bring satisfaction and self-esteem it is because, in fantasy, we still see ourselves as the kingpin of the cradle.

The guilt-ridden person punishes himself and others because he has failed to find perfect happiness. He is frequently unaware of how desperately he wishes to be indulged and admired and of how little he is able to offer emotionally. He is also unaware of how angry he is because his fantasy of self-indulgence is not fulfilled. He mourns the loss of the unattainable. He cannot accept the idea of being happy every minute of the day as illusion. There *is* no Prince Charming or Cinderella, or Jack in the Beanstalk who can climb the highest tree and fell the wicked giant.

The child frustrated too early in life and the child not frustrated enough at the proper time seem to scream the loudest as adults for a happiness they feel due them. Some parents, believing they are raising a happy child, rarely say "no." They indulge the child as they may have been indulged or as they wish they had been indulged. But at the cost to the child of not learning the frustration necessary to control primitive desires. The child indulged too early becomes an unhappy, demanding youngster, often beyond the control of the indulgent parents. Both child and parents will feel guilty.

One mother striving for a life of everlasting happiness for

her child did nothing but gratify her daughter from birth on. She breast fed until the child was three, longer than necessary. She did not toilet train her daughter until she was five, when she should have started at two and a half. She tried to anticipate the child's every demand, fulfill it at once. She constantly hugged and kissed her daughter, especially when the child seemed a shade unhappy.

As a result of this mother's overgratification, the indulged daughter turned into an impulsive, demanding, angry young girl and adolescent. The mother, feeling guilty and wondering if perhaps she did not give her daughter enough, indulged her even more, which made the daughter even more demanding. We could predict that, as an adult, the daughter would be unable to cope with the frustrations of marriage and be unhappy with any spouse, much less bring up fairly happy children.

The college drop-out frequently has been an indulged child, pampered by parents, other relatives and teachers. He goes to a university expecting the same red carpet treatment. Angry if he does not receive it, he rebels. But frequently because he feels guilty at his rebellious wishes, he arranges to drop out as peers and teachers castigate him (the punishment he believes he deserves because of his guilt).

We see overindulgence, masquerading as a form of "making someone happy," not only in bringing up children but between husband and wife, lover and lover, friend and friend, student and teacher. One partner emotionally feeds the other as he wishes to be fed. He fails to understand that part of reality is the ability to say "no" at times, accept "no" other times. In effect he turns the partner into a demanding infant.

One husband who brought flowers every evening to his wife forgot after a difficult day at the office. She reprimanded him, implied he no longer loved her. He felt she had a right to be angry and brought two bouquets a night from then on, wanting her to be happy. He hid his anger at the fact she could not make allowance for his one day of forgetfulness. This anger made him feel even guiltier.

Like Joseph in *The Bible*, who desired at all costs a coat of many colors, we chase the rainbow of happiness. Joseph wanted to be his father's favorite, to destroy his eleven brothers and stand in highest favor with the pharaoh. A very ambitious man, our Biblical hero. Based on his unconscious wishes, he predicted seven years of feast followed by seven years of famine. His desire for such devastating destruction of his fellow men contributed to his guilt at his selfish childlike wishes to be his father's favorite and, later, the favorite of the father of his country, the pharaoh. For these wishes Joseph thought he deserved to starve to death as punishment, hence his prediction of the famine years—not to terrify his fellow man but to ease his guilt. Had he not been overambitious, wanting to be "special" and "first" in all realms, he would not have been consigned to the darkness of a pit as the punishment he undoubtedly felt he deserved.

Many of us feel starved because we do not have enough pleasures and privileges. We feel anger when we face a "no," or when others criticize or attack, stab us in our narcissism. Many group situations, both at work and in recreation, foster our unhappiness and guilt. We all want to be the leader, the chief; it is demeaning to be a plebian plodder. Cooperation as a modus vivendi is not a part of early childhood, when wanting to be the one and only reigns. The power struggle begins with the first cry we utter.

The "midlife" crisis is often described as the years both men and women ask, "Is this all life holds?" They see happiness going down the drain, yearn for a passionate love affair, may take drugs or drink heavily, turning to what they believe a new magic that will bring them the joy they never knew. They look for a drastic change in their lives, perhaps a glamorous career, a more luxurious home.

The midlifers feel their all-too-brief existence is half over and they have not realized their potential in love or work. Spouses leave or indulge in extramarital affairs, men and women seek different jobs, a new city in which to start over. What they do not realize is they still seek to gratify childhood fantasies as they silently scream, "What never? Never the perfect mother or father? Never the perfect sexual partner? Never the perfect job? Never a modicum of fame?"

If we feel desperate about our lives, become promiscuous or seek to change marital partners or jobs, we usually hide rage toward our parents and all others who do not gratify our primitive wish for eternal happiness. We have just as much chance of achieving this as winning the $5,000,000 lottery. Less chance, for there is no one who is going to bring us eternal happiness.

Many who find new sexual partners or change jobs soon discover they are still unhappy. They do not see their unhappiness as self-provoked. They have unconsciously arranged their lives so they will be unhappy because, at some level, they are aware how angry and guilty they feel.

Because of our guilt we seek punitive psychic blows as punishment for our greedy hungers, our inability to accept frustration. This is not to condemn the hunger for we all possess it, we need it to achieve at all. The danger is in being too greedy. The guilt that follows will be tormenting.

Freud wrote that none of us receives enough love. We could obtain far more if we did not feel so unhappy because of our fantasies of perfection and omnipotence. Happiness is each man's dream of the perfect world. We may enjoy many happy moments in life if we do not feel too guilty. If we do not ask too much from others and ourselves.

5

DIFFERENCES IN GUILT BETWEEN MEN AND WOMEN

A WOMAN'S GUILT

When it comes to guilt, men and women do not share equal amounts. Freud once said women have a weaker sense of guilt. He believed there was nothing more physically damaging than for a man to feel unmasculine (impotent, or castrated) and this accounted for man's greater guilt. But current therapists disagree. They have found women possess a more intense sense of guilt than the "stronger" sex.

Freud was referring to the guilt that occurred in the oedipal period when a child first felt a strong passion for the parent of the opposite sex. But since Freud, therapists have explored more deeply the first years of a child's life that precede the oedipal period. New discoveries show a girl faces more emotional difficulty than a boy as she prepares for the oedipal conflict. Out of this difficulty arises her greater guilt.

Why the greater guilt? A girl's first love is her mother, the most important person in her early life before she transfers her love to her father. The mother is also a boy's first love but when he faces his oedipal feelings he does not change the object of his love. The one who has nurtured him also becomes his erotic target as he competes with his father for her love.

But a girl has to switch the object of her love from female to male and risks losing the love of her nurturer and protector. This threat is also accompanied by the wish of the daughter that her mother disappear forever so she alone can possess her new love. The change of loved one from feminine to masculine, from chief nurturer to enemy-rival, causes more guilt in a girl than in a boy. A girl thinks, "How can I compete with the most important person of my early life? I need her so much. And yet I love my father with all my heart and soul." She might also add "body," for her strong sensual feelings for a member of the opposite sex drive her to the new feelings of passion for her father.

An adolescent girl of thirteen, when she first allowed a boy to kiss and fondle her, told her closest girl friend, "Oh, God, what if my mother knew what I was doing?" The boy friend had become the substitute for her beloved father and she felt guilty about taking her mother's place in her fantasized twosome from childhood.

A second reason women possess more guilt is that through the ages in most cultures, men have been considered superior. Because women have been forced to inferior positions, they have felt anger, not dared to show it, then suffered a guilt foreign to men. Women feel discriminated against far more than men do and with good reason, for they have been treated as slaves in many respects.

Also, for decades in this country women were placed in the position of being "teased." The promise of equality in many areas—economic, political, social—was held out to women but never fully granted. For instance, in the 1960s racial riots occurred in which many women, white and black, took part. Just prior to the riots, President Lyndon Johnson and the U.S. Supreme Court had in effect promised women more equality. But it never really seemed forthcoming and women felt betrayed. A few minor advances occurred but on the whole women still remained in a servile state and felt masochistic, furious, then guilty. Rage over an unfulfilled promise is far more intense than if a promise were never made, as parents find out with children.

Despite the advances women's liberation has brought, many women still retain the belief they are of value only if they take care of husbands and children. Though they may be reluctant to admit it, they feel uncomfortable when they assume roles denied their mothers. They also feel an undue amount of guilt if they fulfill roles traditionally ascribed to men. Many a wife provokes punishment from her husband because she feels guilty working at "a man's job."

After a challenging day at her law office, a woman returned home to start an argument with her husband, also a lawyer, then felt guilty. She was trying to convince herself she did not know how to argue a case, that her husband was the more capable attorney. Many a woman denies her abilities as she views a non-traditional role for women as masculine. Feeling like a man in woman's clothing, without realizing it she seeks to be put down so she will not feel guilty at usurping a man's place. It is as though she may now stay in the work place but must not be better than a man.

Today's woman feels guilty for other reasons—reasons that arise out of her new equality. The most obvious guilt is that of the mother who works full-time or part-time. She thinks she fails to nurture her children fully, absent from home much of the day. If she leaves her place of work early to be with her children after school, as many young mothers do, she feels guilty at cutting corners on the job.

An audience of mostly women agreed on this as they discussed Lynn Caine's book, *What Did I Do Wrong?* The book describes the dilemmas of a mother bringing up her son and daughter alone. The discussion was aired on the Phil Donahue show of April 16, 1985 over NBC.

One woman in the audience said, "I am blamed by my husband and my parents for everything that goes wrong with my children. So whether I'm home full-time or working, either way I feel torn. I feel guilty when I'm not working and I feel guilty when I work."

Another woman agreed: "My husband never feels guilty if the children misbehave or fail at school, it's always *my* fault for not controlling them, or making them study. I might as well be a single parent."

Caine commented, "It doesn't seem to matter if you're married and working or stay home. It's a no-win situation for women."

One of the panelists remarked, "It depends on the woman as to what she wants to do—stay home or work. If you have the option, do what you feel is best for you. Many women don't have to work but do so for the extra money, to buy clothes or for other pleasures, or to help out with household expenses."

Someone in the audience asked, "But don't such women feel guilty?"

"Not all of them," said the panelist. "It's a very individual thing. If a woman wants to stay home, she should stay home. If she wants to work, she should work. Every woman is different and there should be no rules."

A man in the audience maintained, "Fathers *do* feel guilty if their children go wrong. Every man who has helped raise a child, or raised a child by himself, will tell you of his guilt. He also feels he doesn't give the child enough time, doesn't listen to him enough, isn't doing his job."

The consensus held that because society says mothers are responsible for the happiness and well being of their children, a woman feels guilty about failing to be a good mother if her child commits any wrongdoing. Throughout life most of us blame our mothers, not our fathers, when we are unhappy and feel sorry for ourselves, unless fathers play the mother role.

There is another reason for women's guilt. The working woman hears the voice of the past: "I, your mother, did not work, I took care of you full-time and you should be like me, don't dare be different, don't try new things, you'll only fall on your face." Many women in our current society persist in resurrecting their mothers' voices, hearing them exclaim, "Serve your husband and children full time." Women feel guilt when they do not obey this admonition of their mothers.

Frequently the woman who works and the woman who stays home are likely to feel guilty when they take the initiative in sex or are aggressive in any way. They feel they are somehow demasculinizing the man. The "ballsy" or castrating woman is a popular concept, originating in condemnation and contempt. But it is possible for a woman to be a top executive without feeling she is destroying a man or turning into a man.

It does not have to be either/or. If a woman has faith in herself, has conviction about her job and is competent, she can be a professional and a housewife, a success in both areas. Her aim will not be competition with men but a chance to be equal in areas where she has met only with subjugation. There are, of course, dominating women who try to run the lives of others. They lack empathy, consideration, respect for the other person's right to make his own decisions. But this also applies to men. Lack of concern about the feelings and vulnerabilities of others is a matter not of gender but of failure to resolve conflicts of childhood around "Who's the boss?"

Women have idealized men and acted as though it was a man's world in which they, the women, were second-rate citizens. Each time women assumed a role traditionally masculine, they exaggerated the damaging effect on men, imagining they were somehow harming men, then suffered unnecessary guilt. Part of this grew out of their repressed anger at men for forcing them to be subservient for so long.

For a woman to enjoy a leadership role, ascend to traditionally top masculine positions, she has to respect herself as a woman. She has to realize no man suffers because she engages in work formerly denied women. A woman may feel perfectly competent as administrator, cooperating with men in the organization, just as a twelve-year old girl can feel competent as a shortstop on a little league team, cooperating with the boys who play other positions. Over the centuries women have felt "beneath" men in most spheres of life and it may take time before they feel less guilty when *not* beneath a man economically, socially and professionally.

One woman who had never worked arranged with a real estate broker to put the down payment on a house for her family. After she returned home from his office she felt depressed, then guilty. That night she angrily asked her husband why he did not take care of the closing. He explained he had to argue a case in court and thought she could handle it by herself. Later she wondered why she had lost her temper. She thought of her mother and how she would never have dared conduct business matters.

The wife realized she had believed it masculine to cement a business deal, then felt guilty as though depriving her husband of his rights. The next morning she apologized to her husband for her burst of anger.

One young wife felt guilty when her husband offered to help dry the dishes, hearing her mother's voice, "I can't stand a man in the kitchen." This wife thought that allowing her husband to help with the culinary chores made her feel unfeminine and him unmanly. Much of women's guilt has to do with her fantasies about what she does, not the activities themselves.

Guilt about abortion, now more prevalent than ever, seems the rule. While abortion has many religious, ethical, economic and psychological aspects, studies reveal that regardless of the complexity of women's motives in getting rid of the prospective baby, many view themselves as murderers. There is a tendency for most of us to view abortion with guilt because we unconsciously think of the fetus as a full-grown child being slaughtered.

Some women feel guilty because they were born girls, sensing their parents, or at least one parent, wanted a son. A little girl may receive the message early in life from a mother or father that she was meant to be a boy and feel confused and unwanted. Such feelings carry into adulthood and influence how she feels about her body and self-image.

Other women view their vaginas as wounds out of which blood flows and consider the bleeding as punishment for wished-for crimes of passion or revenge. A woman may also believe her vagina is a wound because she unconsciously wants to wound a man and take away his penis as a symbol of sexual and aggressive power. Over the centuries natives in some primitive tribes have mutilated their slain enemies by cutting off the penises to symbolize the end of their power.

Many a woman believes her body inferior to a man's—she envies men their power, feels deprived, angry and therefore guilty. A *New York Times* article in April 1985 by Daniel Goleman, stated, "Women tend to distort their perceptions of their bodies negatively." He quoted authorities as saying the body image "is so crucial to a person's very sense of self, that distortions in it can have significant effects. These range from enhancing or impairing one's general sense of well-being to creating a susceptibility to mental disorder."

He also reported, "Several studies have found that women are far less satisfied with their bodies, particularly their weight, than are men." And, "One major difference between how men and women feel about their bodies centers on the middle of the torso, from hips to abdomen, according to a national survey. Women tend to be least satisfied with that zone of their body, while men tend to be more satisfied."

In a phallocentric culture like ours, it is not surprising women envy men. In early primitive societies men and women worshipped the Great God Phallus and our secret hearts still beat at times to jungle tom-toms. Deep within, we are not too different from our ancestors who lived in caves, hunted in forests and fought off enemy tribes with sticks and stones. Instinctually speaking, men and women have changed not one whit through the ages.

Theodor Reik, writing in the 1940s, maintained that women feel as much hostility as men but are "less violent, less inclined and less able to commit violent deeds than men." In *The Need to Be Loved*, written in 1963, he says, "We know there are fewer murders committed by women than by men. Murderous assault and bloodshed, killing and massacres are very rarely consummated by women. No doubt some women are capable of it, are bloodthirsty, but they rarely commit homicidal acts."

He cites as example that "as masculine a woman as Lady Macbeth," tempted to murder the king, "shies away from it at the last moment," and quotes the lines:

> *Had he not resembled*
> *My father as he slept, I had done't*

Reik comments that perhaps these lines "do not give the whole story. Something within her resisted the bloody deed." He believes that women, for biological reasons and because girls are early educated by their mothers to suppress violent tendencies, do not develop "intensive drives of brutal force." Women are not perhaps the "weaker sex" in the conventional sense but use means other than violence to achieve their aims. Because woman is "the perpetuator and guardian of life," allotted the role of continuing the existence of the species, she is less likely than man to become violent—"Lady Macbeth is to be considered the exception that proves the rule."

But times have changed. Studies show that today more women commit crimes and their crimes are more serious. A startling statistic in *Wife Beating: The Silent Crisis* by R. Langley and R. Levy shows that one-fifth of married women now beat their husbands in a turn of the sadistic table. In the book and television film *The Burning Bed*, a wife sets her husband afire (along with the house) after suffering years of brutal beatings.

A new kind of guilt for women was revealed in the espionage case involving John A. Walker Jr. His former wife, Barbara, who married him in 1956 when they were both nineteen and divorced him in 1974, reported him to the FBI which then charged him with spying for the Soviet Union since 1967.

One of the Walkers' daughters, Laura Walker Snyder, told a *New York Times* reporter on June 17, 1985 just after the headlines revealed the charges, that her mother was consumed with guilt, saying, "She doesn't want to live any more. She wants to die."

In a *New York Times* story on June 21, Mrs. Walker explained the reason she finally turned in her former husband. Laura's estranged husband had kidnapped their son and was threatening to expose John Walker if Laura tried to take the boy from him. Mrs. Walker may have felt if anyone was going to expose her husband, she would be the one, the woman scorned who wanted revenge. She later revealed that over the years her husband had been promiscuous. She explained, "He always tried to make me believe that he was going away for espionage but that was a lie: it was a cover," implying he was seeing other women.

The story is a very complicated one but it seems evident Mrs. Walker felt guilty knowing her husband was accepting money from the Soviet Union for betraying high level secrets damaging to the country's national security. When she finally revealed his activities, that guilt must have eased but then, as her daughter said, she felt so guilty at betraying her ex-husband she "wanted to die."

Her long-delayed betrayal no doubt was instigated in part by his "betrayal" of her and the children in the many affairs with other women. It is significant that when she learned her son-in-law was about to reveal her husband as a spy this motivated her to turn him in first, wanting revenge and also wanting to purge her conscience as far as her country was concerned.

Women feel unrealistic guilt on many fronts. In trying to be equal to men, some women think they must display the undaunted courage and physical strength of a man. Women have told their therapists, "I feel guilty when I show my dependency. Or vulnerability. Or physical weakness." Many women believe that to prove they are capable of holding jobs they must not only be like men but supermen. They reproach themselves for not being able to consistently flex their intellectual as well as physical muscles. They demean themselves when they cannot perform all the tasks their husbands or lovers carry out. They feel guilty when they surpass a man on the job, show a superior intellect, drive a car more expertly or earn more money. This guilt comes from their denied wishes to triumph over men in the war of the sexes, waged since Adam and Eve.

A MAN'S GUILT

The contemporary man, the man of the 1980s, tends to feel guilty when he finds himself still wanting to dominate the woman and shows signs of what society now calls "male chauvinism." His father and grandfather could get away with calling woman the "weaker sex" but because of the new liberation of women and the stress on equality, many of today's men feel embarrassed and ashamed if they dare feel pride in their virility. They are constantly urged to renounce the differences between themselves and women. We hear much less the French expression, *"Vive la différence!"*

Though men today are inclined at times to feel guilty when they show strengths their female counterparts lack, they also struggle with a different kind of guilt. While many of the distinctions between man and woman are becoming increasingly blurred, contemporary man is still influenced by the way he was reared as a child at a time differences between the sexes were clear and widely accepted.

Today's man still experiences the voice from his conscience which warns, "Be strong, be tough, never show your vulnerability." When men display what they consider a weakness such as tears they are overcome with shame and guilt. At the same time they feel guilty if they assert themselves. Thus today's man not only worries about appearing vulnerable but is upset if he emerges as too powerful.

Because many men are conflicted about their roles and unsure of appropriate feelings and behavior, more men are reluctant to marry. Said one perplexed single man, "I'm not sure what a woman wants." These were Freud's words seventy-five years ago, though today there is more uncertainty about what a woman wants because she has more choices. Many single men consciously avoid the liberated woman because they fear being trapped into marriage and made subservient.

The anger some married men feel is shown in the increasing number who "batter" their wives and abuse their daughters. Primitive, savage anger is always a part of the battering-wife syndrome and of incest, a violent act toward a child or adolescent. One of the reasons for the increase in wife battering may be the belief of a number of men unsure of their masculinity that a show of violence keeps them from being thought feminine, a threat to the "macho" image. They are unaware the most masculine men of all are tender toward women, not violent.

A husband made supper for his four-year old son while his wife attended a meeting of the Parent–Teacher Association. He felt furious and depressed as he heated the lamb chops she had bought and boiled the string beans she had prepared. When she arrived home at eleven P.M. he accused her of turning him into a woman. She felt hurt and he then felt guilty for his unwarranted attack. On reflection he realized he had overreacted because he felt demeaned at cooking and serving dinner. He asked himself why he felt that way, since many outstanding chefs were men. He then thought of his father who had never stepped into a kitchen, who had warned his wife, "That's your province and don't you dare ask me to wash a dish. I'd rather starve. Cooking and cleaning up is woman's work."

The man's guilt had been excessive because of his identification with his father—men were not expected to carry out the menial chore of cooking or cleaning. But times were changing, he thought, and perhaps he had better get used to helping out in the kitchen. He apologized to his wife, explained why he had lost his temper. She said she was sorry she made him feel so upset. She added she had thought perhaps he felt abandoned when she left him to handle the dinner and that was the reason for his anger. He confessed he had also felt she was deserting him.

Many husbands feel threatened when a wife initiates sex, hearing voices of the past rebuke, "Only the man should indicate when it's time for sex." Men feel women are taking over their prerogatives, stealing their masculinity, forcing them to play the part of the woman. They then feel very angry and guilty.

It is understandable that men, who have been taught the traditional tasks like nurturing children, cooking or cleaning the house belong to women, feel angry and guilty when asked to assume these roles. They believe they *become* women, fail to understand that to cook or to clean does not mean giving up masculinity. In their fantasies they equate the performance of a traditionally feminine chore with castration.

A father felt angry and guilty as he read a bedtime story to his three-year old daughter. He thought of his dead father's voice saying in contempt, "How can a man read such drivel to a child? That's a woman's job." His father had never read to him and he was still trying to act like his conservative father, his image of "man."

Another husband felt guilt at enjoying gardening in his yard. He heard his father's voice saying, "Only women tend the flowers." Still another husband, vacuuming the living room, thought, "If my mother or father could see me now, they'd drop dead of shame." Then he realized his mother had never worked to help support the family as his wife was now doing and he had better accept changes.

A number of men, especially the younger ones, are adjusting to the new roles, find pleasure in them, are willing to share household tasks with wives who hold jobs. A man may find it hard to sit passively by a wife's side as she drives. He may want to criticize the way she handles the car as he tries to buttress his self-esteem. Imagining she is robbing him of his virility, he may accuse her of wishing to be in charge by taking the driver's seat. After his attack, he feels guilt and apologizes. He could spare himself the anger and the guilt if he accepts her offer to help out in this chore with calm and pleasure, realize it has nothing to do with his masculinity. Actually he should feel relieved as she takes over the task of coping with possible dangers so he can, for once, enjoy the scenery without needing to be constantly alert to the recklessness of other drivers. He also should be aware women have felt equally demeaned when forced to be subservient, relegated to the back seat in many ways.

The more a man can accept his masculinity, regardless of where he may sit in a car, the less guilt he will suffer when his wife shows leadership in any way. Just as the more a wife can accept her femininity, regardless of what act she performs, the less guilt she will feel.

Both men and women would be less guilty if they recognized an important psychological truth. Behavior in and of itself does not make one masculine or feminine. Men can be nurses and women airplane pilots and neither has to view the profession as "sexist." If a woman becomes a pilot, in no way is she throwing a man out of the cockpit. If she is promoted to a top position in her advertising agency, she is injuring no man. The unreal reason many successful women feel guilty is because they view their achievement in a masculine world as a hostile act rather than an assertive one. They think of achievement as "getting even" for past subjugation rather than "sharing" a new equality.

In some ways the sexes are merging, they even look alike. An amusement park in California posted the sign, "Guess Your Sex." This referred to the similarity in hair styles and attire of men and women, even unto women wearing tuxedos. "Unisex" beauty parlors exist in most of our cities.

It is natural to feel uncomfortable when roles shift. We especially question who we are as we embark on behavior different from the past. Eric Fromm in *Escape From Freedom* says that as much as we all want to be happier, when we are courageous enough to expand our horizons we face the danger of added guilt because we defy voices that once warned, "Do as I do." Or, "Don't do anything I say you can't do."

85

The new equality makes many more men and women ask, "Who am I?" The search for the "I," or the "real self" seems a quest on the part of many thinking men and women today. They want to end the suffering that has contributed to the hate they feel and the guilt.

NEW BATTLES BETWEEN THE SEXES

As society has changed its attitudes toward sex during the last decades, the status of both men and women has dramatically altered in other realms of life. This century alone has probably brought more freedom to women than all past centuries. As well as new guilts to both men and women.

Formerly a woman had a clearly defined role—to care for her husband and children. Man's role was to provide wife and child with the necessities of life, whether he worked on the farm or, after the Industrial Revolution, in a factory or as a lawyer, doctor, financial specialist, carpenter, corporate exec-utive—areas virtually barred to women until the middle of this century.

The concept of woman as economic, political, social and sex-ual equal to man is new in the history of civilization. It took centuries to acquire even partial equality. But today men as well as women stand behind equal rights. Women are no longer confined to the caring, nurturing role but have become qualified leaders in fields once open only to men. During the 1980s Sandra Day O'Connor became a United States Supreme Court Justice and Geraldine Ferraro was the first woman can-didate for Vice President of the United States. The bottom line is that over fifty percent of married women are gainfully em-ployed full time.

The changes in roles for women has created high tension between men and women. When woman's role changes, so does man's. The gaps must be filled, the changes adjusted to by both sexes. When we are uncomfortable about new roles, unsure of who we are at the moment, we have a tendency to

86

be contentious. Many men and women seem in constant strug-gle, appear to argue more, hurt each other more, feel guilt as never before. Perhaps there is a price to pay for all progress.

One change, from the man's point of view, is that as woman gains more power he loses some of his, as though there were only a limited amount of power to go around. Thus the power struggle is more intense as women fight for some of the power of which they were long deprived. Shere Hite in her illuminat-ing report quoted women as still comparing marriage to serf-dom. But times *are* changing in that more women at least feel entitled to get angry and seek revenge for inequities inflicted on them.

The new anger may appear between husband and wife and between men and women who are not married but live to-gether. Along with women's liberation goes the highest divorce rate ever: one out of every two marriages ends in divorce, one million a year. Not only husbands but wives will no longer en-dure what they consider a miserable marriage. They will walk away from a situation that has caused suffering.

A woman, whose mother had remained with her husband twenty-one years though feeling tormented much of the time, told her mother she was getting a divorce after two years. She explained she could no longer tolerate her husband's drinking or constant criticism. She said she felt sorry her mother had to endure her father's psychological cruelties over the years but she felt she lived in a freer era and did not have to be a marital masochist.

Some experts in human relations urge an unhappy wife to give up a marriage, though others warn both wives and hus-bands that the next time around may be just as unhappy if they do not examine why the marriage failed. Marital history has a way of repeating itself unless we face how we have con-tributed to the dissension, tension and conflicts. We are all too prone to blame the partner even though we know it takes two to tango, emotionally speaking.

There is a tendency in second and third marriages to select the same kind of person as in the first. Most of us are unaware

87

our unconscious conflicts determine the choice of marital partner. If a woman has suppressed anger towards a sadistic father, she is likely to fall in love with a man who will be cruel to her, whom she will then hate. If a man feels angry at a possessive mother he will unconsciously choose to love a dominating woman and may become furious at her domination, find it unbearable.

Marriage never cured a neurosis and never will. Marriage never eased guilt and never will. Marriage tends to heighten anxiety, anger and anguish. Switching partners, like changing jobs, will not make us happier unless we come to grips with what makes us feel guilty. Divorce is frequently resorted to by those who cannot divorce themselves from their neuroses.

One reason for the increased guilt in men is they feel more threatened by women who have become more aggressive sexually. At the same time, single women report that the right to have sex with whomever and whenever they want has not brought happiness nor husbands. Sex is no cure-all for inner misery. Many irrationally blame the men they meet for not following through after sex with marriage proposals. Some say, in sour grapes style, "I wouldn't have accepted the offer of marriage anyhow, he wouldn't have made a good husband." The issue is how well the person knows himself and his partner after the act of sex.

All in all, the battle between the sexes is still waged as fiercely as ever, with guilt rising high on both sides. Few are without guilt when they feel hatred enough to fight. Few have been able to tone down their competitive strivings, which make them turn their sexual partners into enemies.

Guilt recedes only when men and women face reality and recognize that neither sex is superior. Sexual intimacy and love can be enjoyed only when each realizes the limitations of the other that provoke frustrations. When both sexes accept the irrational child in themselves, guilt will vanish, along with the highly competitive spirit that seeks to vanquish the opposite sex.

6

SEX, LOVE AND GUILT

THE CONFUSION BETWEEN SEX AND LOVE

"Against all the evidence of his senses the man in love declares that he and his beloved are one, and is prepared to behave as if it were a fact," Freud said. We are brought up with the illusion there is such a thing as perfect love. Sleeping Beauty, awakened by the Prince's kiss lives happily ever after, enfolded in his arms. Cinderella steps into the proper shoe and love enduring is hers.

Through the ages poets and philosophers have painted poignant images of love's glory and tragedy with words of highest joy and deepest despair. More has probably been written about the passion of love than any other human emotion. "Who ever loved that loved not at first sight?" asked Christopher Marlowe in the 16th century as he proclaimed love a magical spell merging two strangers at first glance.

Love has been described as a desperate, hungry, craving appeased only by the vision of the beloved. Love and death are placed side by side, as though death were the only answer should lovers be torn from each other's arms. Romeo and Juliet live in all of us.

The belief the wild, wondrous feeling of love can be captured for a lifetime propels many into marriage and joy everlasting, as the fairy tales promise. In rare cases, love may endure until death. Sometimes it lasts for years. Sometimes only for months. Perhaps only for days, before the rapture ebbs and turns to rage and indifference. Possibly the question most asked over the centuries, asked in anguish and sorrow, is "What destroyed our love?"

Why does the ecstatic, fiery, all-consuming passion we think of as love smolder into ashes of disillusionment? What causes a man and a woman who have been ardently drawn to each other at first sight to discover all desire has vanished? As a young woman said after six months of marriage, "What happened to that consuming need I originally felt for my husband? I yearned to be near him every moment. I felt possessed."

"Possessed" is the word. Possessed by fantasies so strong they destroy what we call love. Can it be we are looking for the impossible in our search for love? Are we forced to agree with Shakespeare that

> *For to be wise, and love,*
> *Exceeds man's might; that dwells with the gods above.*

We are brought up to believe "being in love" means making another person happy but this is the antithesis of how most of us really feel. We choose someone who, we believe, will make *us* happy, and forever!

Another illusion most of us have about love is that we consider "making love" the same as "loving." A sexual desire and the emotion of love are two different feelings, though often interwoven. Our sexual desire is lustful, erotic, sensual. It represents, we might say, nature's way of making sure the race is perpetuated. Strangers look into each other's eyes, are instantly attracted, embrace, kiss passionately, enjoy each other's bodies in bed. Out of this comes a child. Nature does not care about much else.

Love is a feeling that develops from the day we are born. We first learn the feeling of tenderness when fed (at the breast or by bottle) by our mothers. Most mothers want their babies though ambivalence is usually present to some degree from the birth of a child on. Love is given by caring, tender parents over the years as we grow up. We bring to later sexual experiences a love that has either matured or remains, in large part, infantile. If the latter, the love for a member of the opposite sex may be outweighed by the hate we have felt as a child for unduly frustrating, uncaring parents.

What we think of as "mature" love is different from what a child feels as love. The child experiences love as a strong need to be close to a mother, to merge with her, to be held and kissed by her. To achieve the ability to bestow and receive mature love is no simple matter, given the complexity of human beings. We all have the capacity for mature love but to acquire the ability to love requires a long process of learning the feel of love from our mothers and fathers.

Some parents, as we find out through headlines in newspapers, cannot care for their children, violently abuse them, even kill them if the children demand too much. Why do a number of mothers and fathers, or the live-in lover of the mother, kill a child at the moment he cries and screams? The child awakens the fury the murderer felt as a crying and screaming child when, in all probability, he was struck by his parents. A double fury is operating—fury at the abuse that caused the killer as a child to feel terrified, and fury at the screaming baby who has revived the earlier terror.

We might say the history of civilization is the history of man's capacity to love. Slowly, painfully, over the dead bodies of millions killed out of hate, we have progressed to a more caring stage when it comes to our fellow man. Time will tell whether it is caring enough to prevent the destruction of the world. We have at least made a few steps forward from the caveman, who was capable of sex but probably not of too much love. We try to take care of the needy and we send millions of dollars in aid when disasters such as earthquakes, droughts and floods kill and injure innocent people.

Sexual gratification can be easily achieved between a man and a woman but the desire for the same person seldom lasts if love is not also present. Love includes an awareness of one's own needs as well as the needs of the sexual partner. For, when love is present, our ambivalence—or rather, the hate in our ambivalence that suffocates the love—can be tolerated.

There is no "perfect" love, just as there is no "perfect" being. The idea that love can be perfect contains the illusion the sexual partner can be perfect. No matter how miserable a man's life has been up to the hour he becomes joined "as one," he may hold the fantastic notion the woman he is marrying will enrich his life as it has never before been enriched. By his side, he believes, stands a tender, compassionate, understanding woman, ready to comfort him always. The trouble is that this tender, compassionate, understanding woman in the flowing white satin wedding gown is expecting the same thing from him. She is thinking, "He will give me everything I have always wanted and will understand and comfort me."

Each makes a preposterous demand, a demand no adult can rationally ever make of another. Each believes he is marrying for love but he is really, or unreally, marrying *to be loved* as the parent of childhood was supposed to have loved him perfectly, but did not.

As a rule after marriage neither partner is willing to compromise or accept the sacrifices necessary to love and each continues to make impossible demands of the other. The tragedy is that so many marriages are based on the childish emotion of wanting to be fully and constantly catered to rather than a sharing of love—which means both giving and receiving mature love.

The idea of romantic love, on which we are all nourished, is antithetical to the love that endures. There is a wide chasm between what young lovers expect and what is realistically attainable in marriage. Romantic love holds in it the overidealization of the beloved, who is, unconsciously, desexualized. The chivalrous, romantic lover throughout history rarely demonstrated his passion physically, except perhaps by a fleeting kiss. This courtly ideal may have derived in part from the medieval cult of the worship of the Virgin, the wished-for virginal mother who, like Mary, could give birth without a sexual partner.

In literature, romantic love was not always requited and often not even acknowledged. Many hearts have been touched by the love of Cyrano de Bergerac and Roxanne. Far from confessing his love for Roxanne, Cyrano wooed her successfully for another man. In *Tristan and Isolde*, after consummation the guilty lovers died.

Since the essence of romantic love is the idealization of the loved one, it cannot possibly withstand confrontation with the reality day-to-day married life brings. Seeing his wife of several weeks in hair curlers or brushing her teeth may fill a romantically inclined husband with sudden disgust. Watching her husband clip his toenails or hearing him pass gas in the bathroom may bring feelings of revulsion to a bride. To some, the first show of anger on the face of a marital partner means the marriage is doomed.

Freud likened the psychological state of the romantic lover to madness. The essence of the romantic ideal is exclusive possession, the demand the loved one show no feelings of love or sexual interest in anyone else. Freud said that anything in which we engage excessively carries with it "the seeds of its own destruction." Romantic love is no exception. As the shadow of reality falls on romantic love, the man and woman start to give less to each other, focus more on their own needs and expect more of the partner. It is the juxtaposition of giving less and expecting more that often sets fire to the romantic ideal and sparks the many angry fights that arise. The childish wish remains strong: "If you really loved me you would know what I need and devote all your efforts to meeting my needs."

Also, because romantic love is idealized love and bound to

vanish, sexual yearnings for the partner may diminish. Many couples refuse to acknowledge that a perpetual honeymoon is an impossible dream, that their feelings will not remain as passionate as in the early days of courtship.

The confusion between sex and love lies at the heart of the dilemma as to why we may possess full sexual liberation according to the codes of society and yet seem unable to establish a lasting, loving relationship with one member of the opposite sex. Too many of us are still children emotionally, demanding, "Me first, the hell with you." We are unable to offer mature love because our childhood demands are still too overpowering.

Because many of us are suffused with childish wishes and cannot respond in true adult fashion to another's needs to be understood, love and protected, we feel intense guilt. The adult in us knows when we act or feel like a demanding, angry child we are hurtful to our partners. We often project our guilt on them as we accuse, "You don't love me or you wouldn't be so selfish."

THE SEXUAL REVOLUTION

We have seen sex become a popular commodity in our culture. That sex has long been considered a commodity is shown in the term "the oldest profession," referring to prostitution, the selling of a woman's body.

Men and women use sex like a drug that will create temporary euphoria. But compulsive sex, like any other addiction, is used to escape feelings that are painful and dangerous to self-esteem. It seems easier to the troubled person to flee into the addiction of sex than take on the more difficult task of finding out why he must resort to such a destructive measure to get pleasure.

If we have developed the conviction that for us to obtain any lasting affection from someone is out of the question (because we received so little love from our parents we are unable to give or share love), then random physical contact may serve as shaky substitute for a lasting relationship. Any port in a sexual storm, so to speak. Sexuality may be the only way some can try to relate, it can assume aspects of an addiction.

Dr. Milton Sapirstein, author of *Emotional Security*, wrote that many men and women indulge in excessive sex with countless partners as a way of trying to work out their personal problems. He comments, "Any long-term relationship built exclusively on this premise would become quite unstable." The idea we must be sexually gratified each time we feel a sexual impulse "results disastrously, leaving the individual with very little tolerance to frustration," he warns. It may lead to isolation, anger and guilt.

If we have the feeling of the forbidden about sex, we will find no lasting enjoyment in it because the terror of guilt stands in the way. Guilt rises like an iron curtain between tenderness, needed for mature love, and sensuality which, devoid of tenderness, is a sign of immature love. A man may have no difficulty feeling sensual with a prostitute but he usually feels demeaned. When tenderness is part of sex, self-esteem rises and there is no guilt.

There is something unique about sex that has fascinated, confused, delighted, troubled and obsessed mankind throughout recorded history. No other aspect of human life seems to have given more joy or caused more misery. No other natural bodily and emotional function has been subjected to more divergent means of regulation or given such a profusion of expressions.

Sexuality is part of every human relationship, from the most intimate to the most casual. Sexuality affects our sense of identity and self-esteem. Sexuality is essential to the survival of man and of cultures. Total and permanent sexual anarchy would cause chaos in society and thus regulations are needed.

Some of those regulations have vanished in the light of the sexual revolution. We can hardly open a magazine that does not feature the most intimate details about sexual behavior. Eros has conquered the air waves as conversations about sexual hangups flow freely between the perplexed and the pundit. Some "off the wall" therapists give so-called advice that can only add to the humorous aspects of sex, as well as the distress of the sexually frustrated.

Sexual therapists claim they help thousands learn how to make sex more exciting and fulfilling. Researchers like Dr. Ernest Dichter have studied how advertisers can profit by appealing to the potential buyer through sex—the man who owns a convertible fantasizes the car as his mistress, long sleek lines in a car symbolize the phallus. Or one brand of perfume is heralded as arousing erotic desires in a sexual partner faster than another brand.

Such exploitation of sex reduces it to an act devoid of love, intimacy and tenderness. It ignores the many emotions involved in this most important act of all human contact. In our cold, mechanical computer age where, if we press buttons we produce fantastic results, many sex therapists seem to advocate pressing parts of the body as if they were love buttons in hope the perfect orgasm will be achieved. Sex has become a mechanical maze for the promiscuous, the swingers and switchers, the adulterers. Sex therapists are like the advertisers of perfumes and shaving lotions who subtly claim their products will lead to heavenly sex.

The purveyors of such platitudes conveniently ignore the fact that to enjoy sex we have to be relatively free of guilt. We can try exotic sexual positions, manipulate our partner's body and be manipulated by our partner, but still not get much pleasure out of sex. If we lack emotional involvement, we are still trapped by past fantasies that restrict our ability to feel free in sex and in love.

Sex may swirl around us but many men and women lack the emotional dimension needed for both love and lasting sex with one person. When sex is "sold" as a product rather than treated as a sensuous experience between two people it is viewed more as a "fix" than part of a relationship. When sex is considered a fix, it can hardly be a tender, intimate bond. Fixes give us temporary elation but they are always followed by disillusionment, dissatisfaction, anger and guilt. Whatever emotional involvement exists comes not freely from our hearts but obsessively from our compulsions.

Our society has taken sex out of the closet and talks about it intellectually but with only a slight understanding of its complexity. And with little compassion for those so guilt ridden they cannot enjoy even a few moments of sexual release, fearful of embarking on any intimacy.

Our culture titillates rather than educates, stimulates rather than enhances and frustrates rather than liberates. We watch stars on television and the movie screen go through the motions of sex, look ecstatic for a few seconds. But rare is the movie or television program that helps us face the fantasies involved in sexual desire or eases our guilt. And rarer still in the media is a movie, television program or book that describes realistic love.

But at least we are becoming freer to acknowledge our conflicts and seek to understand them. For the first time in history both men and women can admit, "I have a right to sexual satisfaction and if I don't think I can achieve it, I'll find out why." Until recently, only the man was expected to gratify his sexual desires. The woman existed to satisfy his sexual appetite. He did not care if she enjoyed little or no pleasure. But now women have achieved equality. They claim the right to fulfillment, no longer sexual servants.

In spite of our sexual liberation, we are still very puritanical. President Carter was severely censured when he spoke of sexual fantasies, of "lusting" in his mind for women. Despite our so-called sophisticated attitude toward sex, many condemned a man of whom we thought highly enough to elect president, for admitting a sexual fantasy. This, if nothing else, shows how deep our guilt about sexual feelings and in this case specifically that parental figures like President Carter should not possess them.

The sad fact is that sexual freedom—the *ability* to enjoy sex—is not the same as sexual liberation—the *right* to enjoy sex. The latter gives us license, the former entails our emotional capac-

97

ity to get the greatest pleasure out of sex, both physically and psychically. To fully enjoy sex requires more of ourselves than perhaps most of us are willing to admit. It means knowing the self fairly well and a willingness to know the partner.

The Bible uses the words "to know" when referring to a sexual act. If our advertisers, sex therapists and television authorities on sex pointed out that enjoyable sex requires knowing the self and the partner—particularly to know what creates guilt about sexual fantasies, emotions and acts—we would not only increase our pleasure in sex but feel far less guilty.

It is ironic in this era of the great sexual revolution that celibacy is endorsed. Though as yet there has been no *Joy of Celibacy* there is a book, *The New Celibacy*, by G. Brown, which provides various justifications of celibacy including secular, religious and moral. Even as our society encourages "enjoy more sex," there appears greater emphasis on celibacy because so many men and women are guilty about their sexual feelings. The celibate feels so guilty he rationalizes his inability to accept a sexual partner. Though Brown calls her book *The New Celibacy*, celibacy is as old as mankind, men and women have always been fearful of and guilty about their lustful fantasies and powerful sexual yearnings.

The celibate is afraid of sex in any form. He acts as though he does not possess any sexual desire or fantasies. He sees the act of sex as dangerous. Excessively puritanical parents often are a major factor in the creation of children who become celibate adults.

Many young men and women in our nation are unable to enjoy sex without guilt, afraid to explore the new freedom even though they make tentative tries. They may talk a good case intellectually for freedom in sex but on an emotional level feel and behave like children. We now swirl in the vortex of the sexual sell which has led many to believe any sexual behavior is permissible under the banner of hard-earned sexual freedom. The danger is many believe that what others do in wholesale manner is "natural." They assume if a certain kind of sexual behavior such as promiscuity is widespread, it is therefore normal and healthy: "Everybody is doing it, why shouldn't I?"

They do not realize what is widespread may be emotionally harmful. Promiscuity may be statistically normal but psychologically debilitating and abnormal, an expression of unhappiness rather than new-found sexual freedom. Real sexual freedom—harder to achieve—is enjoyed through a growing exploration of and attachment to one person in more ways than sexual.

Promiscuity today is not confined as in the past chiefly to married men or women. The young single men and women and teenagers appear as promiscuous as their elders. Two-thirds of all the women in this country have had sexual intercourse by the age of nineteen—almost all before marriage—according to a recent study of population experts at the Johns Hopkins School of Hygiene and Public Health. One in five has had sexual intercourse by sixteen and one in ten becomes pregnant before seventeen.

A twenty-three-year old taxi driver, looking for a wife, asked in despair, "What's a 'good girl' today? One who has slept only with ten men, instead of fifty or a hundred?"

There is vast difference between "sexual license" or sex for the sake of sex and "sexual freedom." The latter encompasses the ability to weld sex and love in enduring fashion. Whereas sexual license is the use of sex for purposes other than love. Sexual license brings in its wake increased unhappiness, a sense of demeaning of the self and partner, the deepening of entrenched conflicts and the depressed feeling that sex has failed to solve the torments of life. Sex alone is never enough to guarantee peace of mind.

The promiscuous live with a hungry need for sex which they gulp as a starved infant does food. They cannot look on their partner as capable of and due respect, affection and friendship but as a sexual "object" soon to be discarded. And soon it is, for the promiscuous person carries a guilt he projects on his partner. He *must* abandon the partner after one or a few sexual encounters because he cannot tolerate anyone who arouses his guilt.

It is interesting to speculate about the effect on promiscuity of the recent outbreak of AIDS and other new diseases reported infiltrating from Third World countries. Nature may have its way of restoring a balance in the essential area of human propagation. Perhaps there will be a renewed emphasis on commitment and monogamy in both heterosexuals and homosexuals as the sexual revolution simmers down.

THE EVOLUTION OF GUILT ABOUT SEX

It seems paradoxical to offer a new paradise in the sanction of sex yet to discover few are able to enter it freely. Why? The answer, in an overall sense, is that though our culture says we may indulge in sex, the child within still feels guilty embarking on the forbidden. The voice inside will not be stilled no matter how liberal society's attitude.

It is not easy to acknowledge the child in ourselves, especially the self-destructive part or the part that wants to destroy others. When we want to insult someone or demean ourselves we admonish, "Don't act so childishly." As a child, we heard our parents accuse, "Be a *big* boy," or girl, or "When are you going to grow up?"

The voices of the past that exist in all of us are stronger than the new sexual freedom. We remain clutched by fantasies that keep us from expressing ourselves sexually without guilt. We were taught as children to feel shame over our bodily functions—excretions, sexual yearnings, sexual acts. We absorbed from parents their shame over sex.

We first learn of sex from our mother and father. They may insist they are sexually liberated but if they do not feel comfortable with the idea their guilt emanates in subtle ways that affect children. Most of the guilt adults feel about sexual desire derives from the taboos placed on them as children. Before we can freely separate from parents' "ethical imperatives" we first have to be aware of their influence.

If a parent feels at ease about his body so will his child. One mother walked around bundled in heavy dresses day and night. Her two daughters never saw her naked body. If her bodice by chance fell too low, she would guiltily pull it up and apologize. Her daughters interpreted this as her feeling of shame in her body and its functions—sinful sex and the extruding of urine and feces. The daughters psychologically adopted this attitude (mother knows best) and also felt ashamed of their bodies and guilty at sexual wishes.

Studies of primitive tribes show that in cultures where parents are free from shame, so are the children. In some tribes children are allowed to masturbate freely. Some permit incest as fathers "show" daughters what sex is all about. In France, passionate kissing on the street between lovers is not considered shameful.

Our sexual hunger starts at the breast, associated at first with a craving for food. If a baby is fed lovingly and tenderly he will, as an adult, accept his sexual hunger as a "good" part of his self and not be critical of his partner's sexual hunger. It is important that the baby accept his appetite both for food and bodily closeness as a natural, "good" part of him. If a mother directly or indirectly implies that feeding, embracing and kissing her baby is distasteful, the baby will feel rejected, ashamed and guilty. He takes these feelings with him into later life each time his own or his partner's sexual needs arise.

During the first two years of our lives, which Freud called the "oral period," we need to be kissed and embraced. The therapist and writer Alice Miller refers to this as the "child's right." If a child considers hugging and caressing his "right," he will feel less guilt as an adult, enjoy both initiating sex and his partner's embraces. Erik Erikson refers to the oral period as the "trust–mistrust phase," when we learn, if properly nurtured, to depend on someone else. To enjoy sex as an adult, we have to have successfully passed through this phase.

The endearing terms some adults use about the sexual partner such as "baby," "sweetie-pie" and "sugar" show the connection to the early days of life when our mouth and the "sweets" that went into it were our first sensations of pleasure. If, during the first year of life, a baby has received tender, loving care he is prepared to give tender, loving care as an adult. But if parents feel guilty about their child's appetite for food and love, the child will feel all forms of appetite are "bad." If a baby has not had the chance to enjoy being cuddled, hugged and freely given time and care, frequently his appetite at the breast or bottle is stifled. As an adult he will feel guilty about foreplay such as kissing and other orality in sex.

If parents openly or subtly condemn a child for "touching" himself in a masturbatory act, the child feels he has done something furtive and forbidden and will carry this guilt into adulthood. He will find it difficult to enjoy touching his partner during sex or allowing himself to be touched. A child may ask questions about his sexual organ or exhibit it, only to see a disapproving or fearful expression on the face of his mother or father. Or hear the sharp words, "I don't want to talk about it," or "Stop that at once!" The child will then feel confused, angry and guilty. Or a parent may change the subject quickly, draw the child's attention to something less frightening to the parent. The child will conclude both his sexual organ and sexual desire are "bad" without a word spoken by the parent. The child will feel guilty both at having brought up a matter of which his parent obviously disapproves and for wishing to explore his body. This guilt will influence his adult behavior.

How parents behave sexually toward each other also influence the child's later attitudes toward sex. If he sees them express affection and tenderness, he will be affectionate and tender with members of the opposite sex. If his parents act violently toward each other, he is apt to be violent toward those he supposedly loves. If his parents neglect each other, he is apt to be indifferent to loved ones. A parent who is seductive to a child may turn the child into a seductive adult or one so afraid of sex he will feel uneasy at a kiss or tremble in fear when hugged or embraced.

A man in therapy was compelled to have sexual relations in the dark, unable to look at his partner while making love. He also cringed each time he touched the woman or she touched him. This man was constantly reliving a refrain he learned in childhood from his parents: "To look at your body, to touch your body is a sin. To look at or touch somebody else's body is even more of a sin."

In the unconscious part of the mind looking and touching may be equivalent to hostile devouring—we speak of "devouring" someone with our eyes. A "sexual appetite," if hearty, is frequently repudiated. To engage in foreplay such as touching, seeing, being touched and seen, is equated with a cannibalistic act.

The early experiences that affect our bodily functions are important in shaping not only our later sexual behavior but our personality. They set the emotional stage for such characteristics as stinginess or generosity, optimism or pessimism, the ability to achieve or the wish to fail. And, most vital, the capacity for giving or withholding love and for controlling or expressing hate, thus affecting the amount of guilt we feel. These early experiences relate to our toilet training, which usually occurs during the second year of life, a phase Freud referred to as the "anal period."

The child also learns from his parents the feeling of devotion, part of loving. Not "blind devotion," which is self-destructive because it leads to crippling attachment rather than freely given love, but a devotion that enables the child to gain what Erikson calls a "sense of trust."

Unfortunately, many of us experience mistrust as a result of shame rooted in the early experiences that affect our bodily functions and emotions. If a parent, for instance, humiliates a child over slowness to learn bladder control, the child will feel what Helen Block Lewis in *Shame and Guilt in Neurosis* describes as "humiliated fury."

Shame may inhibit the exhibitionistic wishes all children have if they feel disgust at the wish to show off their bodies. Lewis maintains women are more likely to feel shame and guilt than men. She believes a woman is more apt to grow "red with shame" as blood rushes to her cheeks if she is caught naked, or in the act of urinating or defecating. Perhaps women in our culture feel freer than men to reveal embarrassment and shame, while men try to inhibit shame.

Many children go through shaming experiences. Some adults recall the times as children they "wet" their clothes when they became excited and did not as yet have full control over the urinary tract. There were also times they vomited if they ate food that disagreed with them and, seeing the look of disgust on their mothers' faces, felt ashamed. For many women, shame occurred when, as girls, for the first time they emitted the blood of menstruation.

When adults do not enjoy themselves sexually, they usually feel like children, associating sexuality with bathroom performances. The phrase "put out" implies that unconsciously the speaker views sex as "putting out" for his partner as, like the child, he "put out" on the toilet for his mother. He feels compelled to give and give, with little or no satisfaction. Many a man who suffers from premature ejaculation or impotence is trying to get sex over with or avoid it. He feels a sustained sexual experience is comparable to satisfying a demanding mother who can never be pleased.

Women sometimes refer to sex as a "wifely duty," implying they have to perform, rather than share intimacy. Some sex therapists call the sexual act a "performance." When adults think of sex as "putting out" or "performing," they will resent and dislike their partners before, during and after sex. They may be so guilty about their anger at having to "perform" that they inhibit sexual activity, as the impotent do.

The final stage of our early sexual development, occurring at three or four is the "phallic-oedipal," which follows the anal stage. During the oedipal stage we become aware of sex differences, feel a growing, passionate attachment to the parent of the opposite sex. This prepares us for our later wish to enjoy sex with an appropriate member of the opposite sex. Our wish to have the parent of the opposite sex all to ourselves is accompanied by the wish that our rival, the parent of the same sex, disappear forever. We feel guilt both for the wish to steal the parent from his proper partner and the wish to do away with the parent of the same sex.

If we have not become fairly emotionally free of dependence on parents, we remain too strongly attached to our oedipal wishes. As adults we will unconsciously fantasize our sexual partner as the desired parent of infancy and feel guilty at breaking society's strongest taboo.

The wish to make the later sexual partner into the parent of the opposite sex on whom we bestowed our childhood erotic feelings exists in all of us. We cannot escape it. It is a normal, necessary wish at an earlier stage in our sexual development. Some are not able to transfer their earlier sexual passion to an appropriate member of the opposite sex because they are still too tightly bound in fear and rage, as well as desire and love, to the parent. And of course, bound in guilt.

SEXUAL GUILT IN ADULTHOOD

A wife who turns sexually cold toward her husband is frequently still in love with her father. A man who rejects his wife is often sexually under the spell of his mother. Our highly eroticized culture rarely mentions the most powerful reason we do not have fully rewarding sexual lives—the tendency on the part of many of us to turn our partners into parental figures. We then feel guilty as we experience ourselves as a child engaging in a forbidden incestuous sexual act. We may also think of adult sex as a triumphant, hostile conquest over the parent of the same sex and, because of this forbidden fantasy, become so guilty we no longer enjoy the marital partner.

A number of men are potent with mistresses or prostitutes but impotent with their wives. The reason: guilt. They unconsciously fantasize their wives as mothers. They *wish* their wives to be the mothers to whom they are still too emotionally attached. If another woman does not symbolize "home and mother," she is a safer sex object because she does not arouse oedipal guilt. The same applies to a wife who unconsciously thinks of her husband as her father and seeks men with whom she feels sexually freer.

A young husband after two years of marriage no longer desired his wife sexually and became impotent, though he felt he still loved her. He found a mistress, justifying the affair because he no longer could have sex with his wife. He made the mistress the "bad" woman, the prostitute for whom he felt no love but strong sexual desire, as the wife became the "good" woman, with whom sex did not rear its "ugly head." Then his mistress persuaded him to stay with her for two weeks in a rented cottage on the ocean at Montauk, along the eastern edge of Long Island, New York. There she cooked for him, worried over him, took care of him as his wife did. He hardly recognized the carefree soul he visited during stolen hours when he wanted only sex. He no longer found her sexually desirable when she too reminded him of his mother.

It is sometimes difficult for adults to accept that what activates their sexual inhibitions and guilt is the "child" within who is still in control of their fantasies. This child turns desire into helplessness, independence into dependency and sexual acts into dirty play.

Stirring the guilt of adulthood is another sexual aspect of childhood. Theodor Reik mentioned in *Listening With the Third Ear* a psychological situation that may inhibit us sexually, make us feel anxious and guilty. He theorized that when the sexual act occurred four people were present. The man, the woman, the man identifying with the woman in himself and the woman identifying with the man in herself.

We all have one part that is male, another, female, called "bisexuality." It is obvious in children, who are attracted erotically to both sexes. They want to hug and embrace men and women indiscriminately. They seek the feel of a body close, they do not think in terms of "right" and "wrong," or "moral" and "immoral."

As adults we may feel guilty about that opposite sex within.

A man may be guilty about his feminine feelings, a woman about her masculine feelings. If we are too guilty about our bisexuality, we will not enjoy sex fully. The identification with our partner, the opposite gender, becomes too dangerous.

The normal development of psychosexual growth ends by our becoming a man or woman in the fullest sense—capable of enjoyable sexual activity, capable of giving pleasure to someone else, capable of restraining our hate except when it is justified. We have a long way to go from the complete self-centeredness of our first months on earth to the point where we can freely feel for someone else what was originally self-love.

Two things are involved. First, we have to give up much of our egocentric childish narcissism, replacing it with realistic self-esteem. And, second, we have to accept, then master somewhat, our ambivalence—the great swings between love and hate. Otherwise, to quote Dr. Karl Abraham, a famous psychoanalyst, "Every attraction to another person is, as it were, sicklied o'er with the pale cast of auto-erotism."

"Genital" or mature love implies not only that we use our genitals as the primary part of sexual intimacy but that we have the ability to enjoy the other person as friend and companion as well as lover. We have come to terms with destructive impulses of childhood, both the oral impulses when we wished to eat someone alive if we felt anger, and the anal impulses when we wished to urinate or defecate on someone who infuriated us (at least not wishing to annihilate them, as in the oral stage, only humiliate them).

As we grow up, the early fears, anxieties and guilts should diminish since the dangers of each stage, in reality, lose their force as we learn to use reason. The degree of the lessening of fear, anxiety and guilt depends on how loving and wise our parents, how threatened by them we felt in childhood and how intense the fantasies we call into use as defenses against the pain of our early terrors, rages and guilts.

Many of us live as though the old dangers still swing overhead, the sword of Damocles of daily life. We are not directly aware of the earlier torments but live oppressed by the feeling that something unknown and terrifying threatens us. Something from which there seems no escape and against which we are powerless. We remain childlike in our reaction to danger, fear unreal assassins. But fantasy, which seems to many less painful than facing reality, is often more destructive, otherwise no one would go mad.

The woman who cannot sleep at night fearing a burglar will break in and rape and murder her is more terrified by this fantasy than by any threat of an atom bomb. Her fear is caused by the wish her first love (her father) had seduced her because she loved him so much, and the guilt that followed such a reprehensible wish, which could only result in punishment by death.

Each of us, in our own way, depending on the thousands of emotional experiences in our lives and the shaping of our passions as we relate to our parents and their passions, learns to accept the sexual pleasures open to us. We also try to control our angry impulses, except as they are justified by reality.

Along the way of growth, hopefully, we accept the importance of love. We realize that without love, life lacks an essential quality, one that fills emptiness and assuages loneliness. Hopefully, we also learn sometimes we have to work hard for love. It does not come easily to us as adults if, during our early emotional development, love does not form a large part of it. We may have to face in ourselves feelings we have denied over the years in order to achieve the most mature expression of love of which we are capable.

What is this thing called love? The whole of our lives affects the ability to love, produces the failure to love. We either doom ourselves to a lifetime without love or we learn love can be "a many-splendored thing" when it emerges out of feelings of sensuality, tenderness, respect and trust. Then there is no need for the guilt that corrodes and destroys love.

7

DESTRUCTIVE ESCAPES FROM GUILT

MEA CULPA

We try to avoid conscious awareness of guilt because it is so painful. Guilt plunges us into deep abysses of self-despair and self-recrimination. Guilt holds constant reproach to ourselves and we seize any way open to ease it momentarily.

Guilt wears many cloaks to disguise its presence as we, the guilty, feel desperate. But the ways we choose to avoid guilt are far more dangerous than facing guilt itself. Mistakenly, we try to convince ourselves we must at any cost flee the overpowering oppression of guilt rather than learning its causes.

One way we try to rid ourselves of guilt is to blame others by projecting our guilt on them. Another prevalent method is to flagellate ourselves in a number of ways, some obvious, some disguised. These attempts to deny guilt may ease it temporarily but in the long run are apt to hurt us even more deeply.

THE MASOCHIST

An insidious, subtle and psychically debilitating way of coping with guilt was first described in detail by the famous Baron Richard von Krafft-Ebing, a German neurologist of the last years of the nineteenth century. In *Psychopathia Sexualis*, translated from Latin by Dr. Harry E. Wedeck and published in this country in 1965, Krafft-Ebing coined the word "masochist" to apply to a sexual perversion. He named it after an Austrian novelist, Leopold von Sacher-Masoch, born in 1836 in Galicia.

As a baby, Sacher-Masoch was so fragile he was not expected to live. But he began to thrive when his mother handed him to a robust Russian peasant to be nursed. This was a woman, he later wrote, from whom he gained not only his health but his "soul," according to Krafft-Ebing's story of Sacher-Masoch's life.

As a child he was strangely drawn to cruelty, fascinated by pictures of executions and stories of martyrs. As an adult he dreamed regularly he was chained and in the power of a cruel woman who tortured him. This actually happened, for he remembered at the age of ten he took part in a scene of violence in which a countess, his aunt, played the leading role. It was an experience that strongly affected his later sexuality.

The countess was a beautiful but wanton woman and, as a boy, he adored her, impressed by her beauty and the luxurious furs she wore. She accepted his devotion, often allowed him to help her dress when he visited with his mother and sisters. Once, as he knelt before her to slip on her ermine slippers, he kissed her feet and she kicked him. This act filled him with pleasure, he later wrote.

The traumatic scene occurred one day as he played hide-and-seek with his sisters in the home of the countess. He ran to her bedroom, hid behind her dresses in an open closet. Suddenly the countess appeared, followed by a strange man. The boy did not dare give away his presence. But curious, he peered through the dresses, saw the couple embrace and start to make love on the sofa.

At this point the countess' husband, accompanied by two friends, walked into the room. The countess, instead of being embarrassed, rose from the sofa and struck her husband in the face so fiercely he staggered backwards, his nose streaming blood. She then seized a whip and drove the three intruders out of the room. In the confusion her frightened lover slipped away.

At this moment the clothes rail in her closet broke and, shrieking in terror, young Sacher-Masoch tumbled into sight. His aunt turned on him in anger, whipped him. He recalled the pain as intense, yet also felt "a strange pleasure." (Sharing the sexual excitement no doubt first aroused the pleasurable sensation.)

The count reentered the room, kneeled before the countess like a slave, begged her pardon. Sacher-Masoch took this opportunity to run out of the room but not before seeing his aunt kick her kneeling husband. As the boy closed the door he heard the sound of the whip and the groans of the count under his wife's blows.

With this as his vision of love and sex it is no wonder Sacher-Masoch found the whip and dresses trimmed with fur sexually arousing. He always played the part of a slave in his relationship to a woman. He married a shrew who subjected him to endless insults and humiliations. She lived openly with a lover, refused to let Sacher-Masoch visit his friends, made him give up writing novels and earn money at menial jobs to support her.

He finally mustered the courage to divorce her and marry a far less sadistic woman, by whom he had two children. He spent the rest of his days in comparative peace, according to Krafft-Ebing, though his former wife kept sending threatening and abusive letters.

What Krafft-Ebing described in Sacher-Masoch's life is visible to various degrees in many of us. There is unconscious pleasure in masochism because it temporarily relieves guilt. We punish ourselves psychologically to atone for real and imagined sins. In masochistic sex, where the man or woman arranges to be beaten physically, we see how necessary it is to be punished before, during or after enjoying the forbidden sex. Whenever we find masochistic behavior in ourselves or others, we can be sure we are defending against a wish we experience as forbidden and, at the same time, punishing ourselves for guilt over the wish.

There are myriad forms of masochism. A young television executive compulsively always took a shower after sexual intercourse to "wash off the dirt," as he put it. Holding a young woman's body close, engaging in sex with her, to him was "dirty." The more he enjoyed the sexual act, the harder he scrubbed his body with a soapy brush.

Some marital couples undertake sex only after physically or verbally assaulting one another. They unconsciously arrange to quarrel before sex. A wife admitted to her mother that her husband and she always argued before sex, usually about something trivial. The argument served as punishment in advance for their guilt, giving permission for sex.

In actual perversions the sexual partner may urinate or defecate on the masochistic partner, may strike, knife, even kill him, as is occasionally reported by the press in a heterosexual or homosexual murder. In a recent brutal case, a participant who admitted torturing and killing his partner, also confessed he cut out the young man's heart.

Freud coined the term "moral masochism" to apply to the psychological beating of the self as contrasted to physical beatings inflicted by others. By moral masochism Freud meant the constant verbal barrages we heap on ourselves for feeling unworthy, unwanted, "bad." Moral masochism, like physical masochism, is atonement for feelings or acts we believe reprehensible. Guilt takes over our veins and the masochistic thoughts are an attempt to appease the guilt. If the masochist suffers long enough and intensely enough, he may enjoy pleasure for

THE MASOCHIST

a short while. Then he must punish himself all over again in a vicious circle of masochistic orgies.

Masochism is a human characteristic, allowing us to bear psychic pain, to feel for those who suffer, to be charitable. We are all "morally" masochistic to some degree. The severe moral masochist blames himself for every wrong mankind has inflicted and asks for incessant punishment.

The masochist's *mea culpa* hides the revengeful rage he dare not express. Just as the sadist's brutality hides the cowardly fear he dare not face. The masochist is a secret sadist, the sadist a secret masochist.

One reason masochism exists in so many of us is that parents are apt to make us as children feel that as long as we are helpless, needy and subservient to their commands, they will love us. Once we start to show minds of our own, to question them, defy them in any way, they punish us by withdrawing love. To keep their love, we repress many of our desires and our anger.

Some parents make the child feel he must be their rescuer. A depressed mother may cause a child to believe he is responsible for her depression, only he can help bring her happiness. The child may react to this superhuman burden by struggling to be saintlike. The saint turns the other cheek, believes not only must he suffer for his imagined and real sins but for everyone's. He is the masochist of masochists as he denies his strong natural feelings of aggression and eroticism.

Not only saints, but many others believe it their fault if anything unpleasant happens, even to the extreme of assuming blame for stormy weather. They think, when it starts to rain, "What did I do to cause this?" One man said that as a boy, a sunny day meant he was "good" because his mother became depressed when it rained but felt happy when the sun shone. He, like all children, blamed himself for his mother's depressed state.

There are those who believe if they lose someone close in an automobile accident this was due to something they did wrong. Some sin for which they were being punished by the loss. To such a masochist anything less than perfect behavior brings guilt and the threat of severe punishment. He feels his gain is someone else's loss. If he comes across a deprived child, he feels the need to give money, thinking, "I have money, this poor child does not, in some way I have taken it from him." In fantasy he may feel guilty of robbing a brother or sister of the love of a parent, or stealing his mother from his father in the oedipal battle.

A masochistic spouse is ready to assume the partner's unhappiness is caused by his wrongdoing. This relates to the masochist's feeling of omnipotence—anything that goes wrong with anyone is within his power to cause. Masochistic wives and husbands provoke marital distress. One wife believed every time her husband became upset it was her fault, kept asking what she had done to cause his moods. Her oversolicitousness made him even angrier.

In the sado-masochistic relationship two persons join forces to make each other suffer so both can feel guilty. Reuben Fine in *Healing of the Mind* calls this the "sado-masochistic orgy." It is characteristic of many marriages where adults behave like angry youngsters in a power struggle.

The masochist's guilt is so overwhelming he arranges punishment if others do not promptly inflict it. He may provoke anger in a friend to such extreme he shatters the friendship. The masochist yearns to lash out at all who frustrate his omnipotence. His sadistic fantasies are so dangerous that, instead of allowing himself to know his rage, he feels chiefly the guilt and the need to punish himself.

Masochism starts in childhood with the wish to gain revenge on the mother or father who have in some way hurt us. We then think, "But if I destroy my parents there will be no one to love and take care of me and I will die. For these evil wishes I must punish myself." The song of the masochist goes, "Oh what a bad boy (or girl) am I."

A girl of seven was brought to a child therapist by her parents because she was banging her head against the wall, depressed, and her marks in school had plummetted. The therapist learned the first five years of her life she was permitted to get into her parents' bed at times when afraid at night. Then, without preparing her for the change, her parents decided it was unwise to allow her to do this any longer. The little girl became enraged but rather than hitting her parents she lashed out at herself, hit her own head against the wall. Instead of screaming at them, she screamed silently, became depressed and would not study. Her first wishes were sadistic, she wanted to hurt her parents as she felt they had hurt her. Then she turned these sadistic wishes into masochistic wishes so she would not lose her parents' love. This is masochism.

Another dimension of masochism is mentioned by Theodor Reik in *Masochism in Modern Man*. He points out the masochist always needs a witness. He wants someone to watch him suffer—that is the purpose of suffering, to make someone else pay the price for the hurt inflicted on him. By providing himself with a watcher, he also recreates the earlier scenes with a parent, as though to say, "Look what you did to me, see how I am in pain because you didn't love me enough." In this way he obliquely discharges some of his rage.

Reik gave an eloquent description of a masochist: "The lambskin he wears hides a wolf. His yielding includes defiance, his submissiveness, opposition. Beneath his softness there is hardness. Behind his obsequiousness rebellion is concealed."

Though the masochist punishes himself severely for his sadistic wishes, he is often psychologically active despite seeming passivity. "My purpose is to weaken you as you watch me suffer," he says. "You will humble yourself as you see how much you have hurt me. In the end, I will defeat you by a subtle, insidious victory." Reik called this "victory through defeat." Because the masochist's purpose is to hurt his real or imagined enemy through his suffering, he feels guilt for this subtle sadism.

Some masochistic workers in industry, who resent what they believe their employers' sadism, unconsciously become victims of accidents at work or overlook some of the requirements of the job and arouse the anger of employers. In this way the workers discharge their resentments but also obtain punishment for their guilt. Many a patient in psychotherapy resents his therapist for not being the perfect parent who makes him the favorite child. When his wishes go ungratified, the patient feels fury, then guilt. He may unconsciously arrange to maintain his emotional illness as punishment, feels more depressed and anxious, shows what Freud called the "negative therapeutic reaction." Freud also described how patients act out vengeful fantasies with therapists, then punish themselves.

Some men and women feel little or no satisfaction in the sexual act as they carry out the wish to punish their partners. "I will not allow you to feel pleasure by sexually satisfying me," they think. Like the child who will not eat when angry because this would please his frustrating mother. He wants to deprive her of pleasure as he feels she has deprived him.

Dr. Shirley Pankin wrote of "sweet revenge" in her book about masochism aptly called *The Joy of Suffering*. She recognized the hidden pleasure inherent in masochism. For many centuries women, supposedly more masochistic than men, were forced to be subservient. Physical illness and psychological suffering were the main ways women could take a partial, pleasurable revenge on men. It will be interesting to see if women become less masochistic as they gain more equality with men.

THE PLUNGE INTO DEPRESSION

Psychoanalyst Roy Schafer describes self-esteem as "reasonable confidence in the self." If we do not possess that "reasonable confidence," we will feel depressed. The depressed person has little sense of identity, his need for love has remained unfulfilled and he feels furious and guilt ridden.

The depressed person seeks continued and fervent praise, wants constant attention. Inasmuch as such insatiable needs can never be satisfied, he is always ready to attack those close to him. As he asks less of others, he feels diminished anger and an easing of guilt.

Many of us (more women than men, for women have been taught to repress their anger) may react with depression when, like a child, we cannot have our way. We wish to attack those who keep us from achieving our desires, who do not appreciate our true qualities and capabilities. Then we turn the rage against ourselves. We think, as defense, "I don't amount to much or I would be loved more, noticed more, admired more."

If we expect love to be constant and ever present, we are doomed to anger because constant and omnipresent love does not exist on this planet. A wife who has spent hours preparing dinner, then dressing for an important party to honor her husband's employer, might expect her husband to compliment her on the new, black sequined gown she bought for the occasion. If he says nothing except to prod her to hurry, she may slowly build up a strong anger, then feel guilt at her rage, become depressed. Perhaps if she were not so hungry for compliments she could reason that her husband was nervous since much depended on the evening, including his employer's estimate of him.

The depressed person is very narcissistic, frequently insensitive to others, like the wife mentioned, who placed the missing compliment above all other matters. In a sense, we drown ourselves in misery when depressed, as we wish to drown our frustrations and those who cause them. The depressed person also suffers from the loss of the sadist he has temporarily destroyed in fantasy, a villain he needs. Some body is better than no body. The fantasy of destroying an enemy affords at least slight satisfaction. Such is the power of fantasy—possibly the most underrated psychic process of our mind as it makes possible all things in the realm of our imagination.

The depressed person needs others to fill his emotional vacuums. He has never felt sure of himself, never felt trusted or loved, has experienced frustration as rejection. For some, the rejection was real, the child correctly reasoned his parents did

117

not love him when they refused him certain pleasures. But for others, parents were indulgent and the child distorted their acts and feelings. One little boy was heard protesting to his parents at a fair, "Why *can't* I have my third ice cream cone?" a look of hate on his face. Such a child will be a demanding adult usually attacking others, then feeling depressed and guilty.

Masochism shows itself in many self-destructive ways. The masochist uses addiction, accident proneness, converting of murderous wishes into psychosomatic illnesses, to tell the world he suffers a depression that at times makes him wish he were dead. In effect, the masochist is an angry person who hurls his anger at himself.

THE EUPHORIA THAT DESTROYS

Why does someone become an addict, take a substance he knows will sooner or later harm or kill him? He is willing to face an early death or severe crippling just to "feel good" for the moment. Nothing else matters—the rest of his life is swept away as he seeks to fulfill his relentless craving.

Behind the hunger for alcohol and drugs, or any addiction, lies the need of the addict for a far earlier hunger. He yearns as he did when a baby for nurturing from a mother. He seeks to regain the euphoria he felt after he had been fed, when he lay in her arms and dozed off to sleep. This is our first physical and emotional satisfaction and we never fully forget the pleasure of it. Because no woman or man can later create the emotional climate of this earlier euphoria, the addict turns away from all intimate contact with others. Instead, he resorts to an inhumane substance to bring him that sense of "high." He is defying his mother and all women and men, with the feeling, "Who needs you? I'll get my pleasure from a drug or a drink."

But like all masochists the addict pays a price for his addiction, his wish to yield to an euphoria no longer appropriate. Because of his guilt at acting on a forbidden childhood wish, he punishes himself. After his brief escape from the suffering he feels life has inflicted, he feels hungover, depressed, depleted. But he has successfully found temporary euphoria as he says to the world, "I am victor over those who deprive me of what I need. I feel like Napoleon and to hell with all those who make me suffer." But, like Napoleon, he winds up alone on his special island of Elba—the addict's "morning after."

There appears no dearth of those who wish to drown their sorrows in a sea of alcohol. Alcohol diminishes tensions and dissipates guilt temporarily. Alcohol allows ancient fantasies to bubble to the surface of the mind and, for the moment, makes life less painful as guilt takes a back seat. Alcohol helps our self-confidence, we fear no one, fortified by false courage. One reason drunken men seek fights is to prove they have no fear.

It has long been known that alcohol tempers a strict conscience. Under its influence we may feel more expansive, more friendly, more loving. Alcohol, when taken moderately, may decrease hostility. The hero in Charles Chaplin's *City Lights* when sober became effusively friendly after a few drinks. Too much alcohol, however, may also make a man feel more in touch with his angry feelings as his conscious censors weaken. He may offend others as he humiliates himself.

While alcohol, for a short time, may ease guilt and anxiety and loosen rigid controls, it is debilitating in two ways. Physically, it may destroy the liver and other organs. Psychologically, when an alcoholic realizes the next day what he has said or done while inebriated, he feels guilty, suffers over the exposure of his aggressive or sexual acts. Alcohol may bring about loss of job and income, as well as bodily ills from improper eating, for alcoholics often suffer loss of appetite. The alcoholic also risks the loss of disillusioned loved ones and friends, as well as social ostracism.

Similarly addiction to drugs has been harmful to many, including several celebrities, who pay a high price, sometimes with their lives, for the momentary surcease from emotional torment. Even more than with alcohol, damage to mind and body is a likely conclusion. There is no fast lane to the easing of our inner conflicts, only slow going on the road to self-discovery.

Another addiction gaining attention is that of food, either undereating or overeating and then vomiting to keep slim. The food addict feels guilt about his normal appetites—to enjoy sex, life, love, work—all of which activate underlying wishes of fear, anger and guilt.

The anorexic, by starving herself, makes others worry about her health. Parents show concern and doctors encourage her to eat and stay alive. She is trying to starve herself out of hostility, guilty at her insatiable craving for food, as she also shows her wish to inflict starvation and death on those who have hurt her—a wish she turns on herself as punishment. If we examine the very early lives of anorexics we probably would find they were unwanted babies. One anorexic reported as a child she overheard her mother telling a visitor, "I never wanted children."

The fantasy of bulimics is of "eating up a storm" or "eating up people" in a cannibalistic act. The wish and the overeating produce such guilt that the bulimic has to follow up his over-eating at once with starvation, as though to say, "I'm sorry for being such a pig." The addict tells the world in fairly direct fashion the content of his misery and wishes.

If we believe we escape guilt through addiction, we not only deny our guilt but act self-destructively. The harmful effects of both the addiction and the guilt may bring loss of energy, diminished emotional stability, decrease of creativity, disinterest in sex, physical ailments and, in extreme cases, death.

Many of us are addicted to work. Feeling guilt ridden, we try to placate our punitive consciences by overworking. We become the obedient child who never gives into the wish to relax and enjoy pleasures. By constantly working hard, we obey the bombardment of inner parental voices that say, "I will love you only if you work hard, get the highest marks, beat out everyone else." The workaholic may keep himself busy day and night, hoping to alleviate guilt, to squelch the inner punishing voices.

The overactive jogger, compulsive exerciser in health spas, avid tennis or golf player, may be trying to escape the pangs of guilt. Any activity, physical or mental, in which we overindulge may bring on heart attacks or other physical ailments as guilt eventually takes its toll.

Of the many faces of guilt addiction perhaps is the most tragic. The smoking of cigarettes, causing lung cancer, is an open expression of the death wish. Addiction holds a desperation that masochism, accident proneness and depression lack unless they are extreme. Important to all addictions is emotional deprivation in childhood, then rage at those who withheld love and protection, and following the rage as the night the day, anguish and fierce guilt.

ILLNESS AS A CLOAK

A popular way many of us take to rid ourselves of guilt is through what Freud called "conversion"—the converting of emotional sensations and thoughts into symptoms of physical illness. He arrived at this theory as the result of the famous case of Anna O., a young woman treated by Dr. Josef Breuer, Freud's friend and mentor. Freud was a teaching assistant in the research laboratory of the Vienna Institute of Physiology, awaiting his medical degree from the University of Vienna, when Breuer started his treatment of a hysterical young woman. Her name was Bertha Pappenheim (later called Anna O. to protect her privacy when Breuer made public the case for *Studies on Hysteria*, a book he wrote with Freud—the first book about psychoanalysis).

Bertha, whose mother was related to the Warburg family of bankers in Frankfurt, was stricken suddenly with paralysis of her legs and arms, incapacitating headaches, hallucinations and a persistent cough. She refused to eat and her frightened mother called Breuer, the family physician, asked for his help.

Breuer examined Bertha in her Vienna apartment, thought her suffering due to "hysteria," by which he meant a pervasive anxiety accompanied by many irrational fears. He decided to hypnotize her, employing the accepted treatment of the time for hysterical women. Under hypnosis she started to talk about traumatic moments experienced during several months of nursing her dying father, who lay in the room next to hers. As she recalled not only the events but the emotions stirred by them, Breuer noticed that after she came out of the hypnotic trance her physical symptoms disappeared one by one. Her hallucinations vanished, the paralysis left her limbs, her headaches and cough disappeared and she felt hungry, willing to eat.

One day she laughingly referred to what she called the "talking cure," another time she called it "chimney sweeping." Breuer was pleased he had helped in what he thought a remarkable recovery but he talked so much at home about her that his wife became jealous. She asked him to stop seeing Bertha, according to Dr. Ernest Jones in his biography of Freud. Breuer acceded to his wife's request since Bertha now seemed "cured."

He visited her for a final session only to find her stretched out on the bed in the throes of a phantom pregnancy. She was writhing as though giving birth, claiming he was the father of her baby. He felt panic at this hallucination, for not once during the entire eighteen months had she mentioned love in connection with any man, much less him, as he later wrote in his description of the case. Though frightened, the physician in him took over and, since hypnosis had calmed her in the past when she suffered hallucinations, he hypnotized her, tried to reassure her, then left, never to return.

He spoke of the case to no one until finally telling Freud half a year later. Freud became "haunted" by Bertha's 'talking cure," he later wrote—the relation between her memories and recall of repressed emotions to the disappearance of her physical illnesses. After Freud started to treat hysterical women he persuaded Breuer to co-author an article and the book based on cases of hysteria. Freud publicly gave Bertha Pappenheim credit for starting him on the road to the theory and treatment of what he named psychoanalysis.

Bertha thus sparked Freud's understanding of how thoughts, wishes and feelings that induce guilt may be expressed in bodily ailments. A man who feels guilty about his sexual fantasies may become nauseous and vomit to punish himself for the forbidden fantasies. A woman who hates her harsh employer, instead of acknowledging her hate, suffers migraine headaches. A child who feels guilty about the wish to masturbate, converts the wish into a painful paralysis of his right hand.

In "conversion" we repress our conscious wishes because to be aware of them or to express them causes intense guilt. Since the wishes do not get an outlet, they seethe in the unconscious and may cause physical pain as the body tries to come to the rescue of the mind. Body and mind work together in the interest of our mental or physical survival. Through bodily pain we may try to expiate our guilt and then feel somewhat relieved for a while by the punishment.

One woman, asked by a doctor why she thought she suffered such severe headaches, answered with the flippancy that often conceals truth, "Instead of taking off the heads of those who have offended me, I take off my own head."

A man consulted a therapist because his right arm was arthritic. He could hardly move it and had not been helped by the medicines physicians gave. The therapist encouraged the man to talk about his bottled-up emotions and the man mentioned how unhappy he was with a wife who did not understand him. Suddenly he found he could move his right arm freely.

The next morning the man seized a bread knife from the kitchen table and plunged it into his wife's heart. He had unconsciously paralyzed the arm that might wield a knife, knowing how much he hated his wife. When the paralysis was suddenly removed, without allowing him the chance in therapy to talk further of his feelings of fury and wish to murder, he could not control his rage. This tragic case shows how we may cripple ourselves physically when we are furious to keep from acting out our murderous feelings.

A common symptom among soldiers fighting in the Korean and Vietnam wars was backache. While each soldier had his own vulnerabilities and physiological conditions, they all were "converting" fear and anger into a bodily pain that said in essence to their commanding officers, "Get off my aching back, it can't take any more." Unable or unwilling to acknowledge their fear and anger, which would have made them seem cowards, they psychically swallowed it, punished themselves through physical pain that expressed literally what they felt. This is an example of what Reik referred to as "victory through defeat." By suffering they could at least get solace from physicians and nurses, were removed temporarily from the source of danger.

The child who wets or defecates on his bed after the age of four or five is telling the parent he is "pissed off" or that he would like to defecate on the parent as he expresses anger through the forbidden act at something the parent has done to enrage him. In one way or another the child feels exploited and hurt and is letting the parent know by regressing to an earlier, less controlled time. When we are violently angry many of us use the words "fuck" and "shit" to express rage, indicating the bodily activities that originally caused fear and anger in us.

Conversion reactions are popular among children because children do not dare assert anger when they feel hurt. Rather than disobey parents, they catch colds, sweat, turn red faced, have breathing difficulties, cough incessantly, suffer severe stomachaches. Unable to talk of their wishes to be reassured, praised, held close, they become physically ill and get attention, comfort, kisses and embraces.

THE LITTLE HURTS

Accidents do happen but most are motivated by guilt. Among the most prevalent are car crashes, cutting ourselves with knives or other sharp instruments, losing our balance and falling, misplacing money or jewels, taking the wrong way as we ride to important appointments or functions.

A writer of a column on sports for a national magazine, following an ample raise from the editor, felt he did not deserve it. He promptly went to a bar, downed three scotches, then "accidentally" left his wallet behind with $400 in it. When he returned he found the wallet had disappeared, someone had stolen it. He had punished himself for being rewarded with a raise he felt he did not deserve.

As he thought of the careless act that cost him $400 and a new wallet, he heard his father's voice saying one day when he was a boy, "You'll never amount to anything, you refuse to study and you think you know it all." He remembered how hurt he had felt at these words by the father whose love he wanted, how angry he was at his father for tearing him down. When we feel demeaned, then angry, money and success cannot be enjoyed for our guilt prevents us from taking pleasure in our achievements.

A wife, who hurried home after work to cook dinner for a female visitor she did not like, but whom her husband thought they should entertain for business purposes, discovered she had lost the keys to the house. At first she was angry at herself, then started to laugh. She realized the loss of the keys expressed her wish not to prepare dinner for her unwanted guest as she locked herself out of the house. She was also punishing herself for her anger at the guest and at her husband who insisted on inviting the offending woman.

Another woman was preparing for a large cocktail party at her home in honor of a friend who had suddenly fallen in love and married. While slicing the ham, the hostess dealt herself a vicious cut on her right thumb that bled all over the sink. She ran out to a nearby pharmacy to have it bandaged.

125

After the party she wondered why she had inflicted the dangerous cut on herself, the first time she had ever been so careless. She realized she had consciously felt jealous of her friend, who had been able to find a husband, while she had not. The wound represented her wish to sever her friend's new relationship, a wish she turned directly on herself as punishment for her jealous and hostile thoughts. The mind is very literal when it comes to accidents.

A patient in therapy was furious at her therapist for daring to take a vacation. The fury aroused her guilt and she found it difficult to talk of her feelings. While heading for the last session before his vacation began, as she parked her car she accidentally banged into the car in front. During the session she related this careless act to her wish to "dent" the armor of the omnipotent analyst who was leaving her in the lurch to enjoy the summer sun on some distant beach. (It tells where therapists vacation, to learn of the number of patients who speak of "drowning" themselves in the summer.)

When we carelessly slip on a banana peel, fall to the sidewalk, we may be thinking of someone we wish to "put down." When we are careful of what we do, whether driving a car or sauntering along a street filled with potholes, we avoid accidents. Providing, of course, we do not feel too guilty about sexual or murderous wishes, no longer equating them with evil deeds.

"Evil is as evil *does*," not as "evil *wishes* to do." If we can remember this we will eliminate much guilt and the need to punish ourselves.

8

THOSE WHO SEEM TO FEEL NO GUILT

"CRIMINALS FROM A SENSE OF GUILT"

Does anyone *not* have a sense of guilt? We occasionally hear someone described as "without a conscience," or "devoid of guilt." Many of us believe criminals possess little or no guilt. Or at least show large gaps in their consciences.

It often appears criminals do not know right from wrong. They have no respect for the law. Any of us may dream of committing criminal acts—stealing, cheating, assaulting those who threaten us. But we usually do not allow ourselves to rebel openly against the teachings of our parents and society. We hold to the rules that enable us to get along with one another.

The word "psychopath" is used to describe a criminal, though a person may be a psychopath without committing a crime. "Psychopathic" means without a sense of morality or conscience and, therefore, apparently without guilt. The psychopathic criminal acts on impulse, lacks judgment, assumes no responsibility for his acts. He rationalizes his crimes, appears to show no remorse for inflicting physical or emotional hurts on the innocent. Or, if he confesses his crime, he tries to justify it: he is poor, he can find no work, others mistreat him, he feels the world owes him a living, the country, nay the whole planet, is run by a bunch of thieves.

Is it true, as most of us believe, that criminals suffer no guilt? In his brilliant two-page article, "Criminals From a Sense of Guilt," written in 1916, Freud declared: "Paradoxical as it may sound, I must maintain that the sense of guilt was present in the criminal before the misdeed, that it did not arise from it but conversely—the misdeed arose from the sense of guilt."

He continued: "These people might justly be described as criminals from a sense of guilt. The preexistence of the guilty feelings had of course been demonstrated by a whole set of other manifestations and effects."

He attributed what he described as an "obscure sense of guilt" in the growing child as due to the strength of the sexual and aggressive impulses when he becomes attracted to the parent of the opposite sex. A child's guilt, Freud explained, was as "a reaction to the two great criminal intentions of killing the father," or mother, if the child was a daughter, "and having sexual relations with the mother," or father, if a daughter was involved.

He concluded, "In comparison with these two [criminal intentions], the [actual] crimes committed in order to fix the sense of guilt to something came as a relief to the sufferer."

In other words, the crime committed is preferable to facing the fantasies the crime hides. The criminal chooses to commit a crime he considers far less reprehensible than the one he unconsciously wants to commit. His act of crime gives him temporary escape from the fantasies associated with the earlier, wished-for crime. Though the fantasies will soon return— they disappear only as he is able to consciously face and accept them.

A twenty-eight year old man rapes a thirteen-year old girl but to him this act is less sinful than raping his mother or sister—his fantasies as a boy. He repressed the fantasies when they first came to mind to keep his mother and father's love and respect. But over the years the intensity of these fantasies are so strong he is driven to rape the thirteen-year old girl.

None of us lacks a conscience, though it may appear hardened criminals do. Every child takes in some sense of ethics because, no matter how cruel his caretakers, he wants to gain their love and will accept some rules and regulations. But if a child is treated too harshly by parents, conscience or not, he may rebel. One boy of eight started to hit his classmates in furious outbursts. The teacher discovered the boy was beaten regularly, even for a slight infraction, by his father. The father would say "My father beat me when I did what you're doing." The boy did not dare oppose his father but conveyed his father's cruelty by acting it out in direct fashion with his classmates as he played the part of the angry father. Other children may act out a parent's cruelty on themselves, hitting their heads against a wall, cutting themselves with knives, attempting suicide.

"Many people do not recognize the punitive, scolding attitude which they have toward themselves. Raised in a culture that believes parents spoil the child if the rod is spared, they continue to apply the rod to themselves as adults. This is the way they were taught to treat themselves as children—and the 'child of the past' feels anxious and guilty without the excessive punishment characteristic of his early home."

These are the words of Dr. W. Hugh Missildine in *Your Inner Child of the Past*. He goes on: "Such punitiveness need not have been physical. It could have been endless, strict moralizing— the creation of guilt and feelings of utter worthlessness in a child because of his immature behavior at an age when he is naturally immature."

The child, acting on impulse and forever exploring to discover himself and the world around him, cannot "stay out of trouble" in a punitive home, Missildine says. The child neither recognizes his impulses nor can he understand the need to control them, since he lacks adult knowledge and a view of reality. The harsh scoldings, angry beatings or solemn moralizing tend, in a cumulative way, to convince the child "that deep down, he is really very 'bad.' Is he not always guilty? Is he not always 'in trouble'? Could his conduct not always have been better?"

To a child, the words of his mother and father, but especially his mother in the first years of his life, are as words handed down by a god. Some parents, out of their unhappiness, have threatened to kill, or do kill, or act as though they wish to kill, their child. Children sense the parent's death wishes and become fearful, then angry, then depressed both at their anger and because they are not wanted.

Dorothy Bloch, in her penetrating book *So The Witch Won't Eat Me: Fantasy and the Child's Fear of Infanticide*, writes eloquently of the child's fear his parents will kill him and of his use of fantasy and self-deception to defend himself against that fear. The parent's wish to kill the child may be actually verbalized, or acted out in part by brutal beatings, or unconsciously transmitted by depression, inability to care for the child or abandonment of the child either actually or emotionally.

Bloch reached her conclusion after analyzing her child and adult patients for twenty-five years and finding that all of them, from two-and-a-half to sixty-eight, were struggling to win the love of parents as a primary defense against the fear of infanticide. In varying degrees, depending on the intensity of the hate and the violence in their homes, they all were afraid their parents would kill them, or that they might eventually kill their parents. They pinned their hopes of staying alive on eventually gaining the parents' love, an unrealizable fantasy.

Bloch believes the core of neurosis is the fear in the child of being killed by his parents. This fear is based on the vulnerable child's magical thinking which leads him to believe he is responsible for everything that happens to the parent, good and bad. When parents are actually violent toward each other in words or deeds or violent toward the child, his fear is confirmed and his terror intensified. The parents' violence or violent feelings elicit a violent response in the child. This response produces feelings of guilt and anticipation of punishment: the child expects to be killed.

If the very early relationship to the mother is one of distress, if a "peaceful climate" is lacking, the child will grow up with a feeling of "not-well-being," according to psychoanalyst Annemarie P. Weil. In her article, "Early Pathology," she describes the effect of early nurturing that produces an "unstable fusion with the mother." The mother's aggressive feelings toward her child, her hostile thoughts, affect the emotional climate in which the child grows, Weil points out. These hostile feelings hurt the infant's sense of narcissism, essential at this time, which then does not develop naturally because it is too intensely colored with "fantasies" and "readiness for and severity of conflicts."

If a mother shows undue hostility toward her child in his first year of life, he will have "a basic feeling of worthlessness" the rest of his development, Weil states. The child believes his mother is "bad," has caused his distress, inwardly "feels hurt, attacked (not altogether uninvited), or outwardly compulsively attacks" others. The lack of a "peaceful climate" produces self-devaluation, a basic distrust in others and what Weil calls "the basic distrust in fate" that "renders any decision that has to be made an impossible task."

A loving parent does not worry about his child's fear the parent will kill him for the parent does not convey the threat of death. He knows when he is realistically angry and will not project his unreal anger on the helpless child. He also knows his child is entitled to anger when upset or frustrated and does not retaliate with anger. He sets limits but in a gentle, reassuring way so the child senses the limits are for his own good.

The emotionally mature adult realizes words do not have the impact of a bullet on another adult and also knows he will never die from a violent word hurled by an enemy. For adults, an adage holds the truth: "Sticks and stones may break my bones but words will never harm me." Yet many a person has been murdered because the words he uttered inflamed or offended in some way the pride of the killer, who reacted as though he were still a threatened child.

Some parents care chiefly about their own needs, not the child's. Such a parent may swing back and forth between a possessive love and open hatred in his treatment of the child. "You damned brat!" he may shout one moment, then sweep the child up in his arms and hug him fervently.

One mother demanded to know where her thirteen-year old son was every minute of the day so she could "go to his rescue if anything went wrong." Her fear something *would* "go wrong" mirrored her wish some injury would befall her son and she would be free of bringing up a child she inwardly resented. She believed giving birth to him had halted her career as a concert pianist, not accepting that she could have had the career in addition to the child if she had wanted. She was a carbon copy, psychologically speaking, of her frustrated mother who often wailed that her daughter's birth had caused her to give up all her dreams of becoming a famous opera star.

Many criminals have lived with violent parents, unable to give love, tenderness, protectiveness, as most of us know it. Some criminals have had no parents or only one parent, who has usually been angry or depressed, with little awareness of how to bring up a child without displaying anger. The child's capacity for giving love to others is crippled and fragmented. As an adult, he hears the harsh, punitive voices within threaten punishment almost every waking hour, the voices also haunt his dreams. There comes a time he can no longer tolerate them, rebels and commits a crime that will take him out of society and relieve his guilt.

All of us, criminals and noncriminals, psychopaths and nonpsychopaths, respond to inner voices that order us to "do" and "do not." As psychoanalyst Dr. Charles Brenner states: "Whether an adult be a criminal or an ascetic, whether he be a liar or a truth teller, saint or sinner, he cannot be without a superego," that is, a conscience.

The conscience of a murderer was clearly exposed when seventeen-year old William Heirens of Chicago, a freshman at the University of Chicago, wrote in lipstick on the beige bedroom wall of one of his women victims the appeal:

For heavens
sake catch me
Before I kill more
I cannot control myself.

This message from the "lipstick killer," as reporters named him, revealed a conscience appealing to the world to save him from murdering more women. A conscience so overburdened he could not function at times. Unfortunately before he was caught he was to kill and dismember a six-year old girl he kidnapped one night from the bedroom of her home. He was sentenced to 199 years in prison—three consecutive life sentences for three confessed murders. One month after he entered prison he threw a stone at a guard, calling out, "I want to die," further evidence of his guilty feelings.

Why do so many released criminals commit further crimes and return to prison? Studies show that between sixty and seventy percent are "recidivists"—back in prison before long. Criminologists and other human relations experts have discovered on interviewing these men they often feel safer in prison, kept from committing more crimes. They confess that outside of prison they feel anxious and guilty and these feelings are temporarily eased when they return to prison and serve their terms in an atmosphere reminiscent of the homes without love in which they grew up and were frequently punished.

Thus prison provides temporary relief from guilt. The criminal feels he is punished every hour of every day as he is confined to what becomes a "secure" home, albeit a drab, harsh and dangerous one. Some guards will mistreat him and he must always be on the alert against violence by other prisoners. In recent years some prisons have added therapists to their staffs and have attempted a more humane approach to the treatment of prisoners, many of whom as children lived in abusive homes.

One of the reasons we tend to take a punitive attitude toward criminals is because they act out our secret, most terrifying wishes, both sexual and aggressive. We expiate our guilt for the wishes by punishing those who commit what we, in fantasy, feel guilty about. We call the criminal inhuman and bestial and send him far away to a cell enclosed within an impenetrable stone institution manned by guards with guns. This is just punishment, we say, and will prevent him from further crime.

The wish to understand criminal behavior so we can prevent it is not the same as asking that criminals go unpunished. The protection of society must come first. But if we want to reduce crime and prevent crime, we need to understand the complexity of what lies behind the intolerable guilt that drives men to break our laws.

Even men at the top have given in to the temptation to break the law. President Nixon violated the country's laws and was almost impeached for his alleged criminal activities, resigning to escape trial. Though some writers referred to him as a "psychopath," a man without a conscience, he appeared to possess a severe conscience. He prayed to God when the Watergate scandal broke, then revealed signs of a depressed, guilt-stricken man. He had a harsh father, who beat him as a boy and set high moral standards. President Nixon's alleged illegal acts might be regarded as rebellion against a too-strict conscience that constantly admonished him to be perfect. A rebellion that one day broke out into the open in revenge against the punitive past, as though saying to his father, "Leave me alone, I'll do what I want, even though it breaks the laws of the land I have pledged to uphold."

THE GUILT OF MURDERERS

We might ask why the subject of murder fascinates so many of us—in what we look at on television and in the movies. Take a sample of titles that appeared one day on movie marquees:

134

THE GUILT OF MURDERERS

The Shooting Party, Panic in the Streets, A View to a Kill, Prizzi's Honor—about a hit-man and his wife, a hit-woman; *Fletch*, about a detective who solves a murder, and *Fury of the Mad Monk*.

It is no accident murder draws such a vast, tenacious reading audience. Among the top best-selling books each year a number are about murder. We enjoy murder mysteries or true murder stories because the words and scenes about violence ignite our murderous fantasies, allowing them a harmless outlet as we vicariously enjoy murder. We might say that a murder read is a murder (or at least a murderous thought) uncommitted. As we read, we become both killer and detective, we relish the murderer's deed of vengeance, then the chase which brings him to justice. We identify with both sides of the coin of murder—the committing of the bloody act and the capture of the killer, which eases our guilt over our violent wishes. We can go to bed a happier soul without shedding anyone's blood except in our hearts.

It is perhaps no accident that at a time the world is concerned with the possible mass murder of millions of innocent men, women and children, if not the slaughter of the entire planet by nuclear war, that interest in reading about murder, spies and terrorists has risen to a new high.

Our earliest ancestors (whose first weapon was probably a large stone), if they hated someone, clubbed him to death without a second thought. But we, supposedly civilized, armed to the teeth with nuclear weapons and nerve gas, are forbidden to murder a lone enemy no matter how deeply we hate and desire vengeance. We must be content with the sublimation of our hatred and watch, read about or, for some, write of murder—far better than committing it.

The act of murder releases an unbearable inner tension in the killer. He gives release to a torment that has threatened to annihilate him—dammed-up and damnable fantasies that have tortured his mind since childhood. Our psychic mechanism always seeks a balance. If there is too much rage and guilt within, we must somehow release our intolerable feelings and restore the balance of the mind. Some murderers kill so they will not go mad, or commit suicide. In a sense, anyone who takes the life of another is mentally ill to some degree, whether the murder is premeditated or not. Some murderers are covertly psychotic for years before an explosion in their minds drives them to kill.

That murderers suffer from an acute sense of guilt has been revealed by a number of writers, including Truman Capote who, in *In Cold Blood*, delved into the emotionally disturbed childhoods of two young murderers who wantonly killed a family. One of the most intensive probes into the life of a murderer was recently made by Flora Rheta Schreiber in *The Shoemaker* (Simon & Schuster, 1983). She describes in dramatic detail the emotional suffering, the lack of love, the desire for revenge in the mind of Joseph Kallinger.

Kallinger, a thirty-eight year old Philadelphia shoemaker, along with his son, Michael, thirteen, was arrested on January 17, 1975 for breaking into five suburban homes in Pennsylvania, Maryland and New Jersey. During the Leonia, New Jersey break-in, he held eight people hostage as he murdered a young nurse.

Schreiber spent more than 1000 hours over the next six years interviewing Kallinger, in two institutions in New Jersey and two in Pennsylvania. The most significant interviews were at the Camden County Jail (and the State Correctional Institution at Huntingdon, Pennsylvania). Much of his past was reconstructed through his mother and his neighbors when he was a boy.

Schreiber movingly describes the severe psychological damage inflicted on Kallinger as a child. He told her everything he could remember of his past. He even confessed he had murdered his son and a ten-year old boy. She discovered he had been illegitimate. He later learned from his mother that she had breast fed him for a week in a Philadelphia hospital, then, afraid to take him home (she was married, seeking a divorce and had another child) she placed him in a private boarding house. He remained there two months. His mother gave him to St. Vincent's Catholic Orphanage where at the age of twenty-two months he was visited by Anna and Stephen Kallinger, a childless couple seeking to adopt a son (he would eventually help Stephen in his work as shoemaker).

From Schreiber's account, the Kallingers appeared psychotic, or almost psychotic. Their sadistic acting out of sexual and hostile fantasies was revealed when the boy was six years and nine months old. They took him to St. Mary's hospital in Philadelphia for a hernia operation, which left a six-inch scar on his left side. Such an operation in itself is terrifying to a six-year old, but after they brought him home, they terrified him far more deeply.

They told him the doctor at the hospital had "done something else to you, too." They described it as "fixing your little bird," their word for penis, by "removing the demon who lived in your little bird," implying he would be impotent the rest of his life. His adoptive mother's words, he recalled, had been, "Your bird won't get hard because the demon is gone. Always you will be soft there. So you're gonna be a good boy, a good man. Never get in no trouble. Never get a girl in trouble." To them, sex was evil and the only way they could raise "a good boy" was to convince him he could never use his penis. This was a subtle form of castration.

It would be difficult to imagine a more psychologically cruel threat to a little boy. But, in addition, he received little love, tenderness or respect. His adoptive parents never gave him a birthday present nor did they acknowledge the day of his birth, thus denying he even existed. Once, when he was eight, he desperately wanted to go to the zoo with other children in his class but his mother ordered him to stay home and work with his father. For the first time he rebelled, told her, "Dad said I could go to the zoo and I'm going." Infuriated by his defiance of her command, she reached for a hammer used for driving nails through layers of leather. She hit him on the head four times with the heavy steel instrument and the cuts bled profusely.

His father also frequently flogged him with homemade cat-o'-nine-tails made of leather and rawhide laces, slashing away at his back, arms and head. The cruelty was both physical and emotional, for all physical punishment carries with it an emotional beating as well. Physical cruelty also affects sexual desire which then may take on the characteristics of sadism.

At the age of ten, Kallinger started to defy his adoptive parents. He stole rolls of nickles, dimes and quarters from his parents' bedroom to bribe neighborhood children to go with him to Saturday movies. His parents caught him stealing, took him to the kitchen, turned on the stove burner and placed first the fingers of his right hand, then his left hand, into the flames, as his adoptive father intoned, "This will burn the demon thief out of the fingers that steal." Kallinger kept stealing the coins and his parents kept burning his hands—six times more—until he gave up stealing.

It is severe indictment of our adoptive procedures that the Kallingers' abuse of the youth was never uncovered. Not only violence at the hands of his parents but sexual abuse by strangers became part of his childhood. At the age of eight he was homosexually molested by three older boys in a large empty tank four blocks from his home. He did not dare tell his parents for fear they would blame him for not coming home at once, since they had sent him out on an errand, the only time he was allowed out of the house. He had wandered into an abandoned lot which held empty oil tanks and the three older boys had seized him.

Beneath Kallinger's outward compliance lurked a fierce anger he dared not express at his foster parents, and a corresponding depth of guilt. He had never struck his parents even when they beat him or burned his fingers. But when he reached fifteen and was physically larger, his foster parents started to fear his wrath. They agreed to let him move out of the house and live alone if he would continue to work for his father in the shoe shop. He had become an excellent shoemaker.

He fell in love, married, had two children, then was divorced by his young wife after five years. He married a second

THE GUILT OF MURDERERS

time and had five children. He became involved far more than his wife in his children's activities. When they disobeyed, just as his parents had done to him, he punished them cruelly. He set up a "torture chamber" in the basement of his house where he "disciplined" the children, sticking pins into his daughter's naked body, at times beating two of his four sons.

When his daughter was in her late teens and dated a boy of whom Kallinger disapproved, he burned her thighs with a hot spatula, as once his adoptive parents had burned his hands for stealing. He beat one son over the head with a hammer when he disobeyed, as his mother had beat him.

The children finally went to the police and he was arrested, charged with child abuse. He pleaded for psychiatric help and two psychiatrists and a clinical psychologist recommended he be hospitalized. But the judge sent him home saying he was "a good provider" and the children were "better off" with him in the house.

Kallinger's reason now collapsed as he gave in to delusions. Ruled by them, he expressed the fury held back from almost the day he was born. The distorted fantasies that fueled his crimes were insane to the rest of the world—he heard the voices of God and the devil instructing him to kill—but the fantasies made sense to the abused, tormented child within as he sought revenge for the depraved brutality of his adoptive parents. He copied their violence, built on it by actually taking lives through delusional killing.

One day he and his son set out to commit murder and lured a ten-year old Puerto Rican boy away from a swimming pool under the pretext of hiring him for a few hours' work. They then mutilated him sexually in an abandoned rug factory (as Kallinger had been molested as an eight-year old in an abandoned oil tank) and killed him.

Kallinger's delusions grew wilder and wilder and finally he was consumed by a desire to destroy mankind through the destruction of sexual organs (as he fantasized his had been destroyed). His fury from the earliest stage of life when the mouth is the center of an infant's universe (the oral period), was shown in all its horror when he ordered the nurse in the Leonia home he invaded, to bite off the penis of a young man he had tied up in the cellar, intending to kill. When she refused to perform this unspeakable act, he stabbed her with a hunting knife.

Schreiber shows the terrifying power of the unconscious part of the mind when a child is brought up in such emotional danger he cannot keep his sanity. The very early physical brutality crippled Kallinger's sexual development as well as intensified his wish for murderous revenge on his inhumane adoptive parents.

The world is so dangerous a place because so many homes are so dangerous for children. This is what Schreiber is saying as she describes Kallinger, an extreme example of the lesser rages we all hide. His life held trauma that fortunately most of us are spared.

As to his possessing a conscience, Schreiber has since said:

When he was in a nondelusional state he had a very rigid system of values. But when he was in the grip of delusions and hallucinations, wrong became right and not to commit what we call wrong would have been wrong. He felt tortured when he returned to the nondelusional states and realized what he had done, felt enormous remorse. He said to me many times, "Three people are dead because of me. And for no reason. I am not fit to occupy space."

The self-punishment he inflicted for his guilt was apparent in the several times he tried to commit suicide in prison.

In the case of a second murderer, David Berkowitz, who called himself "Son of Sam," we see the formation of a killer who, in childhood, suffered from emotional problems and was exposed to a subtle sexual seduction by both adoptive parents that impeded his psychosexual development. Like Kallinger, Berkowitz was illegitimate and abandoned by his mother at birth.

The words "guilt" and "conscience" appear again and again

in both Berkowitz's words and those of psychiatrist Dr. David Abrahamsen in his book *Confessions of Son of Sam* (New York: Columbia University Press, 1985). Berkowitz talked somewhat freely to Abrahamsen of his childhood and his criminal acts, including the murder of five women and one young man within a year. The victims were all in parked cars late at night having sex. Berkowitz refused to accept the insanity plea, as his attorney wished him to do.

Abrahamsen presents a complete and thoughtful, eloquent description of the early life of one of New York's most haunting killers. Berkowitz answered most of the psychiatrist's questions during fifty hours of personal interviews that started at Kings County Hospital, Brooklyn, when he was first arrested and continued at Attica Prison after he had been sentenced. Abrahamsen interviewed Berkowitz's family, friends, former teachers, co-workers and others who knew him, and conducted extensive correspondence with Berkowitz.

Berkowitz when he was three days old was adopted by Pearl and Nat Berkowitz, who owned a small hardware store in the Bronx. His birth certificate listed his parents as Betty and Anthony Falco. When he was three years old his adoptive parents told him his mother died in childbirth. They also told him his father had been unable to take care of him.

As a boy he never had a chance to resolve his natural, strong oedipal feelings. There was only one bedroom in the small apartment and from the moment he arrived from the hospital, where his adoptive parents had first picked him up, until he was ten, he slept with his parents in their bedroom, though he had his own small bed. Experts in child development advise that, if possible, a child after birth should have a room of his own to guard against the sexual stimulation induced by watching parents in their conjugal bed.

That they permitted him to crawl into their bed and slip between them for comfort when he woke from nightmares may also have been sexually exciting. Abrahamsen points out that such early, constant sexual stimulation for a growing boy harms both his sexual and psychological development. It produces intense feelings of violence because of the frustration of his sexual desires, and then intense guilt.

Evidently the parents' guilt, when Berkowitz reached ten, was so great they decided he ought to have a room of his own. They gave him the bedroom and they moved to a convertible sofa in the living room. But they still allowed him, when he suffered nightmares, to slip into their bed. By this time, the sexual damage had been done and Berkowitz's natural oedipal desire for Pearl and his concomitant hatred of his rival father was probably fanned to a fury.

It may be harder for an adopted son to deal with sexual feelings for his adopted mother than for a real mother, for the adopted mother is not related by blood. The incest taboo thus may not be as strong, allowing a child's natural desire to flow without the normal restraint.

His adoptive mother, Pearl, spoiled him on the one hand, then overcontrolled him, but had difficulty disciplining him. He played truant from school constantly, eventually she took him to a psychologist. At an early age he was preoccupied with thoughts of death. Starting at nine, he killed fish, poisoned his mother's pet parakeet, made what he called a "torture chamber" for ants, flies, roaches and other insects. He vandalized apartment buildings, broke windows, flooded basements, set fires. Pearl died when he was fourteen and he cried at her funeral, sobbed years later as he told Abrahamsen of her death.

After serving two years in Korea, joining the Army in 1971, Berkowitz returned home and in 1974 attended Bronx Community College. He worked as a cab driver to support himself in a small apartment in Yonkers. When picked up for the murders, he was working as a postal employee in the Bronx.

He had become determined to learn the truth about his biological mother and father and helped by the Adoptee's Liberty Movement Association, found the mother he had been told died at his birth lived in Brooklyn. She excitedly agreed to see him. He was shocked to learn the truth about his life. First,

---

142

that his mother was alive, he had not killed her in childbirth, and second, that his supposed father, Tony Falco, had left home after a daughter had been born and Betty then became pregnant with a man who refused to leave his wife and children to marry her. So she gave away her son three days after he was born.

Berkowitz told Dr. Abrahamsen, "It was all a hoax. I lived with this guilt [of killing her] for so very long. I retained this death guilt for so long."

Two strong fantasies ate away at Berkowitz as he grew up: he had, by being born, murdered his mother and his father hated him because the doctors could have saved her life, rather than the baby's which accounted for his father giving him away. Thus do we carry with us our earliest fantasies, ones that may be far from the truth but which, nonetheless, may drive us to vengeful wishes and create tormenting guilt. This is the child terror that leads to adult terror.

Berkowitz committed the six murders and attempted two others all within the year after his mother's revelations. Abrahamsen commented, "This sudden disclosure of the truth about his real mother had the same effect as a lighted match on a powder keg." Berkowitz's fury exploded into multiple murders for many reasons. He hated his natural mother for giving him away, while keeping his older sister. He also hated her for causing him to believe he had killed her, creating great guilt. A month after his first murder he wrote a poem titled "Mother of Satan," indicating he felt like the devil because of what she had done to him. He described her in the poem as sitting near a cupboard "with a hand grenade under the oatmeal."

His first murder took place within a few blocks of his adoptive parents' home and another of the murders near his sister's home. He shot young couples necking or engaging in the sexual act in parked cars late at night or early morning. Abrahamsen believes Berkowitz wanted to kill couples but especially the young women as he discharged his fury at his natural mother. As though to prevent the young women from having illegitimate children who would suffer as he did from his mother's illicit sexual act.

There is probably not one of us who, at one time or another, has not wished to murder someone. That we do not carry through on our violent wish tells of a more peaceful childhood than those who kill. We are not possessed by such a desperate need to avenge ourselves on those who have hurt us. We can thank the ones who nurtured us, loved us as much as they could, that we are spared the agony of those who cannot control their wishes to kill, so intense their anger and guilt.

THE PSYCHOPATH IN DAILY LIFE

Inasmuch as we all have consciences, at one time or another if we break one of society's minor rules, we will feel guilty, then try to escape our guilt. We may deny guilt or accuse others of acts or thoughts for which we feel guilty, or suffer depression, psychosomatic illnesses, forms of masochism or take to alcohol or other addictions.

Another way of rebelling against a strong conscience is to pretend it does not exist and to appear psychopathic to some degree. Psychopathy in various degrees exists in everyday life since all of us have wishes to defy our guilt-producing superegos. Just as we had wishes as children to defy our guilt-producing parents.

A policeman who resents the voice of a stern conscience that constantly admonishes him to uphold the law at any cost, may rebel by brutalizing a prisoner. The teacher who believes she must strictly mold the minds of the young may, on occasion, strike a recalcitrant pupil. Husbands and wives may indulge in affairs, students cheat on examinations, little children tell lies that belie their innocent eyes.

Resenting the voices that tyrannically command, "Thou shalt not steal," a number of men and women defy the hated voices and surreptitiously slip a coveted item into their purse or pocket in department stores. Diners do not point out under-charges on restaurant bills. Businessmen and women may add to their expense accounts, overcharge for meals, travel, hotel.

But even if we steal only a stamp, we will hear that voice within informing us we have broken a sacred rule of child-hood and of the society in which we are expected to live with honesty and integrity. There is no escape from guilt except to face the truth of what we have done.

Psychopathic behavior may relieve anger for the moment but it increases guilt over the long run. Hardly a fair bargain in terms of emotional exchange. One expression of psychopa-thy is the telling of lies. A woman of twenty-three married a young doctor who, she discovered, would tell what he thought were innocuous lies. He confessed to her he bought an attrac-tive silver mobile that shimmered over their piano, hanging from the ceiling. But when friends admired the mobile, he would admit modestly, "I made it." She was shocked when she first heard him say this, asked after the guests had gone, "Why did you lie to them about the mobile?" He said casually, "What does it matter who made it?" and walked away.

She slowly learned his psychopathy slipped into other areas, that he would lie about the money he earned, subtracting thousands of dollars from his actual income. When he started to lie to her, denying he was having an affair with his secretary, she left him.

We have all met persons who though psychopathic do not appear to be. They seem cool, calculating, rarely show re-morse. They insult others without flinching, they exploit friends without any show of anxiety, they manipulate without guilt—so it appears. But appearances can be deceiving where psychopathy is involved. Such men and women have worked hard at perfecting their defenses against any show of emo-tions, we refer to them as "hardened." They keep such feelings as sympathy, empathy, shame, guilt, so buried it appears they really don't "give a damn" about anyone. Though they arouse anger in us, we admire them to some extent because they seem immune from our anxiety and guilt. But underneath the emotional shell we will find such psychopaths are depressed, hurt and frightened. Often they have experienced such terror and frustration in childhood that they can show only a limited capacity to love. Just as books cannot be judged by their covers, so psychopaths cannot be judged by their cover up.

THE GUILT OF OUR NATION

The guilt of one person is not of much concern to society as a rule. But what of the guilt of the "people," of the jury, the judges, the lawyers, who allow innocent men to be convicted of murder and executed? The American Civil Liberties Union reported, in a story published by *The New York Times* on November 14, 1985 that in a new study on capital punishment in this country, during this century 343 men and women were wrongly convicted of offenses punishable by death and that twenty-five were put to death in "wrongful executions." In thirty-two cases that included some of those awaiting execution for murder, it was reported no crime had been committed, usually because the purported murder victim had been found alive.

The late Edward Mowery won the Pulitzer Prize in 1953 for his series in the *New York World Telegram*, which he carefully researched, proving that Louis Hoffner was not guilty of committing the murder of a New York bartender. Hoffner had served twelve years in Dannemora, wrongly judged by a jury on little evidence. At the age of twenty-six he went to prison for life for a murder he did not commit. A waiter in the bar at the time of the murder was the only one to identify Hoffner, though the waiter confessed the light was dim and he had seen only the profile of the killer. Hoffner's lawyer neglected to summon several witnesses who could have testified, as they did twelve years later, that Hoffner was with them in another part of the city at the time the murder was committed.

How can such miscarriage of justice occur? One reason is that many of us are delinquent in demanding adequate evidence at trials because we wish someone to be punished for crimes we have committed in fantasy, or are afraid we may commit. As criminals are punished, we suffer vicariously their punishment, relieving our guilt. Recently a young woman in Chicago, who had blamed an innocent man for rape (he had been sentenced to prison and served a number of years) admitted, after she joined a religious group, that she had lied. She feared the foster family who had sheltered her would throw her out of their home if she confessed she was pregnant by her steady boy friend. The judge, and perhaps many others, had difficulty accepting her confession. The impulse to rape that exists to some extent in every man and the wish to be raped that exists to some extent in every woman drives most of us secretly to want even an innocent man punished, because of our guilt. There is a tendency in our court system to project guilt on those who stand trial, especially for sexual and murderous crimes—the wishes in ourselves we most repudiate. This is not to say the guilty should escape punishment. Only that the innocent should not be unjustly punished.

And what of the guilt of a nation, the "collective guilt" mentioned by Jung as the guilt we all unconsciously share? A guilt that drives nations to war against each other.

This guilt was dramatically referred to in a full-page advertisement headed "Forty Years of the Atomic Age," the theme of *Newsweek's* July 22, 1985 edition on the fortieth anniversary of the first atomic bomb. Underneath the advertisement's headline were the words: "The bomb that hit Hiroshima forty years ago this summer is still exploding. In our minds." The issue of the magazine contained an article by Peter Goldman and a Special Projects Team that recreated and reflected on the impact of the bomb "on our society and collective psyche."

America feels a special guilt because it was the first country to drop the atomic bomb on another nation, according to psychiatrist Dr. Lawrence J. Friedman, past president of the Los Angeles Psychoanalytic Society. He spent four years in the United States Army, caring for psychiatric casualties of World War II when the first atomic weapon detonated at 6:40 A.M.

on August 6, 1945, killing or maiming hundreds of thousands of Japanese men, women and children.

Friedman later wrote in an unpublished article titled "Nothing Happened, They Say . . . (from Hiroshima to Amchitka)" that "the world changed drastically with the explosion of the first atomic bomb. It started man on his road to extinction; world destruction emerged in religious fantasy, and became reality. It did not change man's relentless march to oblivion. It accelerated it. The accumulated stockpile of destructive weapons is beyond comprehension."

He quoted our leaders as justifying the bomb for halting the war, then asks:

If Hiroshima stopped the war, why was there a Nagasaki? I asked that question innumerable times since, in discussions among politicians, doctors, scientists, lawyers and at public lectures with the same result—a variety of speculations but no satisfactory answers. The majority remembered only Hiroshima, forgot all about Nagasaki. There was the real answer: Guilt.

He added that in 1954, during the presidency of General Eisenhower, "our warlord during the second World War," this nation "added to the pledge of allegiance, one nation, 'under God.'" He then asked, "When do we ask for God's protection?" and answered, "When we feel guilty."

He believes, as he states in his article, that we fought again in Korea, then Vietnam, out of guilt, "our unrecognized, unadmissable guilt at having dropped the first atomic bomb . . . like the criminal we returned to the scene of the crime, seeking punishment by committing new crimes."

He maintains that the guilt in America, "dominated by the Judeo-Christian commandment, 'Thou shalt not kill,' is by all signs overwhelming." He adds, "After all, not the yellow-bellied slant-eyes, nor the godless Communists, but we, the nation under God, ever dropped atomic bombs on human beings. Try as we may to convince ourselves that others would have done it, too, that we stockpile bombs only for peace, only for defense against the worldwide aggression of international Communism, as long as we have to deny our guilt, it remains unchanged, destructive and self-destructive."

He concludes, "No outside enemy, not Russia nor China, and certainly not Vietnam, could have done the damage to us we did to ourselves as a direct consequence of the Vietnam war. And because we refuse to look at ourselves, new violence feeds our guilt, forces us to continue on our suicidal path, all the way to the present danger of world destruction."

Just as children who feel guilty about their unacceptable thoughts, wishes and acts provoke punishment, so do countries. When the populace and the leaders they choose or tolerate feel guilty for their greed, acquisitiveness, envy and wishes to conquer other nations, they unconsciously arrange, just as children do, to be punished—by seeking wars with other nations, sacrificing many lives and being beaten. Then, just as children who are abused protest and feel self-righteous, so do countries.

Political scientists and psychohistorians, who study history from a psychological perspective rather than looking at war as dates of battles, have found the wars of nations are not very different from marital and child-parent battles. Anxiety, anger, anguish, guilt and the need for punishment are also part of the war scene.

Citizens elect leaders who act out the violence, suffer the guilt, then seek the punishment the voters feel they deserve, according to Lloyd DeMause, director of the Institute for Psychohistory and founder of the International Psychohistorical Association. He has explored this relationship between the guilt of voters and the leaders they elect in his books *Foundations of Psychohistory* and *Reagan's America*. He suggests that voters unconsciously elect guilt-ridden leaders so the populace will be punished for the guilt they feel over their murderous wishes. The elected leaders carry the nation to war "as a sacrificial ritual when we feel we are 'bad' and guilty and deserve punishment," DeMause says.

Most opponents to nuclear war agree on one point: the total irrationality of the present buildup. As George Kennan, our former ambassador to Russia, puts it: "We have gone on piling weapon upon weapon, missile upon missile . . . like men in a dream . . . today we and the Russians [have attained] levels of redundancy such as to defy rational understanding."

DeMause declares the reasons we want war are, like the reasons individuals engage in self destructive acts, complex. They involve an understanding of the deepest layers of the unconscious mind. The motives behind past wars have been the subject of study for two decades by research associates at the Institute for Psychohistory. There has been a focus on the fantasies expressed "in the words and images used by national leaders and the media *prior* to wars," DeMause explains.

He reports: "We have been surprised to find consistent patterns of group fantasies which nations share and use as trial actions in the process of finding an enemy and beginning a war." These fantasies, which do not originate in the international sphere, but are circulated in the public dialogue during the early buildup of tensions "include growing guilt over sinfulness, despair about ever achieving happiness, increasing rage and fears of ego collapse, and, finally, powerful wishes to sacrifice youth as representatives of forbidden sexuality and rebelliousness."

He adds, "If one listens to the unconscious messages embedded in the public dialogue, one discovers that people usually tell you in advance what they are about to act out." He maintains the conclusions reached by the research "form a coherent theory of war which is truly *psychogenic*, as opposed to the purely economic theories of war most common today." Among the conclusions are:

1. *War is a wish*, not a response or a "mistake," involving a period of regression similar to the regressions experienced by individuals during psychotic episodes.

2. *This group regression is signaled by violent group fantasies*

that reflect growing rage and fears of national collapse, desires for national rebirth through violence and fantasies of the cleansing of sinfulness.

3. *The regression occurs after periods of prosperity and progress*, when the punitive superego is called forth by a nation's success and by unaccustomed personal freedoms.

4. *War is a delusional solution to these psychotic anxieties*, an ego-reintegrating clarification of the confusions and free-floating paranoid feelings of the earlier period, so that finding an "enemy" is at first felt a release of tension.

5. *War involves grandiose sexualization of inner conflict*, accompanied by group fantasies of rape and orgasmic violence, projected into an appropriate "enemy" who has agreed to participate in a period of mutual sacrifice.

6. *Killing an "enemy" represents killing dangerous inner desires* and is therefore a victory for "good"—the punitive superego—over "evil"—the dangerous id.

7. *War is a sacrificial ritual* in which the blood of soldiers is drained away to cleanse the nation and remove its sinfulness and make it "good" again, so the guilt of the individuals and the nation will be eased.

DeMause proposes the establishment on an international basis of a Nuclear Tensions Monitoring Center. Its purpose would be to describe, measure and publicize increases in violent group-fantasies in each of the nuclear nations and give continuous psychological help in decreasing nuclear tensions. (The latter is already being done on a small scale by various psychotherapists in a number of communities in the United States, as they help primarily children in school and their parents.)

"If the general dimensions of this psychogenic theory of war have any validity, it follows that the most effective help the mental health profession can provide for a world preparing for a suicidal nuclear war is to *make the unconscious conscious*, just as they have been trained to do in the case of individuals," DeMause explains. "Since an unconscious wish derives its power to be acted on through its state of repression, the group-fantasy of having a cleansing nuclear war can only be prevented from being acted out by continuous interpretation of both the wish and its myriad defense systems."

He proposes that psychotherapists, psychiatrists, psycho-historians, political psychologists and other specialists trained in the analysis of unconscious mental life establish the Nuclear Tensions Monitoring Center. Others concerned with the avoidance of nuclear war are asked to take part. Ideally, the center would have a branch in each of the nuclear nations, though it could begin to function with only one center—in this country, where the mental health profession is largest.

The center would concentrate on a continuous analysis of the rise and fall of "violent and paranoid imagery in the speeches and media of the nuclear nations, with the hope that before long an index of national war tensions could be constructed which would be able to warn people when and why nations are escalating their violent group-fantasies."

That nations seek war out of guilt, fear and rage is emphasized by Dr. Otto Kernberg, major contributor to the psychoanalytic literature. He maintains the reason the world has wars is that the leaders of nations do not act out of maturity and thoughtfulness but on the level of raging infants, driven by greed, envy, selfishness, hatred of the stranger, fear and guilt. He compares the psychic state of the world to that of the primitive, savage thinking of the infant. The world has not yet reached the level of emotional development where leaders of one nation are able to think of another nation's needs, or wish to share with other nations, or work with them to avert destruction of the planet.

In the prewar stage leaders use words as weapons—as the saying goes, "Words can kill." Many of our most fearful moments occur when others hurl angry words at us or we hurl words of fury at them. Words have a magical quality. They can soothe or excite and incite. A child learns if he says "no" he

152

may be punished, frowned at or even struck but if he says "yes," he will receive a smile, adulation, a kiss.

The magic a child ascribes to words continues into adult life. We show our hostility even while relaxing and watching sports. In a baseball game we yell, "Kill the umpire!" when his decision goes against our team. We speak of our favorite players as being "robbed" of a homer, or "stealing" a base. The smack of the bat against the pitched ball is a "hit," as we yell, "He smashed that one."

While words do not kill, they may, however, if used by the leaders of one nation to threaten the leaders of another nation, lead to mass slaughter. Freud wrote, six months after the outbreak of World War I in 1915, that the war had brought "disillusionment . . . . It has brought to light an almost incredible phenomenon: civilized nations now understand one another so little that one can turn against the other with hate and loathing . . . . The primitive mind is, in the fullest meaning of the word, imperishable."

Yet Freud also hopefully predicted that "in spite of all difficulties we may expect that one day someone will venture on research into the pathology of civilized communities," which is what DeMause and his investigative group are doing.

Psychopathy and criminality can be found at every level— in the individual, the community, the nation. But it becomes truly a world tragedy when psychopathy and criminality appear at the very top at such a crucial time. A time when our guilt as a nation runs high.

9

MANIPULATING GUILT

INDUCING GUILT IN OTHERS

Guilt is such a devastating feeling, causing us such discomfort and despair, we try in all ways possible to rid ourselves of it. One prevalent way is to manipulate others so they, not we, feel guilty. As though spreading the guilt dilutes our share.

We accuse the other person: "I haven't done anything wrong—you have." In this way we try to cope with both the forbidden wish and the guilt that follows by dumping our unacceptable wishes on others, punishing them for our imagined wrongdoings. Those who have been able to face and accept their unreal guilts do not become provoked. But those who have fled guilt are likely to burst into fury or masochistically suffer without a word in retaliation, hating the accuser and feeling even guiltier.

Husbands and wives find each other easy targets. One wife constantly criticizes her husband for watching wrestling matches on television. She admonishes him for enjoying vicariously what she believes a brutal sport. She thinks anyone who follows wrestling is a sadist. Consciously she cannot tolerate watching one man brutalize another, as wrestlers appear to do, though much of the action is admittedly theatrical.

But unconsciously, as she defends herself against her violent wishes which horrify her, she feels guilty. She then protests against her own wishes, as carried out by the wrestlers, by accusing her husband of enjoying violence on the television screen. It would not matter to her that he relaxes from work by viewing a wrestling match unless the latter touched off a vulnerable fantasy in her. This is an example of "the lady doth protest too much."

Marriage is the setting in which guilt is frequently used to manipulate a loved one. It is easier to condemn in others what we are guilty about. The partner who can admit to a spouse, "I'm sorry about our argument last night, it was my fault, I was in the wrong," is rare. Most marital partners charge guiltily, "It's all your fault!"

Manipulation includes projection, which is a primary way manipulation works. The manipulator does not face the true feelings that stir his anxiety but tries to protect against them by projecting them onto others. Projection is used to manipulate the innocent, trying to cause them to suffer the guilt that really belongs to us.

Manipulation, and the use of projection, may become a vicious cycle as one spouse accuses the other of failing in some respect. The victim feels furious and guilty and promptly lashes back, increasing the collective guilt. Few of us suffer insults to our narcissism gladly or in silence.

A marital partner may accuse the other of resembling a difficult parent. One wife, when angry, says scornfully to her husband, "You're just like my father, who was nasty to women." He retorts, "You remind me of my dominating mother who suffocated me to death." They cannot face the anger at their own parent for which they feel guilty. Instead, each accuses the other of irritating traits.

Some try to manipulate a friend into behaving as they do, so the friend will feel guilty about the same act. An adolescent girl of twelve who had just started to kiss boys urged her clos-

156

est friend, "Why don't you try it? It's great fun." She wanted to share not only the pleasure but the guilt as a way of lessening it.

A father who often shouted at his son would turn to his wife and plead, "I'm tired of trying to discipline him, why don't you help out?" He felt guilty at losing his temper and wanted to share the guilt. He projected it on his wife, thus manipulating her. A nine-year old who stole candy bars from the corner store, in an attempt to lessen his guilt, urged a friend, "You steal some, too." In the 1950s during a basketball scandal over the shaving of points, one player who took part in the dishonest act said he believed all his teammates were involved, wanting them to assume part of the guilt, though most were innocent.

A businessman who felt guilty about underpaying his employees formed an organization of other businessmen to study ways in which employees were taking advantage of their bosses. But he discovered his peers were honest enough to acknowledge their guilt at exploiting employees, rather than censuring them. A student in college felt guilty about his wish to cheat on examinations and approached the professor before a test, warning, "Watch your students, they all talk about cheating." He was, of course, warning against his own wish to cheat. When a child feels guilty about hostile feelings toward his mother and father he may "squeal" on a brother or sister, accusing them of anger at the parents. Or a child who believes he has "dirty" thoughts will accuse another of such thoughts.

The manipulation of guilt is never-ending, almost as prevalent as guilt itself. A woman of twenty-four stood in front of the locked front door to the building in which her therapist lived. Usually she pressed a button and was admitted. On this day the button failed to work and in a fury she banged ferociously on the front door, shattering two panes of glass. She spent her fifty-minute hour on the couch wailing to the therapist about the "lousy" building he chose for his office and insisting he pay for the glass to replace the panes she had broken. She blamed the elevator operator for not showing up to let her in, which he sometimes did. She criticized other tenants for not appearing at her moment of need to open the door. She projected on everyone else her guilt at smashing the glass in her impatience and anger.

The manipulation of guilt happens in large groups as well as with individuals. Republicans charge Democrats with irresponsibility in financing the country's needs, as they project their own guilt. In like fashion, Democrats accuse Republicans of self-aggrandizement at the expense of the poor. The United States accuses the Soviet Union of warlike aims and the Soviet Union hurls the same charge at the United States.

Parents, to rid themselves of guilt may try to manipulate a child. A mother will say accusingly, "You'll be the death of me if you don't behave," causing the child to feel as guilty as a murderer. The mother is projecting on the child her own temporary wish he vanish because he is for the moment irascible. Or the mother will threaten, "I'm going to leave you if you don't obey," her wish projected on the child. He will then feel acute anxiety at the thought of being abandoned.

Parents, out of their conflicts, sometimes play on a child's need for love, knowing how much a child depends on love. Though this is sometimes referred to as Jewish guilt, it knows no ethnic bounds for it is also seen among the Irish, Italian, French, British and other national and religious groups. Jewish guilt is illustrated by the story of a mother who gave her married son on his birthday two ties, one red, the other blue. When he next visited her, he wore the blue tie. She chided, "What's the matter? You don't like the red tie?" She was saying he should feel guilty for not gratifying all her maternal wishes, impossible though they might be.

It is easier for a mother to say, "You're a bad boy," than to ask herself, "What have I done to provoke my child's anger?" Children take parental accusations to heart. There are no "light words" or "words in jest" spoken to a child. His world of words is a literal one. He is sensitive to his mother's every word, every act, every gesture, every facial expression.

One working mother, guilty at not being free to attend her

daughter's dance recital, badgered her daughter to persuade the teacher to hold the recital another day. The daughter, showing rare understanding for a twelve-year old, or any age, said, "Mother, don't feel guilty. I know you have an important business meeting. I don't love you any the less."

A father, guilty for not spending enough time with his children, complained how unaffectionate they were. Finally his wife asked, "And just *who* is the unaffectionate one in this house?" He looked sheepish, admitted, "I guess it's the pot calling the kettle black." He realized he had been projecting his feelings on his children, trying to manipulate them into sharing his guilt.

Sometimes we are slow to recognize someone's manipulation of our guilt. A woman in Manhattan recommended a restaurant in Greenwich Village when a friend from out of town asked where she should eat. The friend phoned the next day, said accusingly, "I got mugged last night leaving the restaurant you sent me to."

The woman replied she was sorry this happened. She felt guilty, wondered if she were to blame. Her friend could just as easily have been mugged outside of Sardi's on 44th Street, near Times Square. There was no completely safe place in the city, especially during the night hours.

A child will often try to manipulate guilt in a parent. One twelve-year-old girl, guilty at receiving Bs instead of As on her report card, said accusingly to her parents, "Why don't you stay home nights and help me with my homework instead of always going out?" She did not want to admit her guilt at watching television instead of studying while her parents were enjoying themselves.

Thousands of men and women are in therapy spending millions of dollars talking about their parents' cruelties and indifference instead of facing their own childish fears, angers and guilts. It is easier for a man to say he cannot enjoy sex because his mother was overpossessive and dominating and he did not feel his life was his own than to confess he feels guilty because in fantasy he makes his partner into an overpossessive, dominating woman like his mother. By projecting his feelings on his sexual partner—manipulating her—he feels less guilty.

Though parents are painted as ogres by almost all of us at times, like all of us, parents are entitled to their imperfections. A young man complained to a friend he had to earn his living as an accountant because his parents had not prepared him to follow a more challenging career. The friend asked, "Where were you in all this? Why couldn't you consider your own wishes?" The man admitted grudgingly, "I was a coward when I gave in to my father's choice of career. I felt guilty at the thought of opposing him." He had been too frightened of his father to speak up, then angry at himself for his cowardice, then guilty.

There is manipulation of guilt, through the projection of one's own feelings, in the educational arena. A teacher who feels inadequate will label his students "unmotivated, unresponsive." One mathematics teacher, after a number of students in her class failed the midterm examinations, told them, "You didn't pay attention when I tried to teach you." College dropouts invariably blame the system or their mentors instead of admitting they do not study enough.

Watching union-management negotiations on television we hear each side call the other "unfair" though neither wants to subject its demands to public scrutiny. The other side is always accused of "failing to negotiate," again a manipulation of guilt at the charge of being biased. Though actually a projection of the attitude of the one making the charge.

When two people collide on the sidewalk or drivers in two cars hit one another each feels guilty but blames the other. Insurance companies understand this need to manipulate and therefore there is "no fault" insurance. A recent book on divorce by Marcia Laswell and Norman Lobsenz is titled *No-Fault Marriage*.

Manipulating guilt works only temporarily for the one who manipulates. After we blame someone for imagined provocations, we still feel guilty because we have not faced the angry, destructive wishes that gave rise to our guilt and, in addition, have tried to shift our blame. When we manipulate others, try to send them on a guilt trip, we fail to keep in mind this is a costly maneuver. Friends are lost, loved ones become angry and opportunities vanish because of our hostility.

AS OTHERS INDUCE GUILT IN US

Just as we may find it expedient to manipulate guilt in others to lessen our own, we are equally prone to be victims of those countless souls only too eager and willing to manipulate our guilt through their own projection.

All of us, no matter how deeply we loved our parents, feel a certain guilt when they die. We wish we had shown them more consideration, done more for them, loved them more. Funeral directors know how to exploit our guilt as they try to convince us to buy expensive coffins and stage elaborate funerals.

Philanthropic organizations capitalize on our guilt to raise money to help those less fortunate. One church, in a daring experiment, asked "Please give money for the cause," without specifying the cause. Almost all the parishioners donated out of a sense of guilt, not knowing or caring what the "cause," was. It could have been to save the Hottentots or dodo birds.

Projection works so often because the one accused usually has the same guilt, of which he is not aware. Wealthy persons often believe they should be punished for possessing more than others. The failure to enjoy riches stems in part from childhood when we wished to deprive siblings of the love they received from our parents, as well as all material possessions thrown their way. We carry this wish into adulthood and irrationally assume we deprive others if we have wealth. It is one thing to donate money by choice and out of conviction. It is another to give it compulsively as penance for guilt. A man who made a fortune in the stock market managed to lose it all because he felt so guilty each time an organization approached him for a contribution.

Many a man or woman serving on the board of a philanthropic organization spends time, energy and money in behalf of the poor because of guilt (or finds a "worthy cause" to support financially). Alfred Bernhard Nobel, who invented dynamite, established the Nobel prizes—five annual awards given by the Nobel Foundation for distinction in physics, chemistry, medicine, literature and the promotion of peace. The famous Swedish industrialist was unconsciously atoning for having invented such a destructive force.

In the early days of philanthropy the duties of the social worker were carried out by wealthy "friendly visitors," women who volunteered to help the poor because these women felt guilty about their unearned riches. Bertha Pappenheim, the patient of Breuer's mentioned earlier, was one of these women. When she recovered from her illness, she returned to her wealthy mother's native city of Frankfurt, Germany to become a volunteer social worker and eventually build and direct the first institution to take care of delinquent girls and unwed mothers in Germany. In recent years, a commemorative stamp bearing her photograph was issued in Germany. Bertha put to constructive use her childhood guilts in spite of her earlier breakdown.

The many pleas for help that come to us through the mail are designed to feed on our guilt. The March of Dimes, the Red Cross, the Hundred Neediest Cases, appeal to us to help the starving children in America, Ethiopia, India, Central America and those who are victims of nature's wrath. The national organizations compete in exploiting our guilt.

The man about to marry is manipulated by jewelers who try to equate the depth of his love with the cost of the ring. Mother's Day permits advertisers to exploit the guilt of children, whatever their age. If we do not buy the entire multivolume set, encyclopedia salesmen tell us we deprive our children of the fullest range of knowledge.

Then there are the life insurance manipulators. A real estate broker whose wife had just given birth to a second son,
was greeted on his doorstep by an insurance salesman who
asked, "Do you love your family?" The broker, though a devoted husband and father, knew he was not the perfect husband and father. Feeling guilty, he showed no resistance to the
salesman, who knew he could capitalize on the average man's
guilt.

Manipulations often occur at the hands of peers. A freshman in college, the top scholar in most subjects, was manipulated by his classmates who told him to stop "showing off" and
making it so difficult for them. To get their approval he deliberately failed some subjects. A college professor who had received acclaim for successful articles and books was informed
by a few colleagues he admired that the dean had criticized
them for not writing as much as he did. Frightened at the
thought of their ostracism he stopped all writing. A mother,
jealous of the close relationship between her husband and
daughter, told her husband he was harming the daughter's
emotional stability. Feeling guilty, he withdrew love and attention from his daughter, who then became so confused and
troubled she sought therapy.

Most of us easily accede to manipulation by others because
of our guilt. We would not compulsively buy costly coffins,
lavish wedding rings, expensive gifts on holidays if we did not
feel so guilty. We may pay thousands of dollars for funeral
arrangements for a mother or father but this will not ease our
guilt. We may buy expensive presents for those to whom we
feel close but this also will not ease the guilt we feel for not
loving them enough, or for our anger at them for not being
perfect. We can buy large insurance policies to provide for our
families after we die but this will not make our lives on earth
more enjoyable.

Whether guilt comes from real or unreal causes, we cannot
expunge it by paying off others or allowing ourselves to be
manipulated by others, whether it be an insurance salesman,
a spouse or a child. Only by facing our guilt can we ward off

predatory salesmen, artful hucksters and all others who would manipulate us.

Of all emotions, perhaps guilt is the most difficult to own and to own up to. This causes the strong wish to manipulate others and also explains the ease with which others manipulate us. Many marital fights could be avoided if husband and wife did not wish to inflict guilt on each other. Many a parent-child confrontation would cease if the parent took responsibility for his guilt, since a child as yet cannot. Many an advertiser would have to promote the real qualities of his product rather than our fancied reaction to it if we felt less guilty.

One recent advertisement for ice cream flashed these three words across the television screen, "Enjoy Your Guilt!" A woman was pictured in half-apology to her husband for having devoured the entire pint of this brand. Perhaps better that we enjoy our guilt than to manipulate others. We do not achieve any easing of guilt if we attack the innocent. Guilt is a boomerang. What we hurl at others speeds back at us with even greater force. And when we let others manipulate us, we do not expiate guilt because we have not dealt with the forbidden wishes and unrecognized anger that created the guilt.

Tossing one hundred or one thousand or one hundred thousand dollars to our favorite charity might raise our self-esteem for a few days but will not help us face our guilt. Buying off someone we love with a costly string of pearls or a tie of the finest silk may ease our conscience for the moment but not the guilt felt in our bones for years.

When a beggar asks for money to buy a cup of coffee many of us oblige at once. We feel comfort in the thought it is the beggar, not we, who is so destitute. Then we feel guilty at enjoying our superiority at the cost of his helplessness and plight, and for being so easily manipulated by him.

When we face with greater honesty our forbidden sexual fantasies and violent angry wishes, we are not so easily exploited or manipulated. We have less need to manipulate others, knowing that both manipulating and being manipulated is part of the punishment we seek for our guilt.

The only way we can stop being manipulated by unscrupulous advertisers, exploitive charities, tantalizing advertisements on television or in the newspapers, beggars and devious projections of guilt by our dearest friends, is to understand the roots of our own guilt and not let others use it against us.

PART II

LETTING GO OF GUILT

10

STOP DENYING GUILT

WHY YOU DENY GUILT

How can you rid yourself of the needless guilt that may be crippling you emotionally and physically? The guilt that causes you sleepless nights, fatiguing days and endless punishing of yourself?

The first step is to stop denying your guilt. The very reason guilt is so devastating is *because* you deny it. You use denial when the truth seems so terrifying you have to put it out of mind to keep your sanity. Or to stop committing an act you would regret the rest of your life.

Denial is one of your chief defenses against any forbidden wish that looms as dangerous to your self-esteem. If guilt were not such a pervasive, tormenting feeling our religions would not provide so many outlets for it. Protestants and Catholics hold their confessionals and other rituals that help men and women admit guilt and feel relief for the moment. Lent, for instance, is a period of penitence for Catholics. Jews fast one day each year, Yom Kippur, to ask God for forgiveness for sins.

Because you believe guilt brings a loss of love and self-esteem, and fear humiliation (if not ostracism because of what your friends and society might think if they knew of your guilty feelings) it is less painful to deny guilt than to face its origins or admit you even *feel* guilty. When you banish guilt from the conscious part of your mind you believe you banish wishes for vengeance, wishes to kill all those who have hurt you throughout life. Wishes to be the dependent child once again in times you feel troubled. Wishes for pure and everlasting love without a tinge of hate. Wishes to break all the rules and regulations imposed on you by parents and society—to have sex with anyone to whom you are attracted, to run away from the life you lead and start over, as Gauguin did.

Such wishes are hostile, greedy, envious, murderous and lustful. They do not take into consideration the feelings of others. You expect to be punished for them, as you were when a child, because acting on them might cost you your mother or father's love. Loss of love is anathema to your very spirit, a kind of pale death.

So to escape what you consider the worst possible fate, you are willing to bear anxiety, deny anger and suffer anguish—the terrifying trio that precedes their fourth and most deadly companion, ominous guilt. You hasten to rid yourself of a guilty thought the second it flashes to mind, believing it hides something sinful.

The fallacy in your thinking is that an emotion, a thought, a wish, can be "wrong" or "sinful." Only monstrous *deeds* are sinful in the eyes of society. Yet you imprison yourself in a dungeon of despair to expiate for a mere forbidden wish, denying the wish and the guilt.

But denial will never help ease your guilt. Instead, it puts you even more in the grip of guilt. You may push guilt out of mind but still punish yourself without being aware of it. The wish that causes the guilt remains as strong as ever and keeps driving you to greater depths of depression and rage. To deny guilt is like hiding your head, ostrichlike, in the sands of the unconscious.

Freud said it best: "To be completely honest with oneself is the best effort a human being can make." Or, to quote Polonius' famous advice to his son Laertes:

This above all: to thine own self be true,
And it must follow, as the night the day,
Thou canst not then be false to any man.

Perhaps neither you, nor anyone else, can ever be "completely honest" for that is a wish for impossible perfection in the self. But you can try to understand why you feel guilty and whether it is reasonable to feel guilt under the circumstances or whether you are reacting to old fears and angers that should by now be powerless.

You may deny guilt by putting it out of your conscious mind but it will seek partial outlets in many ways that have been discussed at length earlier. You may try to dispel your guilt by projecting it on others. When you fail a task at work, you may blame it on another employee, or the employer. You may blame a marital partner when you do not feel sexually aroused.

An easy way to discover what you feel guilty about and are denying is to become aware of what you criticize in others. This will be the guilt you cannot admit to yourself. One woman complained to a friend, "You're always attacking me." The friend stared at her in amazement, for this woman was the one constantly criticizing and condemning her friends. She was blind to her need to tear down everyone else so she could reign supreme. Instead, she projected her propensity for caustic attack onto her innocent friend. An ancient Yiddish proverb says (transliterated, of course): "On someone else you can see a flea; on yourself you can't see an elephant."

You may try to justify a forbidden wish by rationalizing. One wife, disillusioned with her husband after six years of marriage, wished she dared have an affair with the attractive married man next door who had made several advances. She felt guilty at the idea of becoming unfaithful though she had not permitted the neighbor to do more than kiss her at parties. She did not want to risk an affair, though, she thought, she would not feel any more guilty at indulging in it than imagining it. Suddenly she realized her guilt had less to do with sexual desire for the neighbor than with her forbidden wish for revenge on her unfaithful husband. As she became aware of her hostile feelings for her husband, she no longer desired the affair. To become sexually involved with the neighbor would have increased her guilt and she preferred to face its underlying cause and deal with it. She talked about her feelings with her husband and they decided to seek therapy in the hope of saving the marriage.

To release yourself from psychological imprisonment by guilt you need to realize wishes and fantasies will not harm you. Accept your so-called darker self for what it is—the repository for your most primitive, wildest, evil desires, not wicked deeds.

To remove the shackles of guilt, when you first feel anxious try to understand and face the forbidden wish that stirred your anxiety. Did you want to gratify a sexual fantasy? Did you hate someone so intensely you were speechless with rage? Did you wish to compete in some game but thought if you won the losers would hate you? Did you want to depend on someone but felt such show of dependency would demean you?

To rid yourself of guilt you have to stop denying you are human and realize that to be human means to possess the ability to hate as well as love. As much as you may detest yourself when you hate, and as much as you may deplore the reasons you hate—usually childish reasons—you cannot free yourself from guilt until you acknowledge your hatred and become aware of what propels it to mind.

You have to accept you are not a saint though you may try very hard at times to be. You believe if you act saintly you do not have to feel the pain of guilt over something "bad" you have thought or felt. Ultrareligious celibates, the saintly among us devils, shut themselves off from all temptation so they will not commit evil, their lives dedicated to "good."

But saints deny their natural impulses. They receive immortality at the cost of giving up all natural sexual and hostile desires. To be human, to a saint, is to be a sinner. Saints dwell in a world dichotomized into saints and sinners, not of flesh and blood. That we extol saints tells of our wish to be saintly as well as our knowledge of how difficult it is to be. St. Augustine's great guilt over his self-indulgent, hedonistic life drove him to the opposite extreme of seeking purity.

It is not easy to confess to yourself your so-called sins: unfaithfulness to a spouse, neglect of a parent, betrayal of a friend, cruelty to a child. Whether it be an unpaid bill or a hostile act, you prefer to deny guilt rather than say those three words, "I am responsible." Or these other three, "I am sorry."

A woman of twenty-six found she was getting little pleasure out of life—sexual, recreational or creative. She told a friend that, as a child, when she misbehaved her mother gave her a different name. If she were bad, her mother would say, "This isn't my Sally, this is the stranger Susan." As an adult, each time this woman sought pleasure, she thought of herself as the wicked Susan. Being saintly was a way of denying the evil part of herself.

The multiple personality is a very frightened, angry man or woman (usually a woman) who imagines many (anywhere from two to more than 100) persons within who serve, as Susan did, to speak for the forbidden wishes of the "core" personality. The multiples are created to protect what the person feels as threats to his survival, usually at the hands of a cruel, insensitive parent. A large number of women who suffer multiple personalities reveal that as little girls they suffered incest at the hands of their fathers and, in rare cases, a vicious incestuous attack by a mother as in *Sybil*. Such a child has to deny the intense guilt that follows the fury at these devastating assaults on mind and body.

The pain of repressed guilt however, does not subside with denial. If you want to achieve at least some of the happiness to which you are entitled in a world Lucy Larcom in her poem "Three Old Saws" calls "a vale of tears," you should try to admit guilt and understand why you have wanted to run away from it. If you face your guilt you will be more in control of your life rather than let your repressed feelings control you.

A prominent gynecologist felt increasingly guilty as he examined his women patients. He believed he was performing a valuable professional service but felt depressed at work and at home. He knew he was an honorable, respected citizen who loved his wife and children and had many esteemed friends. But he felt that what he did to earn $200,000 a year was somehow "wrong" and "evil."

By chance a colleague helped him understand his feelings. The colleague confessed over a lunch that included two glasses of white wine, "I get a certain sexual thrill even at my age" (he was sixty) "from examining the 'private parts' of my patients. I feel I'm in forbidden territory but I enjoy the terrain, so to speak."

Then he added, "I'd have to be an automaton if I couldn't admit I enjoyed my work."

Hearing his colleague so freely confess his sexual feelings gave this gynecologist permission to become aware of his. He started to feel less guilty over his voyeuristic wishes satisfied in acts whose main purpose was to relieve or prevent pain and suffering. He realized too that lack of pleasure in his work related to the guilt he felt as a boy of six when he and the pretty seven-year-old girl next door acted out "doctor and nurse." He thought, with a smile, "I really started to be a gynecologist at six when I first played doctor."

From then on he enjoyed his professional skills as the depression abated. He no longer felt guilt over his sexual fantasies and feelings. He was grateful to his frank colleague, sent him a bottle of white wine with the note, "I owe you this. I'll explain at our next lunch."

One husband stopped regularly at a bar near his home after work. He could not admit to his wife this was the reason he was sometimes late for dinner because he feared she would be angry and stop loving him. Instead he felt guilty, like a child who expected punishment.

His guilt would have disappeared if he had been able to admit to his wife, "Just as you see your friends in the afternoon for a cup of coffee to relax, I like to spend some time with my friends before coming home. It doesn't mean I love you any the less."

When you stop denying guilt you free yourself from the childhood wishes, thoughts and acts you believed deserved punishment—some of which brought you punishment. It is humiliating and humbling for you, a chronologically mature adult, to admit, "I feel like a child." But every irrational guilty feeling means there is a small, not-so-still voice within repeating, "You'll be punished for what you are thinking, you bad child, you," haunting you beyond all reason.

THE TRUTH SETS YOU FREE

You are no doubt afraid that if you confess to a spouse, friend or colleague that you have acted irresponsibly, hostilely or neglectfully, you risk losing their love and respect. Therefore you deny guilt because the child in you feels the cataclysmic fear of abandonment. Not really by current loves, friends or colleagues but unreally by the all-controlling parents of your past.

One businessman, facing an early morning appointment, forgot to set the alarm clock when he went to bed. He overslept by one hour. He rationalized it was his wife's fault, he had told her he had to get up early and she should have reminded him about the alarm.

He called the executive with whom he was supposed to discuss a new project, apologized, saying the alarm had failed to go off. They made an appointment for the following week. During the week he remained angry at himself for forgetting to set the alarm, felt guilty. He realized he was afraid of being asked to put up a large sum of money for the new project, not sure he wished to take the financial risk. He also was afraid the executive would think less of him for his mistake about the

---

175

alarm clock. He recalled how his father berated him for making "stupid" mistakes as he grew up. Forgetting to set the alarm was a "stupid" mistake.

The day of the second appointment he decided to be honest with his colleague. As they ordered breakfast, he confessed why he had missed the previous appointment. He also admitted he thought he forgot about the alarm because he was worried as to how much money he would have to invest in the project. His colleague said he understood this all too well, he had forgotten to set his alarm many times, then added with a laugh, he usually blamed his wife for not waking him.

The two men had a serious hour-long meeting. The businessman decided to invest the money needed and eventually the project brought him a fair profit. By telling the truth he had earned the respect of his colleague and, more important, of himself. The truth always increases the esteem we receive from others as well as ourselves. When we stoop to lie we give ourselves a psychic downer.

Perhaps you do not have friends as understanding as this colleague. If you told the truth your friends might feel hurt, react angrily. But if you masochistically accept their rage and rejection, using it to punish yourself further, you deny the fact that human beings make mistakes. You learn from your mistakes if you can admit them and thus avoid similar errors in the future.

A young woman who worked on the night shift of a newspaper as rewrite reporter, and slept during the day, occasionally made social appointments after her shift ended at eight in the morning. One day she scheduled a nine o'clock breakfast with a friend but forgot because she had worked hard that night writing a number of late-breaking stories and went directly home.

She woke at noon with a shock, realizing she had missed the breakfast by three hours. She called her friend, said, "I'm sorry, Nan, for not showing up this morning. I worked like a dog through the night on important stories, including a murder."

Her friend, a widow whose husband had left her a comfortable inheritance, snapped, "I waited a whole hour for you, starving to death in that dreadful hotel lobby. I finally left, wondering if you'd dropped dead!"

Her words showed her fury: "starving to death," what she hoped would happen to her friend, and the wish her friend had "dropped dead."

The woman reporter repeated, "I'm sorry. I didn't do this on purpose. You know how hard I work and those night hours are tiring."

The friend said angrily, "I don't care about your excuses. I never want to see you again," and hung up.

The woman realized her friend was more punitive than her own conscience. She thought, "I don't need friends like this. I would forgive her if she were in my position and had to work nights and I had nothing to do all day but spend money left by my husband."

She realized she had not looked forward to breakfast with her unpleasant friend, though she did not admit it to her friend. It was enough she knew. She had forgotten the breakfast to avoid discomfort—the barbs she expected her sarcastic friend to hurl at her. Unconsciously, she had been seeking to free herself from the relationship with a woman whose hostility she had felt directed at her. Our unconscious often takes care of us in ways that prove beneficial as it seeks to rid the mind of pain. Pain related to the destructive patterns of the past. Like her friend, this woman's father was often sarcastic. She grew up shedding tears at times because of his unfair, critical remarks.

She had not consciously meant to hurt her "friend." There is an important distinction between doing something consciously on purpose and unconsciously on purpose. You may hurt someone, neglect someone or provoke someone, know you do so and take responsibility for your provocation, hurt or neglect. But it is more difficult to recognize your unconscious provocations. When you unconsciously forget an appointment you should try to discover what really troubles or angers you and what revengeful thoughts follow. There is no such thing as simple forgetting. Some unconscious motive is always at work trying to keep pain at bay.

Many times the accusations by your unconscious are more powerful than anyone else's conscious accusations. If the unconscious part of your conscience is too harsh, you will seek extreme punishment. When your superego is unduly punitive, you are possessed by an unusually powerful sense of guilt, one too painful to be allowed to enter consciousness. You feel like the overwhelmed child who does not know what to do.

If you face the truth about your guilt you will be less likely to berate your loved ones or allow them to browbeat you. If those close to you continually tear you down, refuse to accept your imperfections, you need no longer tolerate such denigration. As an adult you do not have to take verbal beatings.

A wife snapped at her husband after he dropped coffee grounds all over her newly mopped kitchen floor, "Can't you be more careful?" He looked at her thoughtfully, said, "If you wanted a perfect husband, you shouldn't have married me." She burst into laughter, realized he was entitled to mistakes, as was she.

If you grew up with a sarcastic, critical parent, you are apt to seek a sarcastic, critical spouse who will continue the familiar pattern. There is something about the familiar, even though it hurts and demeans you, that is reassuring. The unknown terrifies you more.

One woman married a man she knew was a con artist who had served a short prison term for one of his frauds but had convinced her he had reformed. After a year of marriage, she realized he was once more involved in a scam. She berated herself for not having accepted he could not change. After the divorce, when she was able to think through the reasons she had married him, she became aware she had always thought of her charming, irresponsible stockbroker father as somewhat of a con man. She had unconsciously sought a man like her beloved father.

When you wish to give up someone who causes you more

mental anguish than you can bear, you should not feel guilty about leaving him. Some, rather than face their guilt, provoke the other person to reject them, as the woman reporter did her angry friend by forgetting the breakfast appointment.

But note that you should not expect your denial of the truth to evaporate all at once. It takes practice to make perfect—or at least as perfect as humans can be—the telling of the truth to yourself or those to whom you are close. You really do not deceive anyone else. Most people know the truth about one another. A truth revealed in subtle ways. The sincerity of a touch. The passion of a kiss. The falseness in a voice. The uneasy expression in the eyes.

When you feel guilty it is helpful to ask, "Am I trying to be perfect or am I trying to make someone else perfect?" With all the attention to perfection in our culture it is not surprising that finally a movie called *Perfect* was released in June 1985. It was set chiefly in a health club devoted to perfecting the woman's body.

You are entitled to a fair amount of love and respect and so are your loved ones and friends. But you would feel less guilty if you did not expect yourself to be a perfect spouse, perfect parent, perfect friend, perfect colleague, perfect employee. Or expect yourself to fulfill all the needs of others. You are human, not divine. The concept of the "divine" person may have arisen from the thought of yourself when an infant as "divine", projected onto your mother who granted your every wish. The creation of such an imaginary superpower is an achievement. But it is even more of an achievement—a realistic one—to understand why you needed to maintain the image of perfection within and to give up the fantasy you or anyone else can be perfect.

Becoming aware of the fantasy of perfection in yourself and others will reduce guilt and produce more of that valuable feeling known as self-esteem, a quiet, honorable pride in the self. Guilt emanates in large part from your desire to be without flaw. As you understand the wish to be perfect is unrealistic, though natural to childhood, you ease demands on yourself and lessen guilt. You no longer have to victimize others and then punish yourself. Or allow yourself to be victimized because you chase a rainbow fantasy.

The administrator of a college realized much of his depression and guilt arose from his unreal expectations that all his faculty would greet him daily with enthusiasm and carry out pronto his slightest request. He overlooked the fact that each faculty member possessed his own limitations, needs and wish for a perfection that lay beyond human reach.

He decided to expect less of the faculty, made fewer demands, gave each member a longer time to carry out his requests, tried to greet everyone affably. He discovered his faculty smiled more at him, granted his requests far more swiftly than before. He realized an understanding attitude speeds up pleasurable results, a dominating one impedes. He also became aware the faculty had been jealous of his power and were afraid of their anger at his success. As he became more genial and accessible, the faculty discovered he too was human, with failings and imperfections, and felt more comfortable with him. He was surprised and pleased when they gave him a birthday party, something they had never done before.

An adolescent girl who despised school felt less angry and less guilty when she could accept that her teachers were mortal and did not have all the answers to life's questions, though they were qualified to teach Latin or trigonometry.

Since so many of us in this age of narcissism expect too much and then fail to get it, a large number of men, women and children live in a constant state of simmering fury. Demands are excessive, rage extensive and guilt overwhelming as it becomes more difficult for us to consider the needs of others.

It is unrealistic not to expect rejection at times. No one can earn everyone's love. Even saints are reviled by some. But you can reduce the anger that precedes guilt, as well as the guilt, if you assure yourself, "Nobody is perfect, I am not perfect, and no one can love me every minute of the day, cater to me the way my heart desires, for I am asking the impossible."

If you do not give up the myth of perfection you will lash out at its eluding you. The rebellion will not bring what you want and you end up depressed, wondering, "What did I do wrong? Why didn't I marry the perfect partner? Why am I not famous, rich as Croesus?" You have been in search of paradise, where all is perfect.

As you face the truth about yourself you will like yourself more and others will admire you more. Truth cements friendships, rather than destroying them. If a friendship is easily dissolved, it is not a very trusting one. The adage, "Truth will win out," usually proves valid though it may take some of us a long time to face the truth about ourselves or others. Truth is often difficult to know but the alternative is self-destructive— the pursuit of fantasies that are false.

You will encounter resistances. Part of you will defend in a tenacious way against becoming aware of thoughts and wishes you have been taught are taboo, defiant, wicked. But tell yourself thinking does not make it so, only acting on the thought. And that everyone has "evil" thoughts, it is the denial of them that is destructive. As you face them, they no longer haunt you and the guilt will tend to disappear.

One woman realized all her life she had idealized her tall, good-looking father, a man highly critical over the years of her and her mother. One day she asked her mother how she had stood his contemptuous manner. Her mother replied she knew it was his way of showing he felt afraid, hurt or angry. She added he was unusually penitent and sweet after he said something critical so she waited for those moments which, to her, outweighed the unhappy ones.

The daughter realized she had seen her father with stars in her eyes. She thanked her mother for helping her to be more aware of him as human, prey to the demands of his wishes. The mother then asked the daughter if she knew how closely she resembled her father when she was angry. The daughter became upset, answered defiantly she did not want to be like her father in that ugly respect.

Her mother then asked whom she expected to be like, since

she grew up knowing chiefly her mother and father. The daughter admitted her mother was right and if she did not like herself when she copied certain traits of her father, it was up to her to change, not feel angry, then guilty.

If you love someone, if your love outweighs the hate always present to some degree (we can never escape ambivalence), you allow the one you love the right to feel unreal guilt. It is enough for you to know the reasons for your own guilt. Honesty is contagious and as you are able to be more honest with yourself, those close to you become aware of this and are more honest about why they feel guilty. Honesty strengthens your spine, so to speak—you stand straighter, in a psychic sense, deal more fairly with yourself and others.

In addition to words, you transmit the honesty through unspoken thoughts, emotions and attitudes. Not everything has to be uttered. Sometimes the most important feelings are never verbalized yet they are deeply felt by another.

Honesty with the self automatically raises self-esteem, your inner resources strengthen. The higher your self-esteem, the more likely you are to choose as a partner someone who also possesses self-esteem and is less apt to inflict anger and guilt on you. It is no accident many masochistic women marry men who beat them, tear them down verbally or flaunt affairs in their faces, further lowering their opinion of themselves.

It is important not only to raise your self-esteem but help raise the esteem of those you love. There are women who destroy a man's self-esteem to the point where he is driven to kill them. Many a wife would be alive today had she not sneered at her husband, "You're not a man, you can't even find a decent job!" Accusing a husband of not being "manly" or a wife of not being "womanly" is one of the most insulting indignities one person can inflict on another. It not only feeds the low self-esteem in which the object of contempt holds himself but accuses him of being a sexually impotent baby, not a passionate adult.

Self-esteem is founded on a certain love of the self and trust in the self. Out of these feelings comes your ability to love and

---

182

trust others. Guilt and self-esteem are mortal enemies. As you face guilt, your self-esteem rises. You no longer blame others for your failings, you have less need to flail out in anger and thus less need to feel guilty.

THE GREATEST COURAGE

It takes courage to say to the self, "I am less than perfect, I have done or thought something sinful, selfish and inconsiderate." But in the long run you will feel more at ease, more honorable, than if you tried to sweep the truth under the carpet of guilt.

It is ironic many easily muster courage to undergo physical pain, including surgery, but when it comes to the pain of the mind, deny it exists. But, like the body, if ignored, eventually the mind exacts its price, perhaps in bodily illness, perhaps in mental illness of varying degree.

When you lack the courage to face guilt, you punish yourself more than you realize. The Biblical claim, "The truth shall set ye free," could have as corollary, "And the denial of truth shall enslave ye even more." The denial of the truth of the once-terrifying thoughts and wishes that whirl below the surface of your mind.

Freud implied that to be human is to have the capacity for guilt and you should be able to say, when you feel angry and express it mildly, "I was hostile but I didn't kill." Or if you neglect someone you love, "I was thoughtless but I didn't destroy." Or if you do not get a promotion, "I may have failed but I am not worthless." Or if you achieve a certain fame, "I am successful but that does not mean I have hurt anyone to reach the top."

The more you fail to face your anger and guilt, the more you leave courage behind. Not the courage that inspires men in battle or to discover ways to reach far planets. But perhaps the greater courage—to know the truths about yourself. Such truths as that, as an adult, you no longer desperately need your mother's love. A child needs a mother but an adult should be able to survive without asking others to take care of him as his mother once did.

The man who cannot tell his wife, "I admit I was insensitive when I forgot our eleventh wedding anniversary and I am very sorry," because he feels he has committed a crime, is reacting like a ten-year old who has forgotten his mother's birthday and believes she will no longer love him.

You should be aware, however, that confessing the truth to others is not always practical or expedient but may prove unnecessarily cruel. In the play *Nothing But the Truth*, the hero decided to speak only the truth for twenty-four hours. It proved the most painful experience of his life for he lost all his friends. When a woman he had known for years asked if he liked her new hat, he said it was hideous. When he failed to show up for an appointment and his friend asked why, he told his friend he really did not want to meet him. When his wife asked what he thought of the dinner she had carefully planned and cooked, he said it was tasteless. The author of the play wanted to show that to tell the truth all the time may be destructive to others.

But the ability to tell the truth to yourself is an admirable, too-rare quality. The self can listen without rancor and as you hear from within your own truths, you are less likely to make provocative attacks on others that produce guilt in you and bring punishment both from yourself and others. When you do not attack, you promote love, rather than calling forth hate.

If you know the truth about your feelings, you will sleep more soundly, feel better physically, not punish yourself by tossing away the night reviewing how you have hurt others or they have hurt you, then feeling guilty. You will not experience your guilt through psychosomatic symptoms. You will live more at peace with yourself—and it is with yourself you *must* live, twenty-four hours a day, seven days a week, from birth to death. This new peace will not only be reflected in your daily activities but in your dreams as nightmares disappear. They are no longer needed in view of the new daytime awareness of what you believed unspeakable terrors—the unreal ghosts of childhood.

One woman, able to be more honest with herself as she explored the wishes and fantasies that made her feel guilty, examined her relationships with those she loved. She became aware she had stopped obsessively making cutting remarks. She might think of them occasionally but no longer uttered them. You do not have to verbalize every thought. Only a child does this, unless he is too terrified to talk.

This woman no longer needed to hurl the verbal spear. She realized the caustic wisecrack had served to try to rid herself of hostility. As she slowly developed more of an empathy for others, aware of her need to be center stage, speak lines that would bring shocking attention but little love from family and friends, she felt less guilty.

Consideration for others, awareness of how they too suffer, reduces your guilt as you feel less angry at them. This is not to advocate always turning the other cheek, for you need to defend yourself when unjustly attacked. If you have been oversubmissive, afraid to assert your rights, mistakenly equating assertion with assaultiveness and violent anger, it is a step forward toward greater self-esteem to speak up when you feel exploited.

A woman writer lived in a large apartment house on the same floor as a concert pianist and the two became friends, respecting each other's privacy. One day the pianist asked the writer if he could borrow her typewriter for a few hours to send letters to professional musical organizations. He did not want to write by hand as he did to friends. The writer did not want to refuse him anything reasonable but felt angry, thought this request unfair. She told him he could borrow anything in the apartment *but* the typewriter on which she depended for her living. Her friend said he did not feel that way about his piano, she could use it any time she wished, but he understood her decision not to lend her typewriter.

The writer then wondered whether the use of the piano equaled that of a typewriter and feeling guilty asked another friend, a psychotherapist, if she had acted reasonably. He told her she had a perfect right to refuse to jeopardize her livelihood. If her friend damaged the typewriter she would suffer loss of income.

The writer realized that though her refusal might hurt her friend, if she had given in she would hold back an anger that might produce such intense guilt it would destroy the friendship, in that she would likely end it. As it happened, the friend called someone who had a portable typewriter and carried it to his apartment. All concerned managed to solve the conflict with the least possible distress because the writer had faced her angry feelings honestly. She had not erupted in wrath, as she always believed she would if furious (as she had seen her parents explode in her childhood). Instead, she quietly explained how she felt to her friend, who then accepted her decision calmly.

This experience spurred memories of guilt in the writer over earlier times when her mother had forced her to lend her brother her most cherished toys or ordered her to take care of him when her mother was busy. The woman realized her anger was not directed at her innocent friend, who could accept a refusal, but at the mother of childhood who made her relinquish to her brother an object or precious minutes she wanted for herself. She also admitted to herself she had been jealous of her younger childhood rival because she felt he was her mother's favorite. As they grew up, he, the boy, was accorded privileges she was refused such as staying out late at night.

Thus do feelings of which you may not be aware, have not been aware of for perhaps decades and continue to deny, cause your current anger and guilt as they are stirred to the surface of your mind by what you believe a trivial word or occurrence. As you have the courage to face these buried feelings and assert yourself when you are in the right—no longer fearing justified assertion as an act of murder—you will lose guilt. You will find you have been punishing yourself for crimes purely imaginary. The voice of guilt is the voice of implied punishment. The "conscience that makes cowards of us all" becomes less punitive as your unrealistic fear and anger evaporate.

You will acquire a new peace of mind when you do not have to repress so much guilt at such cost to your mental and physical well-being. The peace comes from not having to deceive yourself. You cease looking at yourself as either saint or sinner and accept yourself as a vulnerable mortal.

To face the inner self requires the true courage. For that inner self contains what Freud referred to as "the demons of hell" he was loosing through his discoveries of both the content of the unconscious part of the mind and the method of reaching and releasing the "demons" safely. As you face these demons, they lose their pernicious power, disappear like a puff of psychic smoke. You wonder how you ever thought them so terrifying. Then you realize how vulnerable the child, how full of fear the child, and how powerful the parents' edicts on control of the strong hungers against which you, as a child, struggled.

You forgive yourself for what you thought horrendous wishes, ask "Why am I giving myself such a hard time as an adult?" You assume a more benign conscience. If you can become your own best friend, why can't you become your own benign conscience?

You, like everyone else, need courage to live—the greatest courage of all is to face your deepest fears and wishes. This is the real war. You have to make peace with your hidden enemy—the only enemy that really counts. The destructive voices within from the past.

The truth about yourself will not hurt as much as your denial of it. Denial can prove your psychic executioner, your self-inflicted sentence of death. Only you can change this verdict.

Life is no bed of roses, no cup of tea, no bowl of cherries, no lasting party. If you think of life as simple, if you do not give space to the idea that each of us is very complicated in thoughts, fantasies and feelings, you make your life that much harder. You increase your guilt as your defenses against knowing the real causes become more and more rigid.

It is an illusion to believe we must live torn by guilt because we cannot face the hidden truths. When you feel the touch of guilt, ask yourself, "What am I really feeling guilty about? What am I denying that is the cause of my guilt?" As you discover the guilt stems for the most part from unrealistic causes you will feel new pleasure in life.

11

CHANGING YOUR INNER SCRIPT OF GUILT

UNDERSTANDING YOUR INNER SCRIPT

You need to know the "inner script" of your life to lessen anxiety, anger and guilt. You have to understand what the voices within still say that has caused your unhappiness over the years.

The voices include both your own and those of your parents, voices that keep on controlling your thoughts, acts and fantasies. An essential part of the truth about yourself centers on distorted fantasies that, as a child, you were bound to concoct about yourself, your parents and the world outside.

You need to become aware of these twisted impressions and how you tended to magnify small traumas so that many of your feelings were intensified beyond what reality demanded. You looked at yourself and your mother and father at times as though you all were images in the crazy mirrors of the "fun houses" in entertainment parks. Your imagination ran wild about the witches and giants in your life. As did your ideas of the excessive punishment that would be inflicted on you for thoughts of revenge when the witches and giants hurt you.

Your unhappiness is perhaps more self-created than you wish to admit. True, your parents left their emotional imprints as they tried to guide and protect you but sometimes, instead, threatened you, causing you to develop a punitive conscience. But in essence you write your own inner script. You are responsible for the anger, shame and guilt you feel. If you wish to ease guilt you have to become aware of and take responsibility for this script. You have to change some of the self-destructive action and the false lines.

Your inner script appears in your daydreams and nightdreams. In your daydreams you plot ways to get even with those who hurt you or imagine sexual intimacy with someone you find alluring. In your nightdreams your wish is disguised because it holds a fear and terror you do not want to face openly. You may not realize it but in a dream you arrange the plot, write every scene, choose the cast. You play all the roles—the corpse on the floor and the one who has committed murder, the demanding boss and the subjugated hireling, the abandoned lover and the one who abandons.

Dreams tell you the hidden truths about yourself. You are an oft-amazed author but you have to take responsibility for what you have written, no one else has had a hand in your dreams. The wishes that dominate your dreams and are given partial release in the images and acts you imagine while asleep are the deep wishes that dominate your daily life, causing guilt.

Your inner script is writ slowly over the years, starting at birth. Some experts in human behavior believe it begins at your conception, since the fantasies of your mother and father about their unborn child influence the way they will later act towards you and how you will eventually cope with life's problems. The young pregnant woman who takes drugs makes it clear she does not care much about her baby, since she knows drugs cause physical damage to a fetus. Nor does a reluctant expectant father, who has married a woman to give the baby a name but plans to leave both wife and baby right after the birth, care about his infant.

The inner script contains your earliest guilts. The guilt that stems from your jealousy of a brother or sister. Jealousy of the parent of the same sex as rival for the parent of the opposite sex. Passion for the parent of the opposite sex. Secret exploration of your body. Anger at rejection by a parent. Inability to accept frustration. Any threat to your omnipotence.

The eternal Greek chorus to your script contains the voices of your parents carried into adulthood. Voices that command, reproach, praise or intimidate. What Dr. Joseph Sandler, renowned psychoanalyst, calls "dialogue with the ghost mother," goes on within you during moments you are lonely, in pain, confused. There is no reason why you may not indulge in this slight regression to a time you received comfort, if the use is not excessive. Every mental process of which you are capable exists for your use in a moderate and reasonable way.

You can hear this dialogue with the ghost mother as you walk the streets of any large city. A homeless person talks to himself and, if you listen, you will hear, usually accompanied by curses, both commands of his angry parent and his retorts as an equally angry child. These emotionally overwhelmed men and women have never learned to control their childish primitive impulses, at least not in public forum. Emotionally needy, intensely angry and guilt-ridden, as may be seen in their faces, especially their eyes, they live out our nightmares as they lurch along the streets or slump in doorways, clad in rags, sometimes carrying a few tattered possessions wrapped in old cloths.

They still search for the "good mother" they never had. To some degree we all lack that "perfect" mother though many of us possess what Dr. D. W. Winnicott called "the good-enough mother." In the inner script of our lives we never give up our demand for the perfect mother but most of us avoid becoming "homeless" because we are not as angry, deprived or guilty as those who make their beds at night in parks or doorways. We have been able to emotionally separate sufficiently from our mothers so we function without demanding substitute mothers take care of us.

Our mothers allowed us emotional separation from them so

we were not doomed to a dependency that crippled us unduly. You pay a high price for independence if it has not been granted early by your parents. Independence does not mean the freedom to do as you rebelliously wish but the ability to think clearly and choose wisely when you act.

In your inner script you may rage at your mother for frustrating you at times, for not always being available, but you have received enough strength from her so you can take care of yourself, at least when it comes to shelter, food and cleanliness. The homeless do not possess this strength, they have so little sense of their identity that, as their monologues show, they are still emotionally merged with their mothers, conduct angry dialogues so the world knows of their misery.

To ease guilt you have to become aware that the words you heard and uttered as you grew up helped form your inner script. Some of the reasons you give to explain your feelings of guilt may be rationalizations that cover the truth. A truth that will emerge only if you understand the inner script and how much you have been influenced by it.

Your script deals with two main themes. Almost always you will find persistent guilt hides behind the partially closed doors of childhood that defend against your two strongest drives—sexual and aggressive. The emotion of love is seen in the tenderness and caring that accompanies raw sexual need. The emotion of hate causes you to want to get even with those who threaten your physical or psychological survival. Love "makes the world go 'round" in pleasurable ways and hate makes the world seem dangerous and painful.

THE FIRST THEME: SEXUAL DESIRE

The first theme of your inner script deals with your sexual desires and the guilt they arouse. Erica Jong described the dilemma the guilty feel in *Fear of Flying*, when the heroine declares, "The man I love I cannot fuck, the man I fuck, I cannot love." When sex is devoid of tenderness and respect it remains just a "fuck," with little chance of a warm, tender bond between the partners.

You have to be able to enjoy your tender feelings for love to be part of sex. Tenderness permits you the exploration of the "touch" and one of the requisites of sex without guilt is the ability to enjoy touching and being touched. Sexual play is now accepted in society but to be able to "play" with your partner sexually, and to be played with, you must feel free of the guilt of childhood masturbation. You know you do not demean yourself for wishing a partner to increase your pleasure in sex by the touch. Nor do you think of the partner as a helpless child if he wants to depend on you for his greater pleasure through the touch. This entails the right to explore in ways prohibited in childhood.

All the exercises Masters and Johnson provide, all the staring at photographs in *The Joy of Sex*, does not free you to explore new sexual techniques if you still hear the command, "Don't touch yourself there," as though you would damage yourself beyond repair by the slightest touch in a forbidden part of the body.

If you cringe at touching or being touched, you are reacting to guilt about masturbation. To masturbate at an early age is a natural act for a child and the wish to engage in it never completely disappears but becomes revived as part of adult sex. You may also cringe at the touch of another person because you had a mother or father who drew away from you when you sought to touch them as part of your expression of love. You will think of the touch as distasteful if, as a child, you have not received gentle, loving touches from a parent or been allowed to bestow them.

Your adult sexuality recapitulates in part your earlier psychosexual development. It repeats the sensations, feelings and fantasies you experienced growing up. These emotional aspects of sex are not discussed fully enough in sex education courses nor in the popular books about sex, which feature mainly the mechanical aspects. All the sex exercises in the world, all your reading about sex, will not reduce your inhibitions if you still view your sexual partner in fantasy as the cold, aloof, demanding parent of childhood. You may be able, through the sex exercises, to be more proficient physically in the act of sex. But the critical voices of your past still haunt you and limit your pleasure because you feel so guilty about the earlier fantasies that rule you.

You have to learn to accept your sexual fantasies as natural. They are part and parcel of your every relationship from the day you were born, starting the moment you opened your eyes and first looked into your mother's face. As you grew up, you had sexual fantasies about all the members of your family. After all, they were your first loves, models for all subsequent loves.

When you feel irritable, depressed or unhappy you may be repressing your sexual fantasies. A married man in an advertising agency found it impossible to start a project he was assigned. His co-worker was an auburn-haired, blue-eyed woman of twenty-five, beautiful enough to be a movie star. He kept postponing a meeting to discuss the project, saying he was still void of ideas.

He talked at dinner with a male friend of his reluctance to meet with this woman. The friend pointed out that perhaps he wanted to have sex with the young woman but dared not admit it. The friend suggested that if this man could face his amorous feelings and accept the decision either to pursue her or give up the idea of sex with her, he would feel far more at ease in her presence. The man took his friend's advice, decided he would remain true to his wife and found he had no trouble working with his lovely colleague. They created new ideas for the advertising campaign, putting the "libido" (sexual energy) into their livelihood. He could admire her as men admire attractive women without feeling unfaithful to his wife.

A woman administrator of a hospital who found herself attracted to a male subordinate fifteen years younger felt guilty. To admit she wanted sex with so youthful a man made her feel like a mother seducing her son. Many mothers have sexual fantasies about a son during his adolescence, sometimes ear-

194

THE FIRST THEME: SEXUAL DESIRE

lier. This is a natural wish hardly ever put into action, though studies show a number of cases of incest between mother and son but far less than between father and daughter.

You may have all the sexual fantasies you wish without danger of becoming a pervert. Such fantasies are part of your sexual development and they do not stop until the moment you draw your last breath. Not a fantasy is lost to memory. Fantasies never hurt a soul other than those who feel needless guilt at having them.

When you suffer irrational guilt you are apt to be repeating the irrational attitudes toward sex possessed by your parents, your role models. One woman recalled her father warning her when she was in her early teens not to have sex with a man, predicting she would become promiscuous if she allowed this before marriage. She took his advice, as she had taken his advice about all the important decisions of her life, and waited until marriage for sex. It proved an unhappy marriage that lasted only a year. She wished she had been able to explore her sexual desires with a few men instead of marrying a very rigid man who evidently knew as little as she about sexual intimacy.

Another woman copied the sexual behavior of her promiscuous father, a man she had revered, rather than the sexual behavior of her reserved mother who had never been unfaithful to her husband. This daughter grew up afraid she would be like her cool, aloof mother, preferring to imitate her affectionate, carefree father. She never was able to settle for a lasting relationship, unsure of her feelings, unable to trust herself or a man. When you unknowingly imitate the wanton sexual behavior of a parent, you usually will be unhappy. But by realizing you imitate a parent, you then free yourself to make your own pattern. It is the unconscious repetition of an irrational act that keeps you in bondage.

As you are able to view your parents more realistically, you can detach yourself more emotionally from them and achieve your own sexual identity. With this courageous act you also will project on your parents far less your concept of perfection and omnipotence. Unfortunately, parents may make it difficult for a child to separate from them because they emotionally need the child almost as much as the child needs them.

In the writing of a new script for your adult life you can arrive at your own convictions as to what sexual intimacy means by examining the stereotypes you have carried from the past. Have you identified with your more sexually aggressive parent or your more passive one? Or identified sexually in some ways with one parent, in other ways with the second parent? The answers depend on the complicated emotional web of love and hate woven between your parents and you in your early years.

Perhaps unknown to yourself at the moment, you are repressing sexual wishes you never dared act on. The crusader who openly condemns vice is often secretly only too eager to study pornographic films, articles and photographs in magazines as evidence for his campaign against vice. Such as the Reverend Alfred Davidson in Maugham's *Miss Sadie Thompson*, the short story that depicted the suicide of a married minister after he found himself sexually hungering for a prostitute who, under his influence, had reformed.

Those we choose to condemn for their sexual behavior usually act out the sexual desires we have been taught not to tolerate in ourselves. We would not need to accuse others of being licentious ("dirty old men" or "lascivious young flirts") if we were more accepting of our sexual wishes. Many of us would like, at times, to have several sexual partners perhaps, or to attend orgies. To admit lust does not mean we have to act lustfully. It means only that we accept our natural instincts. Accept too we may have to restrain them by understanding, not repressing them. We are all born hedonistic but parents and society ask us to be less pleasure-seekers and more responsible as spouse, parent and working member of the human race.

You have to accept it is not abnormal to have an occasional homosexual dream since dreams hold memories of your entire sexual development—your wishes from the day you opened your mouth to take in nourishment. Frequently in fantasy you may lust after members of your own sex. The wishes relate to early adolescence when girls had crushes on girls, boys on boys and early childhood when you were attracted to members of both sexes.

You need feel no guilt if you have a warm, loving relationship with a member of the same sex, one in which there is no sexual acting out. Many a man feels guilty about liking another man, fearing to face his childhood feelings of wanting love from his father. This yearning is frequently denied as men fail to get along with male colleagues, not aware they are guilty about secret wishes for a father's occasional reassuring hug.

In the Army, where men spend much time together, mental health experts find that many signs of emotional distress in those who come for help are based on guilty wishes to be accepted, admired and esteemed by other men. Like children, who feel if they admit their secret wishes they will act on them, these men become depressed and tense as they deny feelings that are human.

You also should try to come to terms, though this is difficult, with your first wish when, as a baby, you wanted to lustfully devour every object in sight, including toys. This ravenous, cannibalistic wish exists in all of us as infants when we start to relate to the world solely through the mouth. At this stage your sexual and aggressive desires are not integrated but eventually will be, as you know reality.

It is not easy to accept that you are insatiable, have sexual fantasies about those of the same sex or sexual fantasies about innumerable members of the opposite sex. But if you can become aware of the fantasies that lie beneath your anxiety, beneath your anguish, beneath your anger, you will break the vicious circle that ends in guilt. These fantasies have been seething for years in the storehouse of your mind and are the cause of much of your unhappiness.

To reach the sexual fantasies that cause your guilt it helps to relax and let your mind "wander." Your mind does not actually wander. There is always a direct emotional connection

197

between your thoughts as they follow from one to another. They may seem nonsensical, irrelevant, crazy, but if you trace them to their hidden sources, they make sense in terms of the forbidden wishes and primitive desires they both reflect and hide.

One of the ways to reduce guilt and make life more pleasurable is to allow yourself not only to enjoy sexual play but play in work, in recreation, in creativity—to engage in what psychoanalyst Heinz Hartmann called "regression in the service of the ego." When you permit yourself to regress in a way that puts yourself in touch with the "good" child within, you increase your pleasure. Such as playful behavior on a vacation. There is truth to the adage, "All work and no play makes Jack a dull boy." Whoever wrote those words was trying to be a benign conscience encouraging you to relax and help lessen your guilt about the time you take for play.

To enjoy sex without guilt you also must be able to enjoy your sexual appetite. Many of us who feel guilty hear the child within accusing, "To hug, to kiss, to want sexual gratification is a sin." Some feel so guilty they vomit at the thought of sex. Many prefer getting drunk as a way of avoiding sex. Addiction is less fearful to them than intimacy with another person. Addiction is also a way of stopping the self from what is felt as the challenge of sex.

When you enjoy someone you love sexually, you are saying in a sense your partner "tastes good." Partners taste good when each as a baby has experienced his mother's breasts or the milk she provides from a bottle as "tasting good"—the aura of the oral period has been a "tasty" one. Some who become nauseous in restaurants or find certain sexual partners "distasteful" are reliving the "distasteful" experiences of their first months of life. Others speak of a sexual partner as "unpalatable," as "leaving a sour taste," implying they have no appetite for sex.

A woman in therapy became nauseous every time her husband tried to penetrate her in sexual intercourse. Her dreams and fantasies revealed she unknowingly equated her hus-

198

band's penis with her mother's breast. To her, taking in a penis was the same as taking in her mother's "cold, unkind" breast and she wanted to vomit, rather than enjoy the experience.

To get the full pleasure of sex, you have to feel some of the love toward your partner that a baby feels toward a mother. If you have unresolved hateful feelings toward your mother, sex may become like forced feeding. There follows the wish to regurgitate the experience or to give up sex completely.

You also feel less guilty if you become aware at times you would like to turn your marital partner into a parent so you would be loved and protected far more. This universal wish, which becomes intensified in marriage, may create marital stress. You may prefer to deny such yearnings, pretend they do not exist, repress your desire to be embraced and fondled. Without realizing it, you begin to hate your partner for withholding love. You do not face or understand the hatred because you do not know why you are angry. You feel guilty, whereas you could ease guilt if you admit you want your partner occasionally to be a mother.

To enjoy sex without guilt also means you no longer feel like a frightened, angry, guilty child rebelling at your parents' restrictions. You do not use your sexual partner as outlet for your childish wishes of dependency. You feel dependent on the partner in an adult way, emotionally separate from him. Some yearn for a relationship in which they psychologically merge with their sexual partner and for this feel guilty. If there is too much fear and guilt they may flee from one sexual partner to another, overwhelmed by the desire to be abnormally close, physically and emotionally. Or they shun a sexual relationship completely, not daring to get involved even temporarily.

Guilt prevents you from experiencing not only the full physical pleasure of sex but the equally important emotional pleasures of love, caring, respect, tenderness, friendship—all part of fulfilling sex. To achieve the emotional pleasures, you need to see your sexual partner in his own right, not endow him with the magical qualities of either the all-giving or all-frustrating parent of a bygone era.

199

Then you will be able to share love, to give it freely and accept it freely, rather than demand what no one could give— a feeling of confidence in yourself as a man or woman. That comes only from within.

As Dr. Karl Menninger says:

> Most of us spend a lifetime finding out what love really is. It is surely little wonder that, with the start they receive in childhood and adolescence, many people reach adult life without the faintest conception of what love is, or of what it might be for them.

If there are conflicts in your marriage, remember it takes two to tango, psychologically speaking—the dance of the wits. If a wife controls a husband, he has unconsciously invited her to do so by his choice of a woman who wants to be boss of the home. Unhappy marriages show a collusion in which partners act our ancient childhood battles. Most of the time marriages are made not on the basis of the real or conscious wish but the unreal or unconscious one.

When there are complaints by a husband or wife, those complaints hide unspoken, unrecognized wishes. If a wife stays with a husband who beats her, in all probability she wants to be beaten for her forbidden thoughts and for her guilt. If a husband complains, "My wife treats me like a child," part of him wants to be treated as a child, even as he consciously resents it.

A chronic marital complaint usually masks an unconscious wish that will keep guilt at bay. A wife complains, "My husband's sexual desire is low. He rarely wants sex." She unconsciously *wants* a husband who seldom asks for sex because she feels guilty about her sexual wishes and can escape the guilt by berating and blaming him. A husband says, "I married a cold bitch, she's as unresponsive as a wooden Indian." He unconsciously *wants* a cold woman. A sexy one would make demands he is afraid he could not fulfill and he would feel guilty.

To enjoy a sexually rewarding life you have to be relatively

free of the guilt connected to dependency wishes. Some husbands, though dissatisfied with their wives, do not embark on
an extramarital sexual spree. They are afraid if their wives, on
whom they are excessively dependent, found out, they would
leave home. It is not morality or fidelity that binds the husband but a symbiotic tie to the "mother-wife."

Some wives voice their unhappiness at such dependency, as
do some husbands about their wives. The common complaint
is, "You don't give me enough space." This means, "I am afraid
you will emotionally overwhelm me, and to survive I must have
more time to myself or I will go mad." Each partner feels anger, then guilt, for being part of an extremely dependent twosome. Many a marriage breaks up because of an overdepen-
dency that demands too much emotional investment from the
partner.

A convenient and expeditious way of easing guilt in marriage when you feel uncomfortable is to ask, "Why do I secretly want it this way?" The answer will always prove psychologically on target. You have chosen a partner who provides
what you unconsciously wish for.

If you want a happy marriage and free sexual intimacy you
will engage in a mutual dependency different from your earlier dependency on your mother and father. This mature dependency allows you and your partner to regress in fantasy
and action so there is mutual sexual satisfaction. Enjoyable sex
involves both cooperation and, at times, acceptance of frustration. No two people always want the same amount of sex at
the same time. You have to adjust to your partner's desires as
well as possessing the freedom to state your own. Your coop-
erative spirit will result in warm feelings from your partner
and relative freedom in both of you from competition with or
destructive fantasies toward imagined or real rivals.

You have to be able to tolerate at times sexual tension without immediate gratification. You should not feel pressured to
provide instant gratification—for yourself or for your partner.
As one man put it, "I don't want to be rushed through the act
of sex nor do I want my partner to feel rushed. If I feel urgent

about sex this destroys much of my pleasure. It becomes an obsessive act rather than an act of choice."

You should try to keep hostility out of sex. The man who speaks of the sexual act as "banging away" is showing hate, not tenderness or love for the woman. One man said, "I'm afraid if I lie down naked with a woman I will act like a savage beast. I might physically hurt her." He felt guilty about his violent wishes, fantasized the sex act as fulfillment of those wishes, as a hostile triumph, "savaging" the woman. A woman may resist sex because in fantasy she imagines the man as the father she wished as a child would "penetrate" her. Guilt runs deep at such fantasy, it is less painful to negate all sexual desire.

If you feel too vulnerable, too dependent, too weak, you may compensate by a facade of toughness, look on sex with hostility. Like the child who throws rocks at another child to deny his strong sexual attraction, then feels guilty for the assault. If as a boy you felt deep anger at your mother, this feeling may emerge in the sexual act either in violence, inhibition, or guilt after the sexual act.

For many, sex becomes restrictive and constrictive, as they withdraw after foreplay or are unable to progress beyond mutual masturbation. In an old joke a man says of masturbation, "It's easier than having to get dressed and go out and find a woman, bring her home, then have her complain sex wasn't good enough." He is saying he does not trust a woman to enjoy sex with him, or he with her. For sexual pleasure, he goes back in time to an earlier stage of his sexual development when he could bring pleasure to himself without depending on anyone else. He feels guilty at this regression but he also feels a lesser fear than if faced with the challenge of sex with a woman.

If you are a "Don Juan" or a woman who is promiscuous, you feel guilty about remaining true to one partner. You equate the one partner to a sexually taboo parent. The Don Juan is trying through sex to gain constant reaffirmation of his sexual prowess. He cannot love or be loved because of his guilt and he compensates by a behavior that tries to prove his sexual adequacy. Many men believe, as Casanova did, that if they have sex with hundreds of women they are the epitome of virility. They do not understand that to them sex has become a compulsion, rather than an enjoyable, loving, mutually enhancing intimate experience.

If you are a woman who cries after an orgasm you may feel you have taken part in an act your parents have forbidden and are ashamed. Your tears are those of a child who feels anxiety and anguish. Sometimes a woman sheds tears instead of having an orgasm and experiences the relief of sexual tension. Or she may cry because the man does not satisfy her fully and leaves her, as one woman described it, "on the edge of orgasm—the most frustrating of all feelings." A woman who cries a great deal, not only during sex but at other times, feels little pleasure except through suffering.

In our society fidelity is often considered a weakness rather than an admired trait. While many marital partners stay together out of anxiety and guilt, researchers on the extramarital affair have found that those aware of their conflicts have happy marriages while those unaware of why they feel troubled are the ones who experiment sexually outside marriage.

If you fail at marriage, not only all the person-to-person guilts are aroused but also the guilts from infancy on. You may wake each morning filled with guilt and not lose the conscious feeling until you fall asleep that night. Then you continue to feel guilty in your dreams.

You are part of a society which shows the highest rate of divorce ever, as men and women try to escape their guilt over unhappy marriages. But there has never been a time, starting with Adam and Eve, nor a civilization, where the majority were happily married. Even the ancient Greeks tried "open marriage" and the Romans engaged in "swinging" couples. In spite of our contemporary life styles we have not progressed any further than our forebears in ridding ourselves of the guilts inherent in betraying the promise, "I do."

Today's more liberal attitudes allow you to separate and divorce more easily. In one way this is healthy for it means an end to hypocrisy if your marriage is loveless. But the underlying issue remains hidden and thus rarely dealt with: The same conflicts will be perpetuated by both husband and wife in the next marital relationship and the same guilt will result unless each faces the reasons for his previous incompatibility.

Freud called the lustful, passionate feeling of "falling in love" akin to a "psychotic" state out of which the couple emerges into a reality that often proves painful. During that psychotic period, there is little or no awareness of the other person as a human being who possesses his own fears, needs and hates. Rather, he is hailed as a god who will fulfill all his partner's wishes.

Because of the emotional blindness we all feel to some degree during courtship, you will later feel anger and guilt, then self-hatred, because of the guilt. Your former "god" or "goddess" is now perceived as no more powerful than the fallible self. You bring to marriage the guilts of childhood and project them on the spouse, as he projects his guilts on you.

Guilt among married couples runs high, as proved by the fact marriage all too often does not seem to work. Among married couples, statistics show, suicide has increased, as has alcoholism, drug addiction, promiscuity, violence and depression.

How do you reduce guilt in marriage? So you do not have to destroy the marriage or remain married and function as though fueled by an undercurrent of despair and rage, hating to face the night knowing the spouse is there. Overcoming guilt in marriage means facing and accepting your hostile fantasies and wishes. It also means recognizing the depth of your dependency—the wish the spouse be the parent of childhood. This wish is openly shown in the way husbands and wives call each other "mommy" or "daddy" or "papa" and "mama." The wish is right out in the open—that not-so-unconscious demand, one bound to produce great guilt.

You may also sabotage your chance of a successful marriage because of your guilt at believing you will be happier than your parents. Many a woman cannot enjoy sex with a lover or husband because she fantasizes, or perhaps it was true, that her mother did not have a fulfilling sexual relationship. Children sense whether parents are sexually compatible, no telling words need be heard.

Success at marriage entails knowing when you feel guilty and why. A young wife insisted her husband be inordinately clean. She followed him around, emptying ashtrays, picking up anything he dropped, cleaning the bathtub right after he took a shower. He had grown up with a mother who also did this, one reason he unconsciously sought the same behavior in a wife. But now he became furious at his wife, as he had been afraid to be with his mother. When his wife commanded, "Please pick up your socks and put them in the drawer," he roared, "I'll do as I damned please!" and flung them at the wall. He heard in her voice the hated domineering tones of the past and felt guilty at his anger.

He apologized and she said, in good humor, he did not need to, she was too compulsive about neatness, she had no right to tell him what to do. Over time, as they understood each other's needs—one to be neat, the other to be sloppy—their guilt disappeared. They had been dominated by voices from the past, now had to consider the needs of each other.

If there is a common denominator for guilt feelings that keep marriage from being a success, it is that we view marriage through the eyes of the child within. We forget we are not as powerful as our fantasies would have us be, nor as evil as we appear in nightmares that tell of our wishes to lust like Casanova, annihilate like Attila the Hun and cling to our spouse like a leech.

You have to accept the spouse not as a stand-in for the voices of the past but as a warm, loving, sometimes ambivalent soul—same as you are—capable of accepting the realistic demands of marriage but not expected to fulfill the unreal ones. Able to live and let live, knowing there may be some things you will never understand, both about yourself and the one you love.

But you can keep trying to understand why you feel guilty. Irrational guilt rarely raises its formidable head when there is a reasonable love for others and a sense of fair play. Guilt appears only when you wage battles based on fantasies, often romantic fantasies about the marriage of your parents. You have to face the fact that one of the reasons success in marriage is difficult to achieve is that too few of us have witnessed consistently happily married parents.

Sex without guilt means you have been able to add tenderness to erotic feelings and will not be plagued by anger or remorse. If you can be tender toward the one you love, and he is tender toward you, if you desire each other sexually and respect each other, there is good chance you both will enjoy monogamy, able to cope with its frustrations. If you are guilt-ridden about sex, you are more apt to be a philanderer, a bisexual or a celibate.

You will gain little comfort by trying out sexual partner after sexual partner, then feeling guilt. Sexual clinics will not help you feel free about your sexual feelings. That free feeling comes not by edict from without but approval from within. No advice can set you free sexually. Attaining such freedom is more complex than the written word.

If you possess severe sexual conflicts you can tell yourself you are feeling guilty about childish sexual acts, childhood sexual fantasies and childhood sexual wishes. You unconsciously want to engage in incest, be a member of the opposite sex, give yourself incessant physical satisfaction and are furious because you are thwarted in carrying out these primitive desires.

Mature sexuality implies you have faced at long last all the thoughts and wishes you have believed "sinful." You now discover them for what they are—unnecessary mental torment caused by memories of days when you did not know what love really meant.

THE SECOND THEME: AGGRESSIVE DESIRE

Equally as important as the sexual theme in the dramatic action of your inner script is the second theme—the role of your forbidden aggressive desires. The feelings of hate and wishes for vengeance you may find difficult to face. Yet if you wish to lessen your guilt you have to become aware of how angry you have been over the years at enemies you wished dead. Each time you felt a spark of hate for someone this automatically carried with it the wish he die. The feel of the death-wish is alien to no one, no matter how strong the denial.

The action of your life, in a psychic sense, takes place in large part on a field of battle where phantom bodies pile high, as your guilt mounts even higher. The cause of your angry, often violent feelings is the result of your "punctured narcissism" or blows to your self-esteem, according to Dr. Gregory Rochlin.

In *The Masculine Dilemma*, Rochlin speaks of masculine narcissism as "especially vulnerable." He quotes Joseph Conrad: "A man's self-esteem remains precarious and demands that he put out of sight all reminders of his folly, of weakness, of morality; they all work against efficiency—the memory of failures." Rochlin adds, "In these characteristics the boy was never more father to the man."

He also points out that, "precariously rooted self-esteem being the condition, masculinity is besieged—prone to injury, sensitive to and fearful of limitations. Aggressiveness and at times a ready hostility, typical of ever-vigilant masculinity, issue easily to its defense."

In fantasy, we automatically wish to kill anyone who rejects us. Rejection is the cruelest of blows. You, like everyone on earth, wish to be loved beyond human possibility, praised lavishly every moment of the day, suffer no rivals. If you are overlooked, ignored or abandoned, you will feel like committing murder or suicide, the opposite side of the coin of murder.

Your feelings of frustration cause your fury. Your rage will diminish as you accept that life contains innumerable frustrations. You will *never* get the idolatry you feel you deserve, nor the fame and fortune you covet. But if you know your aims are unrealistic and your anger at frustration disproportionate, you will not suffer the guilt that arises from the robotlike defense of denial. The cheerful optimist often hides his pessimistic psychic plunge into anger and guilt.

Our anger is fueled by our narcissism, envy, greed and jealousy—the "deadly" sins. But they are par for human intercourse, otherwise they would not be so forbidden. We all wish for what we do not have—fame, success, possessions of others. Though we may deny our competitive spirit and envy of those who have more than we do, such feelings are natural. If we do not accept them as such, we punish ourselves with needless guilt.

A young woman writer was intensely jealous of, and thus angry at, an older, far more successful writer for her financial success and public plaudits. One day the younger writer learned of the personal life of the older writer. She had been divorced from two sadistic men and her only child had killed himself at nineteen. The younger writer lost her jealousy and anger. She thought that though she would like the fame and fortune of the older woman, she would not wish the anguish of her emotional life. She preferred taking her chances on a less traumatic existence with a man who was not sadistic and live without wealth and fame.

It helps to appease guilt to realize you may wish for more than you can achieve. You may feel a cannibalistic anger when your fantasies are not fulfilled (overeating is a civilized sublimation for your cannibalistic wishes from the oral stage of development). As a child you exaggerated the differences between your parents and yourself, thought of them as gods while you were as an ant struggling for survival. The more envious you are of someone with possessions and power, the more you make him into a hero and the more you turn yourself into the miserable, cringing insect.

You would feel less guilt, be far less angry, if you accept that the similarities between king and peasant are much greater than the differences. Most of us look on the important figures in our adult life such as employers as though they were deities. You need to become aware that the gods of your present and past also possess conflicts, limitations, failings and, like you, eat, sleep, go to the bathroom and have difficulties with intimate relationships. When you realize no one is a god, you are less inclined to hate, to feel murderous.

Freud realized the important part repressed anger and its companion guilt played in the mind's script as a result of his self-analysis and his analysis of patients. One of his first was an eighteen-year old girl he called Katharina (he disguised the names of patients to preserve their anonymity). This had to be one of his shortest cases for he saw her only twice. But it was a very important meeting, both he and Katharina probably never forgot it. She helped him realize the importance of becoming aware of hidden rage so guilt would disappear. She had good reason to be a furious young woman.

Freud was on vacation in the Alps walking along a mountain trail, when stopped by Katharina, a waitress at the inn where he was staying. She had followed him up the mountain after learning he was a famous man who helped unhappy men and women find out the cause of their distress.

Freud was accustomed to seeing patients on his vacation (some rented houses near him for the summer so they could continue their analysis). He sat down on a bench with Katharina and listened.

She told him she suffered severe headaches, "like a hammering in my head," shortness of breath, dizziness and such a weight pressing against her chest that she had difficulty breathing. She felt at times she was going to die. She was also troubled by the vision of a man's angry face staring at her.

Freud encouraged her to talk freely about her feelings and after initial reluctance she did so, with the words, "You can say *anything* to a doctor, I suppose." (All of her quotes are from Freud's report of the case.)

She said her physical symptoms had started two years before on a day her mother had left the house to shop and she and her younger brother went to their father's room. They found the door locked. It seemed strange to her he would bolt the door during the day.

She decided, with the curiosity of the young, to go outside and look in the window. She saw her father in bed with her young cousin, a girl her age, who lived with them and served as cook.

Freud asked what she felt as she stared at the scene. She said, "I came away from the window at once, and leant up against the wall and couldn't get my breath—just what happens to me since. Everything went blank; my eyelids were forced together, and there was a hammering and buzzing in my head."

Freud asked if she told her mother what she had seen and Katharina replied, "Oh, no I said nothing."

But her behavior was so queer in the next few days that her mother suspected Katharina was concealing some frightening secret. When her mother demanded to know what it was, Katharina described what she had seen. The mother then confronted her husband with the story, he confessed it was true and she left him, taking her two children with her.

Under Freud's questioning, Katharina further recalled that when she was younger, she had traveled with her father one winter on a trip into the valley where they spent the night at an inn. He stayed up late, drinking and playing cards, and she went to bed in the room they were to share. Sometime during the night she awoke suddenly, "feeling his body" pressing against her. Alarmed, she hopped out of bed, demanded, "What are you up to? Why don't you stay in your own bed?"

"Come on, you silly," he said. "You don't know how nice it is."

"I don't like your 'nice' things; you don't even let one sleep in peace," she rebuked him. She stood by the door, ready to run out into the hall should he persist, but he fell asleep.

Freud commented that from the way in which she told of defending herself, it seemed she had not clearly recognized the attack as sexual because she was too young. When he asked if she knew what her father was trying to do, she replied, "Not at the time."

She recalled another night at home when she was forced to run out of the house because her father became very drunk and made advances. She remembered other scenes of intimacy between her father and her cousin.

As a result of this session, finally able to talk of her feelings—though not relating her intense anger at her father to the sexual threat against herself and for fulfilling his sexual desire with her cousin—Katharina briefly reported to Freud several days later that she felt healthy once again. Her headaches, dizziness, pressure in her chest and shortness of breath had vanished.

She also realized, she told Freud, that the "angry" face she sometimes saw staring at her was that of her father. She remembered he had glared at her in wrath, knowing she had told on him, when her mother had accused him of seducing his niece. The "angry" face had remained with Katharina so persistently because it also mirrored her violent anger. An anger she had been unable to admit or express at feeling both betrayed and assaulted by the one man in the world supposed to protect her from sexual attack. The anger of the daughter whose father forces her to commit incest has been well-documented by psychoanalysts. In a recent case the daughter, fourteen years old, shot her father, who had forced her for four years to submit sexually to him. She was finally unable to contain her fury over his repeated sexual molestations.

Listening to later patients, Freud concluded that, like Katharina, if a child were subjected to sexual assault or undue sexual stimulation the child could not emotionally or physically handle, even if this produced no apparent effect at the time, it could gain traumatic power over the years because of the child's repressed rage and guilt. In later life it might result in symptoms of physical or mental illness.

While you were not likely to suffer this severe a trauma in childhood, you can ease much guilt if you become aware of the inner script of your life and understand how much child-hood anger you have repressed. The anger may be due to un-kind acts and provocations of your parents or to your narcis-sism which resented all the "no's," or both. It helps to ease guilt if you realize your darkest desires are never lily white. Your strongest instinct is to survive and thus the emotion of anger is always near at hand, or rather, near at heart. This allows you to take quick action at the first sign of danger—physical or psychological.

You have to face the fact that your emotional survival may, at times in childhood, have been so jeopardized that your adult life is filled with a hate and guilt that will disappear only as you become aware of the old wounds. You would do well to face them, at long last, so you can write a happier inner script for the rest of your life.

12

IF GUILT PERSISTS

SEEK FURTHER TRUTHS

After you start facing your conflicts, if your self-esteem still remains low you may have achieved only partial answers as to why you feel guilty. You have to explore those "depths beyond depths," as Emerson so aptly described it.

Dig deeper you must. You have to keep asking, "What forbidden wishes am I evading?" "What blows to my pride am I not acknowledging?" "What losses and rejections am I not admitting?"

At first it may take work to start to ease your guilt—work with the self and on the self. In psychotherapy there are two main concepts: transference and countertransference. Transference refers to the irrational, subjective unrealistic feelings of childhood that the patient "transfers" onto the therapist. "Countertransference" alludes to the unrealistic, distorted feelings the therapist may possess toward the patient that reflect the analyst's unresolved conflicts. No therapist is perfect though he is expected to be by every patient, representing the all-powerful parent of childhood fantasy.

IF GUILT PERSISTS

When asked, "Does self-analysis work?" Siegfried Bernfeld, internationally known psychoanalyst, once replied, "No, the countertransference gets in the way." Meaning the part of the self that acts as therapist. Asked the same question, Freud once said that when people analyze themselves they are too satisfied with partial answers. But a partial answer is better than no answer and may lead, with enough probing, to the whole answer. As you keep trying to discover the more deeply hidden answers, you often succeed. Sometimes they emerge when you are least trying. You cannot force the truths of the mind, they have a pace of their own at which they reveal themselves.

LOOK FOR BLOWS AT SELF-ESTEEM

Frequently when guilt persists you may not be aware you feel hurt, angry and guilty about your punctured narcissism. Blows to your self-esteem may wound deeply as you feel rejected, inadequate, less than human. Narcissism will turn into self-esteem if you understand the causes of your guilt.

One woman felt rejected because her husband worked six nights a week at his law practice when she wanted to be with him at parties or the movies or at least have his company watching television at home. At first she denied her hurt feelings, squelched her anger, then felt depressed and guilty. If she had been able to admit she felt unloved and wanted more attention, had a right to be angry at his neglect, her depression and guilt would have diminished.

Then one night she quietly told her husband how she felt, asked if he could spend more evenings at home. He said he knew he had been neglecting her, apologized. He explained he and his partner had been working overtime on two difficult legal cases and reported his partner's wife had also objected. He promised in three weeks the cases would be argued in court, he would have his evenings free and take her out every night. She said he would not have to go that far, she would be happy just to have him home.

He kept his word when the pressure of writing the legal briefs ended. He came home every night for dinner, took her to the movies or watched television with her. She had been able to speak in a calm way of her feelings, he had appreciated her right to feel resentful over his extra work at night. They had avoided what might have been a wide rift by talking frankly of their feelings instead of nursing imaginary blows to self-esteem.

Another husband became upset when his wife suddenly became famous as an artist. He could not admit he felt threatened as the breadwinner but instead lost his temper. He criticized her as a wife and mother, asked why she spent so much time on "silly art work." She felt angry at this attack but said nothing, knowing he felt threatened. If he could have admitted he was jealous and competitive, resented his wife making more money than he did, he would not have attacked her, then felt guilty. He also resented, without being aware of it, that she now had a life of her own. Sometimes the issue of a wife's financial income exceeding her husband's is far less a threat than his wishing to be the complete boss whose every demand must be met if he is not to feel less a man.

This husband's narcissism was injured. In its pristine form narcissism properly belongs in the nursery. It is the forerunner of self-esteem if all goes well psychologically, if we do not feel too threatened by our parents. When narcissism turns into a quiet pride in achievement and faith in the self, it becomes self-esteem, an admirable quality. But if narcissism remains in the childhood stage, it is likely to bring little self-esteem as we act selfishly, unable to share ourselves in an open way with anyone.

One face narcissism wears is the eternal complaint. Narcissists accuse others of neglect, of hurting them, of keeping them from happiness, as they demand endless attention. The hunger of narcissism can never be adequately fed for it is insatiable. If you face your narcissistic wishes and come to terms with them you will not be victimized by those who try to make you feel guilty out of their narcissism. The person with self-esteem lacks the guilt on which another's narcissism feeds.

Incessantly going over the wounds of your childhood, in and of itself, will not ease your guilt. You have to be able to forgive those who inflicted the wounds, by commission or omission. You no longer wish to punish them. You reduce your guilt by accepting others and their limitations. In other words when you obsess about old wounds, guilt will not recede. But when you accept the fact that those who wounded you are not the sadistic criminals they appear in your fantasies, your anger will ease, your wish to punish will vanish, and your guilt will evaporate.

One man experienced as a deep wound from boyhood the fact his mother obviously preferred his sister. "My mother has made no bones about liking girls better than boys," he said in anger to his therapist. The therapist asked, "But why are you still angry at her after all these years?" The man laughed, said, "I guess it's time I stop wanting to punish my mother for something she couldn't help." Facing the wound was the first step, giving up the wish to inflict hurt on his mother as he once believed she inflicted hurt on him was the second step. The one that would enable him to finally accept his anger and free his guilt.

In other words, do not harbor hate. It is a hate, in large part, that stems from your secret wish to still be a king or queen. Just as this man had to accept his mother had limitations, ruled by her fantasies of childhood, you have to accept you have your limitations and so do all others. Rare is the spouse, relative, friend or employer who wants you to reign supreme. They want you to be mortal with faults and you will feel less guilty, give up the wish to punish them if they fail to bow down to you in tribute, as you give up your wish to be idealized.

This holding on to unreal anger for not being treated as a little dictator causes much of your guilt. When you can allow someone important to you to look upon you as equal, perhaps even inferior at times, accepting this as part of his need, you will not feel angry and wish to attack, then guilty. You will become a more loving person and a more lovable one.

You have to accept there will always be those who will never love and admire you because of their jealousy, envy, wish to be the one and only. If you try to get their love and respect, you will remain in a frustrated rage. Your misery recedes only when you stop making demands on others. It is particularly hard when someone you love and respect cannot return the · feelings. But you have to accept that, as the saying goes, "You can't win 'em all." If you try to win them all, you will fail and continue feeling guilty.

THE CHILD WITHIN

Perhaps nothing is more important in the easing of guilt than acknowledging the child in you, for this frees guilt, allows you to become more mature. Once you are aware of that child, the more at home you become with your sexual and aggressive feelings. When you deny the child in you, you are apt to be victim at times of the helpless child. It is a paradox of life that to enjoy adulthood you must become better acquainted with the child within. If you bury that child, you not only kill adult spontaneity and spirit but chain your later years to a punitive past.

When you greet the child within, understand how he feels, you become more tolerant of yourself and more loving to others. Human relations experts, regardless of their point of view, usually agree on one issue: the child in the adult must become better known if the adult is to ease his guilt.

You will free much guilt if you can say to yourself, "Part of me remains a child and sometimes thinks as a child but this does not mean I will act as a child or that I *am* a child. As I know the child-part better, I am freer to think for myself as an adult." You can never get rid of the child in you but you can make peace with the unhappy experiences and thoughts of childhood by bringing them out into the open and seeing clearly how they caused anger and guilt over the years.

The child within still equates the forbidden wish with the deed. Still believes the chant of childhood (undoubtedly some angry child thought it up), "Step on a crack, break your mother's back." This implies an angry wish can lead to a calamitous act. To ease your guilt you have to accept that a wish is only a wish, far from the evil deed. Wishing does *not* make it so. Many of us, however, are reluctant to give up the wonderful world of childish omnipotence where heads fall at our slightest whim and we fear our own may fall at the moment of a forbidden wish.

It is the child within who maintains your excessive wish for dependency on others. To survive, you depend on others to love you, to help make life bearable and pleasurable. It is a psychological truth that if you do not receive love, you may develop psychosomatic illnesses or turn to addictions. Just as the baby needs love to be physically healthy, an adult deprived of love may fall victim to physical ills that tell directly of his suffering.

Actions may speak louder than words when words are unavailable. The actions tell of concealed words of terror and are a plea to the caretaker to be more loving, more tender, more protective. An asthmatic child may be telling a mother or father, "You take my breath away," an indication he is so frightened of them he dares hardly breathe. The person prone to inflict accidents on himself is saying to those he loves or has loved, "You hurt me too much." A lonely, depressed man of fifty who suffers a heart attack may be accusing a wife who has left him, "You're breaking my heart."

People say to each other in many ways, "Sometimes I feel like a motherless child," as they convey the wish to be comforted. There is nothing wrong with this wish, we all have it to some degree. Admitting it to ourselves reduces our anger and guilt. If we do not condemn ourselves for the wish to be somewhat dependent on another person, we will be more likely to find someone who will offer emotional nurturance when we need it.

The honesty of admitting to yourself what you wish, regardless of how preposterous or shameful you believe it to be, is a large part of the battle to reduce guilt. You feel a new freedom of spirit as you finally become aware who you really are, what you really want. "Really" means searching below the rocklike defenses and knowing the voice of the self apart from all the other voices you took in during childhood—some alien, some friendly, some loving, some hateful.

Whether you can realistically get what you want is less important than knowing, "I want this and I am not depraved for wishing it." One woman with two children and a full-time job suddenly felt very depressed. She could not understand why, for she loved her husband and children and enjoyed her job as vice president in charge of advertising for a large department store. One day she thought, "I wish I could give up work, forget I had children, sleep all day, have sex with my husband every night."

Then she laughed, knowing a more mature part of her wanted to achieve at work, enjoy her children. She realized if she gave up the job she would be miserable after three days at home, that her wish to do so was only pure fantasy on a morning after a sleepless night. She could enjoy the dream of freedom from responsibilities even as she knew it was that of a child.

To expose the child within is no easy task but if you accomplish it you are on your way to the easing of guilt. The new awareness becomes part of you as you now automatically continue to delve into hidden wishes and fantasies. This process goes on for a lifetime—the exploration of the self is endless—and once started, extremely gratifying.

First, you must picture yourself as a child, feel the child, not the adult you are. Then ask, "What wishes do I want gratified? Do I want to be loved by my mother? Admired by my father? Praised by my teacher? Looked up to by my brothers and sisters?" As you get more in touch with your childhood wishes, you feel an easing of tension.

But further tasks are necessary. You then have to ask, "How have I been wanting to punish my parents and others for not giving me the love, admiration and praise I deserve?" You may allow yourself a few moments of silently telling off those who have hurt you. As the child within gets even in fantasy, you are likely to accept, "Yes, I *am* angry because others did not love and admire me fully."

The last step, and the hardest is to say, "No one let me be the child I wanted to be, granted all my wishes." This is difficult for it includes, "Yes, I still often want to be the most loved child in the world, get my way all the time. But I must accept this can never be. I must recognize others too do not accept the child in themselves. But I no longer have to punish them for not being omnipotent gods who refuse to grant my every request." This last step entails your taking responsibility for everything that happens in your current life, good and bad.

To a certain degree we all resent taking responsibility for ourselves yet this is a sign of maturity. The irresponsible person who refuses to take command of his life, pay his way, but looks to others to be the "good" parent, does not possess much pride or self-esteem. We have to grow up not only physically but emotionally. Leave behind the wish that someone will always be there to take care of us in all respects. The severely mentally ill, too wounded by childhood trauma, cannot assume responsibility for their lives but seek others to house, clothe and, in some cases, even literally feed them.

LISTEN TO YOUR OWN VOICE

When guilt remains rocklike, you still listen too intently to the voices of parents. You have to listen more carefully to your own voice. And, at the same time, see yourself in the struggle with the mother and father who have been the gods of your life. Realize how your own voice may have been subdued or at times choked off in childhood but now no longer need be.

To reduce your guilt and heighten self-esteem is to differentiate between the voices of your parents and your own voice. Often you will hear their voices in opposition to yours and feel guilty because you want to still their voices. Then you punish yourself for your daring defiance. But if you hear your voice as the loudest and clearest, if you act on your voice alone, you will be more in possession of yourself, rather than by parents possessed.

You feel great guilt because, as Harry Stack Sullivan once described it, "We are who we are because of those we have internalized." To "internalize" means to take in psychologically those characteristics and attitudes of our parents we acquire as part of ourselves. Some internalizations are constructive, others destructive. It is the latter that cause a large part of our guilt.

A girl with a controlling mother may "take in" and copy this trait and in later life it will keep her from getting close to men because they usually resent controlling women. A boy with a father who is a Don Juan may, as an adult, copy his father's sexual behavior, believing this the way to be a man. But the son will be unable to love one woman for any length of time because of identification with his promiscuous father.

It is important, in the easing of guilt for you to be aware of how much you were influenced by your parents' behavior, words, thoughts and wishes, both conscious and unconscious (which you sensed). One father was surprised to see his eleven-year old son pacing back and forth as he talked to a friend on the telephone. When the father asked why he did this, the son said, "I don't know, dad, but you do it, every time you're on the phone." The son had unconsciously copied his father, internalized an aspect of his behavior the son admired.

If you had a father who often shouted in anger or a mother who burst into tears when frustrated, you, as an adult, may do likewise. If your parents coped easily with life's ups and downs, so will you. Such internalizations, when they are destructive ones, may feed your guilt. Whether you are aware of it or not, you feel guilty if you behave differently from your parents even when you know better. One husband who treated his wife with love and compassion had difficulty enjoying his pleasurable feelings. He felt guilty at being a traitor to and betrayer of his father. He grew up seeing his father treat his mother with arrogance and contempt, finally leaving both wife and son. That men could treat women with love and consideration the boy had learned from his uncle, who took an interest in him, played baseball with him, encouraged him to be a top student.

A wife who enjoyed her husband sexually and emotionally felt guilty because her mother had always been contemptuous of her father. If this woman admired and loved a man it seemed as though she were untrue to her mother's image. As a girl, however, she had been close to her paternal grandmother who enjoyed a harmonious relationship with her husband and encouraged her granddaughter to find a man with whom she could be happy.

To reduce guilt you have to stop feeling like a religious heretic if you defy what you think a parent's unfair behavior or judgment. You have to be aware of the close connection between the way you think and feel and the way your parents thought and felt. The more you are aware of the connection, the more you can change your defeatist attitude, diminish your destructive behavior and enjoy available pleasures. Much guilt is dissipated by daring to question the internalized instructions you have memorized from your parents' sometimes distorted viewpoints. You also have to catch the distortions in which you engaged that misrepresented things your parents said or did, since childhood is a time of great distortions—a child does not as yet know reality too well.

You should also examine the moments you act provocatively or with hostility, then feel guilty. When you find yourself in trouble with others, you are often initiating, identifying with and repeating your parents' ways of trying to handle their conflicts, which may have proved unsuccessful for them, as well as for you.

A young man in his first year of college genuinely enjoyed his professors and peers but on occasion suddenly threw temper tantrums that antagonized those he admired and liked. He could not understand why he suddenly rebelled, seemingly without cause. He felt so upset by his behavior that he consulted a psychotherapist in the mental health clinic.

The therapist asked if he liked those he attacked verbally. The student said he liked them very much and could not understand why, at moments, he turned into a Mr. Hyde. The therapist then asked if he admired the story of Dr. Jekyll and Mr. Hyde. The young man said he particularly enjoyed Stevenson's short story because the hero reminded him of his father who was also a doctor. He recalled his father often shouting at him, using sarcasm to make him feel inferior or wrong, and at such moments he would think his father had temporarily turned into Mr. Hyde.

The therapist pointed out how the student's behavior—when he turned on professors and classmates with bitter, sarcastic remarks—was much like his father's. While it was natural for him to copy his father as a boy, he was now an adult with a mind of his own and did not need to continue the destructive word attacks. Understanding his hidden wish to be like his father, he was now able to hold his tongue, found he no longer had the need to verbally attack.

A minister consulted a psychologist because his adolescent son was caught stealing cars. Overtly the minister was shocked and shaken by his son's criminal acts for the minister preached law, order and honesty every Sunday to his large congregation. But as he described his son's wanton behavior to the psychologist, the minister's eyes widened in excitement, as though he had been on the scene. He exulted in and praised his son's act, said admiringly, "Can you believe that boy got away with it and would never have been caught if some stranger hadn't followed him in another car, trying to play detective?"

IF GUILT PERSISTS

The psychologist pointed out the "stranger" was the owner of the stolen car who saw the boy drive it out of the yard. The owner had hailed his neighbor who offered his car in which they both followed the boy and caught him. The minister muttered this was unfortunate. The psychologist then asked if the minister, perhaps, had not vicariously enjoyed his son's stealing. The minister was shocked, demanded to know what the psychologist inferred. The psychologist explained that the minister talked about his son's act as though it were not unlawful, one for which he should be punished, but admirable. All the minister said seemed to point to his enjoyment and approval of his son's behavior, the psychologist added.

The minister was outraged, asked the psychologist how he could possibly make that conclusion, insisted his life was dedicated to what was "good and right and lawful in the eyes of the Lord." The psychologist asked, "But what about in your eyes?" The minister did not answer.

The psychologist sensed how much stolen pleasure this man, who undoubtedly lived a very narrow life with few pleasures, had received from his son's criminal acts. And also how the son knew the pleasure his father derived whenever his son broke the sacred laws of church and society. The son was obeying an unconscious mandate from his father to steal. The stealing would not stop, the psychologist knew, until the father faced how much he had unconsciously encouraged it. The psychologist helped the minister understand this and also helped the son realize he had unconsciously obeyed his father's wish that he steal.

It is difficult for a child to take responsibility for what he does that endangers him or anything dangerous that happens to him for he expects his parents to protect him from all evil. A little boy of six, standing ankle deep in the Atlantic Ocean off East Hampton, did not see a large wave roll in. The wave knocked him to the sand. He stood up, turned to his father and said angrily, "Why didn't you stop that wave?"

Because children feel so powerless, they ascribe all power to the parent. This fantasy continues in adulthood as we blame others for the accidents or small tragedies that may befall us. We have not as yet learned there are forces other than our parents that may knock us temporarily off balance.

Though many of us think we are vastly different from our parents, there is no way a large part of our personalities will not resemble them. One example in fiction is Herman Wouk's *Marjorie Morningstar.* Though Marjorie rebels for a while against her mother's wish that she marry a Jewish man from Scarsdale, a wealthy community in Westchester County, New York, eventually she does just that. The story of Wouk's life parallels this. As an Orthodox Jew he defied his parents and married a non-Jewish woman, then insisted she observe the Jewish rituals and turned her into the woman his parents wished he had married.

You will feel guilt in part because of your deep need to act, and to react, in the fashion of your parents, those who cared for you and loved you as much as they could. Though you may consciously fight their edicts, as Wouk did, you will end up obeying them unless you become aware of how much you have copied them in ways that make you unhappy.

Why is it so hard to separate emotionally from parents and honor your own values, free of guilt? Because you interpret separation, autonomy and independence not as liberation and growth but as rebellion against and hostility toward your revered parents. It is as though you repudiate them when you strike out on your own. You fear they will hate you for differing from them.

You have to become aware that differing from your parents' values does not mean you are destroying your parents. You are entitled to disagree, to be different from parents. Your happiness depends on your ability to think for yourself, to be free to make the important decisions of life—who to marry, where to work, where to live, choice of friends. You have to believe your values are more healthy and constructive than your parents' values, or at least serve you better. You have to refuse to live in the shadow of the fears, angers and guilts that reflect your parents' fears, angers and guilts.

Possessing your own ethical, social or moral codes and ideals does not mean you are an infidel. The child psychiatrist Peter Neubauer stated: "It is a parent's solemn responsibility to set rules and to enforce them and it is a child's solemn responsibility to break them."

He meant children should not merely acquiesce and obey but test and question, try things out on their own. Unfortunately, too many children fear to question a parent's commands or acts. They feel guilty either way—if they question and the parent is then angry, which most often happens, or if they do not question and hide their rage. If a child questions a wise, loving parent who understands the questioning as a healthy act, the child feels no guilt. But parents may make outrageous demands of the frightened child and if that child, as an adult, does not believe he has a right to his own judgments and decisions, he will hate his parents all his life and feel commensurate guilt.

As you are able to know yourself better, recognize attitudes and characteristics you do not like about yourself that you have unknowingly copied from your parents, you will not only be more independent but freely love your parents more. They no longer haunt you as arbitrary, angry umpires and you are no longer the innocent victim of their unreasonable commands. You are free of the frozen guilt that in the past bound you to them in fear and terror.

GUILT OVER LOSSES

One area in which almost all of us need to "dig deeper" into memories, emotions and thoughts is that of our losses. As Swinburne so evocatively put it, "Time remembered is grief forgotten." Many haunting moments of the past reflect repressed sorrow, grief and anger connected to losses. Because of the anger there will be guilt.

We are usually aware of the sadness and grief we feel when

we lose someone we love through death and feel bereft. An extreme example was described in a 1985 newspaper story about Gustav Heinrich Schwegler of Regensberg, West Germany, who, at thirty-four had lost his mother, father and two sisters. He felt so stricken he sold the family property for $300,000 and lived as a hermit in a tiny hut in the woods. Dressed in rags, he begged for scraps of food, ate at soup kitchens. For necessities he walked five miles to town, not speaking to anyone. He lived this spartan life for four decades, then was found frozen to death one winter day at the age of seventy-eight in the hut, which had no heat or electricity. Documents showed he still possessed the $300,000 he had placed in several banks, never spending one cent on himself.

About one year of mourning for the death of his parents and sisters would have been natural. But four decades indicated Schwegler felt such guilt at being the one survivor—the same guilt concentration camp survivors said they felt—that he gave up all the pleasures of life to become an impoverished hermit, punishing himself beyond mere mourning. He felt in intense form what everybody feels after the death of a loved one: "I must have caused the death. What could I have done to keep my beloved alive? I have no right to enjoy life because I didn't prevent him from dying." In Schwegler's case, his hermit existence was his way of saying, "I'll be as miserable as I think I made my family. I will suffer and atone for my guilt."

One wonders from what guilts Howard Hughes suffered to end his life also as a hermit, with the obsession that the germs in the air would kill him. What losses was he mourning as he virtually shut himself off from the world? He died a lonely, ill, old man with all the money he needed to give himself the luxuries of life though unable to enjoy them.

Most of us do not feel as guilty as Schwegler when a parent or relative dies, though we mourn deeply. When strong guilt persists beyond the traditional year of mourning, more than sorrow at the death of a loved one is involved. Much of the self-flagellation that accompanies the death of a mother or father is guilt over not having done more to make the parent happier. In reality, a parent has to provide his own happiness. Though many a parent unconsciously or consciously asks the child to rescue him from depression to provide the love and care the parent's own parent failed to give.

After parents die, we also mourn as a way to keep them alive in our minds, to hold on to their love and support. We berate ourselves for neglecting them when they were alive, punish ourselves through our suffering and believe the more we suffer the better chance we have for their forgiveness. Many religions have formalized this process, claiming if we suffer during the mourning period, we will be a "better person." Instead, we usually feel guiltier.

To resolve this guilt we have to recognize we are not as powerful as we think we are and no matter how much we neglected our parents or how hostile we felt, we did not cause their deaths. We no longer need to be guilt-ridden children unrealistically resurrecting our loved ones and suffering with their images before us. Guilt will recede when we accept the fact we cannot relive the past and that condemning ourselves in the present resolves nothing. At this moment in our lives, as the existential philosopher Sartre said, "The NOW is the importance."

We now have to be our own rescuers and nurturers, as our parents had to be theirs, and we can best rescue and nurture ourselves by casting out useless guilt. Parents will always be part of us but if we have the courage to face our guilts about not having been a "good enough" child, we can emotionally let go of these guilts and of our crippling dependence on the parent even though he is dead.

Many of us do not take the time to mourn other losses that occur during our lifetime. Losses not as dramatic as the death of a parent but that also cause deep anger and guilt. Psychoanalyst Dr. Margaret Mahler, famous for her studies on how a child emotionally separates from a mother, once said, "Growing up is a continuous process of mourning losses." We face many and varied losses in infancy, childhood, adolescence, marriage, middle age and old age. The way we meet each loss is determined by how we have met the losses of the past. If we were not able to fully mourn previous losses, we continue to carry with us through life the repressed sorrow and anger at all the losses we have never accepted.

Mankind's first recorded loss was of Paradise and the loss of a personal paradise *is* our first loss as a baby—the paradise of our every need taken care of by a warm, loving figure. Perhaps the paradise started before birth, when we were snug and warm inside our mother's body until forced out into a cold, strange world where we emitted our first cries at the discomfort of it, the need to breathe and to struggle for ourselves. Possibly the cruelest cut of all is that of the umbilical cord.

Every step of growth carries with it some sense of loss. As Emerson put it, "For everything you gain, you lose something." Or, as a more recent saying goes, "You pay a price for every pleasure."

A difficult loss to admit—for any adult to confess to himself—is the loss of the sense that infant and mother are one. This sense of merging is our first feeling as a baby, what has been called an "oceanic" feeling. We do not have a responsibility in the world, afloat on a sea of self-indulgence.

At times in later life, especially when the going seems precarious, our infant-wish for merger with our protective, caring mother will encompass us. Usually the feeling is one of grief and pity for the helpless self. To be able to acknowledge this wish for merger, to realize it is a very primitive wish (possibly at the bottom of the well of all our infant feelings) helps us gain more of a sense of identity apart from our earliest caretaker. We will feel the burden of guilt lift, as it always does when we accept a forbidden wish.

The emotional loss in childhood of the mother with whom you once felt merged, is a severe one. Throughout your life you never fully accept the loss but to face it will ease its pain and the guilt you feel because of your anger at the loss. Bowlby also discovered that when children lose parents their self-esteem wanes and their guilt increases.

229

Many other losses also result in loneliness and anxiety, leading to anger, then guilt. Anyone who causes you to feel humiliated, demeaned or unloved causes you a loss of self-respect. When you lose money at gambling or carelessly misplace a valued piece of jewelry, you feel unworthy and irresponsible. As Freud pointed out, whenever we lose something (a material loss) or suffer an indignity (a psychological loss) we wonder what we did to deserve the blow, what sin we committed to warrant such punishment. Any calamity sends us straight to that personal courtroom where we will be judged guilty or not guilty.

One woman lost her pocketbook as she raced from store to store buying food for a dinner party of twelve. She could not recall in which store she lost it and had to run from one to the other in what proved a vain search—someone had undoubtedly stolen it. There was only twenty dollars in it but also her house keys and three credit cards. When she returned home, where the maid let her in, she had to phone the credit card companies and persuade the locksmith to come to the house to install new locks on the front and back doors.

All this extra work was punishment for her guilt at the loss of her pocketbook. She thought of herself as "a damn fool" and "crazy." She recalled her very strict mother would use these phrases to describe her when, as a little girl, she lost a schoolbook or a toy. She now told herself she was entitled to occasional mistakes, she no longer had to be perfect to please an imperfect parent. She had allowed enough time to shop for dinner, there was no reason she had to rush from store to store and she would, in the future, try to enjoy shopping, not think of it as an annoying chore.

To get rid of guilt over losses, you have to become aware first, of your sorrow, then your fury, then your guilt. The repressing of any emotion after a loss keeps you from accepting the loss. It is a natural reaction following a loss, large or small, to go through this mourning process of sorrow and grief, then anger, then guilt. If you do not complete the process, you never fully give up mourning the lost person or object and remain depressed, angry and guilty. The completion of the mourning process allows you to detach your feelings from what has been lost.

If a person is involved, the process includes becoming aware of both your grief at the loss and your rage at the abandonment. As you accept both the grief and anger, you then relinquish the idea the loss can never be replaced and seek another love, a new interest. You invest your emotional energy, formerly bound up in the person lost, in someone new.

Some of us are unable to follow through on the mourning process. A woman artist never married because, she explains, the only man she ever loved died on a Korean battlefield. She keeps his photograph on her desk, his letters within a drawer. She wears daily the pearl necklace he gave her before he went to war. In a sense, she is married to a corpse. She never completed the work of mourning that would allow her to separate emotionally from her lost love. She never relinquished the grief, anger or guilt she felt because he died.

If you feel excessive guilt about the death of someone you love, you hide the rage you feel because you believe you are abandoned. The artist described cut off all desire for someone else, a love that might have brought her happiness, because of her denied rage at the death of her first love. To emotionally separate from him was experienced as killing him, because of her rage, a thought she could not tolerate. So she hung on to him in memory and also clung to her anguish and guilt.

Not a day goes by but that you are apt to feel a loss of some kind. A friend snarls an unkind word. Someone you love breaks an appointment or fails to call when he said he would. Or you lose a treasured ring, a wallet, opportunity for advancement on the job. Or, in today's violent cities, money or jewelry is snatched from you by an angry stranger armed with knife or gun.

With each loss you feel shock. Then you feel sadness and despair, as though you have parted from something valued.

Then a surge of anger either at the one who inflicted the loss or at yourself for causing it. Then guilt at the anger or at your imagined complicity.

The word "loss" appears often in our thoughts. We suffer a "loss of dignity." "A loss of faith." "A loss of time." "A loss of self-esteem." "A loss of spirit." At times we are "at a loss for words." We speak derogatorily of a "loser." We tell someone we dislike, "get lost." When we forget a name or a line of poetry we feel for a moment "loss of mind."

Guilt is closely related to a most important loss—loss of self-esteem. Frequently you lose esteem after someone criticizes or rejects you. Usually you feel immediate guilt for not living up to what was expected of you. But was the expectation real? Is the rejection to your advantage? Is the criticism valid?

You should ask yourself if you were really to blame. Perhaps you were, perhaps unconsciously you antagonized the person who criticized you, or the lover who walked away. But perhaps you were not to blame, perhaps you were rejected by someone who could not tolerate anyone getting close. Or the criticism was hurled by someone who uses a sharp tongue as his chief weapon, with nothing personal intended in the attack. Or someone was projecting on you his own felt inadequacies. Or lashing out at you after being criticized by his superior.

If you can be honest about a loss of self-esteem, you will not feel guilty at rejection or criticism. You will know the ability to reject or criticize exists in everyone and you are not responsible for its use by anyone other than yourself. The loss of the admiration of the person who has rejected or criticized you is not a loss to be mourned but examined. As you understand how perhaps you invited the rejection or criticism, your sense of loss disappears, you no longer feel guilty.

If you are the one who rejects or criticizes, you will also feel guilty and you should look at the reasons for your need to hurt others. Why are you so angry you must criticize those you love? Why are you driven to reject someone close? Do you reject him because he fails to meet your impossible demands?

Or because you fear he will reject you first and you want to beat him to this psychic punch?

Perhaps when you suffer a loss you are unable to shed tears as a release of feelings. You are given the capacity to cry to relieve your sorrow, anger and guilt if it becomes painful. Unfortunately, most of us are taught as children not to be "cry babies," especially boys, who dare not shed a tear even when severely hurt on the football or baseball fields. Men are supposed to conceal tears at any cost or be considered weaklings.

One man, attending a dinner party, was called to the telephone. He returned to the table, his face white. He explained that his best friend, whom he had known since the age of nine, had just been killed in a plane crash. The other guests expressed polite, restrained sympathy and he sat down to resume eating. But his grief was so overwhelming he burst into tears. Everyone, including his wife, was embarrassed to see a grown man cry, except for one guest. He walked over to the grieving man, put an arm around his shoulders and said, "Cry it out. You obviously have lost someone you loved very much."

When someone close to us dies, we will feel ambivalence. Part of us experiences a devastating loss and we mourn. We need to cry as part of accepting severe losses. We should shed tears when someone we cherish is lost to us. We need to be aware of the appropriate emotions that ease losses in life so they will not torment us and cause guilt. We cannot avoid some of life's conflicts and blows but we can influence our reactions to them so they will not cause undue anguish, anger and guilt.

Sometimes you must probe deeply into your mind and heart to find the causes of guilt connected to losses but it is perhaps one of the most valuable searches you can make. By becoming aware of still another of the golden nuggets of truth, you eradicate guilt. You no longer have to blame yourself for the small losses, that of a wallet or jewelry, or for the large losses, the death of someone you love. You are entitled to moments of carelessness, in the case of the small losses. And you are not to blame when someone dies, no matter how many times in fantasy you have wished to kill them.

233

GUILT AS A PARENT

If you are a parent who on the surface wants the best possible life for his child, you should be aware of ways your guilt influences your child. A guilt-ridden parent will produce a guilt-ridden child—it is as simple and as complex as that.

Each time you, as a parent, lose your temper at a child, try to find out why. Is it something your child has done that reminds you of yourself as a child when you defied your parent and were punished? Is it something that threatens your authority? Why do you feel so punitive—is your child perhaps impinging on your privacy?

Therapists who work with parents have discovered that when a parent can express his guilt more openly, understand the anger behind it, his child will act with less guilt and feel emotionally freer. The parent becomes able to look at his child as a vulnerable, small human being, not a savage out to destroy him.

As a parent, you can create guilt in your child through physical beatings, for instance. A parent who has to strike his child lacks the ability to face the punitive child in himself. Perhaps you were beaten by your father as a child and are repeating the cruelty to show what you suffered, unable to control your hidden wish to inflict the cruelty you knew. The need to repeat your suffering, to scream to the world, "See what torture I endured!" may be stronger than your need to be kind to your child. The violence you endured at a young age obliterates your wishes to be loving to your child. Until you face your buried anger at your parent, you will continue to create guilt in your child.

Guilt will also weigh heavily if you do not permit your child to separate emotionally from you, tying the child to you far beyond the years when you should be helping him gain his independence. You are using the child to fulfill your fantasies, treating the child as part of yourself.

One mother said to her daughter when the daughter was seventeen and leaving for college 300 miles away, "Remember to call me every night so I know how you are and what you are doing." Showing more understanding of her daughter's need to become independent, another mother told her daughter, also going off to a distant college, "Call me whenever you feel like it. I'm here if you need me."

It is important you tell your child honesty is vital. We all would feel less guilty if we had learned as children the value of honesty with the self and others. Not the honesty that has to do with dollars and cents and stealing other people's possessions but honesty in knowing what we think and feel.

You should tell your child, "You may say, feel and wish whatever you want as long as you do not act on it if it will hurt you or someone else." Rather than ordering, "Don't you dare talk back to me! I know what is best for you. You'll be punished if you don't obey!"

But even if you are the best parent in the world you will be bound to frustrate your child many times and the child will momentarily hate you from the bottom of his aggressive instinct, so to speak, and feel guilty. However, your child has the right to feel anger and to tell you when he is angry and why. You would feel less despair and guilt as an adult if, as a child, you had been given that right. It is tragic, psychologically speaking, that more parents do not say to a child, "You have the right to be angry at me and I won't punish you. You may tell me your angry thoughts without being afraid I will love you any the less." A parent who can listen without being judgmental is showing love and understanding of a child and the child will be grateful instead of guilty.

An aunt earned the lasting love of her thirteen-year old nephew one afternoon as they sat on the beach at Montauk, Long Island where she visited his family. He had suddenly reached out, seized a wandering insect, took a match from his pocket, lit it and burned the bug alive. She was horrified, asked why he wished to kill an innocent creature. She knew he had repressed fury for years at his very controlling mother and father, who spoiled him outrageously one moment, screamed at him the next. She had once heard his mother shout that she wished he had never been born. This is the insult of insults to a child, meaning she wished he were dead (his killing of the insect was a reenactment of this fear).

He did not answer his aunt's question and, though somewhat upset by his wanton slaughter of the bug, she tried to be accepting of his violent impulses. She knew she would not help if she scolded him. So she said reassuringly, "I love you, no matter what you do. If you feel hate, that is something to be understood, not condemned." He looked at her gratefully.

Ancient cultures realized how deeply man was dominated by hate. The *Koran* held: "If God should punish men according to what they deserve, He would not leave on the back of the earth so much as a beast." Or, as Hamlet said, "Use every man after his desert, and who should 'scape whipping?"

We learn along the way of life to hide anger to escape those "whippings" as we automatically hate anything that or anyone who frustrates our wish for pleasure. A child who has looked forward to an afternoon outing at an amusement park or the beach and is then told by his parents the skies are overcast and the pleasurable jaunt is postponed, will protest, possibly cry, and hate his parents at that moment for what he considers a devastating deprivation.

Out of your guilt, because of your repressed anger at your parents, your child learns of guilt as he represses his anger. And his wish for revenge—his killer feelings—will emerge in subtle, devious ways when *he* becomes a parent, unless he is aware of the reasons for his anger and guilt.

You should not feel guilt at setting limits for your child. Though you should set them not by tyrannical orders but with explanation of why they are needed. There is all the difference in the world between a harsh "Do as I say!" and a gentle, "I ask you to do this because it is in your best interest." Usually the way we do something, not what we do, makes the difference between arousing anger, then guilt, in the other person or gaining his love and respect.

You have to help your child acquire a realistic sense of guilt so he will not be destructive to himself and others. Little boys cannot be permitted to bully their sisters with words or slaps. Little girls cannot be allowed temper tantrums to express their rage at not getting their way nor should they be permitted to strike their brothers.

You also impose an extra burden of guilt on your child when you are overstrict or, the opposite extreme, when you are so permissive the child is allowed to do anything his little selfish heart desires so he will never learn to set limits for himself and will demand the impossible of others. If you want to help your child avoid unnecessary anguish and guilt do not frustrate him excessively or indulge him too liberally. You will then provide an atmosphere of easy communication between your child and you. In later life, your child will find it easier to get along with both men and women, especially members of the opposite sex. If there were fewer guilty children, the future battle of the sexes would be a less furious one.

You do not always have to be right in the judgments that affect your child. It delights a child to hear a parent, that godlike creature, admit he is wrong. The child then knows he does not have to feel guilty at being wrong occasionally. He learns tolerance of himself as he sees this displayed by you.

As a parent, you should accept the ancient prescript, "Know thyself." If you are aware of your own emotions and thoughts, principally your anger and guilt, you will be less likely to inflict that anger and guilt on your child. This is the greatest gift you can bestow, for it will lead to far more happiness in the child's later life. Though thousands of books have been written to guide parents in the raising of children, few stress the essential need for the parent to understand his own life, both its torments and its joys.

Your ability as a parent to understand your feelings and acts will make the difference to your child between a guilty life and a life that is fairly guilt-free. Both you and your child will benefit—you will live with a happier child and the child will not be burdened with heavy guilt.

13

EASING THE GUILT TRIP

GUILT: REAL OR UNREAL?

We all take what might be called the "guilt trip." As we travel its path from childhood on we feel like the tourist who has embarked on an automobile journey from New York to Iowa but loses his way and finds himself in Utah. Just as the traveler needs to understand where he went astray, when you feel guilty you need to examine the map of your life and see where you made wrong turns because you were too full of anxiety, or too much in a hurry, or took someone's mistaken directions.

You can do away with much of your guilt if you realize there is vast difference between the guilt you feel that is appropriate, based on what society demands of you, and guilt that is unnecessary and unreal, caused by your fantasies. Real guilt is necessary, part of being civilized. Unreal guilt is a result of the needless suffering you inflict on yourself.

You need to feel real guilt so you do not needlessly hurt others or become a criminal. But you do not need the emotionally costly unreal guilt that keeps endlessly tormenting you.

When you accidently or deliberately hurt someone you

should feel guilty. If you act belligerently or provocatively and do not feel guilt you should ask, "Why am I *not* feeling guilty?" If you are selfish and greedy in the business world or in your personal life you should feel guilty. If you do not, you may be slightly psychopathic and in need of therapy.

The guilt you feel if you inflict hurt on others should lead you to probe into what has caused your wish to be sadistic. Try to explore more of the hidden part of your mind by letting your thoughts flow freely instead of quickly banishing them to the unconscious. The unconscious, as you reach it, is direct in what it keeps trying to tell you to explain why you feel guilt.

Guilt is a result of something that "burns" in your mind, an emotion felt as smoldering. Studies of arsonists show they are driven to set fires as an outlet for the "burning" emotions, usually hostile or sexual, they can no longer bear to keep buried.

Much of therapy focuses on the literalness of the patient's words. When a patient says he feels "pissed off" he usually has the childish fantasy of angrily urinating on someone who has offended him. Or when he describes his employer as a "pain in the rear end" he feels like a child spanked by his parents, now symbolically spanked by his boss.

The unconscious is also a punster. We may in a dream, as we order fish in a restaurant, use the word "sole", then discover, as we think more about the dream, we are speaking of our "soul". Or we use the word "fowl" in a dream to refer to a chicken but our thoughts that follow on the images in the dream lead to a "foul" insult we have received from someone we thought loved us.

In the search for unreal guilt it is necessary to explore the self in all its complexities. Know when it is realistic to be guilty and when it is not. So you do not torture yourself when you have not committed a crime or torture others when they are innocent.

To know yourself is to ensure wise decisions. For instance, if you know yourself before marrying, you are more likely to choose someone who will not make unreal demands of you or you of him. You will not bring the unexamined child within to the marriage, the child that still cries out, "Me, first! Me first!" A husband or wife who enters marriage demanding unrealistic goals is inflicting an impossible burden on the partner.

In marriages where there is little unreal guilt, each partner is aware of his childish feelings and able to show tolerance for frustration in himself and his partner. Each feels he can compete without wanting to destroy and that he may achieve without fear of envy and retribution. Each enjoys his sexual identity, considers his own and his partner's needs and realistically tries to meet both.

Unreal guilt is caused by hidden, forbidden wishes and fantasies you have not permitted yourself to know and may often lead to destructive acts. You are less likely to hurt yourself or others if you know yourself better. You will not feel misunderstood, indignant and self-righteous. You can enjoy intimacy and devotion without the fear of engulfing or being engulfed. You will be capable of mutual commitment to a relationship, rather than an obsessive, possessive attachment that does not endure.

As you distinguish between real and unreal guilts you feel entitled to anger if someone attacks you unfairly in word or deed. If you become enraged and fight back, you need not feel guilty. If, however, you meekly submit to unfair attacks then you are masochistic, punish yourself for not asserting your rights, repress appropriate anger.

As you face unreal guilt you will defend yourself when you are right. To do so is part of self-esteem. There is no reason to deny righteous rage, far different than childish fury. There are times and places you have the right to anger—when someone breaks an appointment without notice, fails to keep a promise or makes unwarranted hostile remarks about you or those you love and admire. If you cannot express resentment when you *should* feel anger, you are ascribing too much power to your antagonists. In fantasy you make them the parents of infancy and turn yourself into a child.

To distinguish between unreal and real guilt you have to

examine that inner script by which you automatically read your lines and act your part in relation to others who read their lines and act their parts. Such "behavior by rote," so to speak, leads to unreal guilt.

For example, many people who believe their employers are treating them unfairly or who accept unfair treatment are simply reliving their need to act the robot victim, as they did in response to their parents. One secretary did not know how much longer she could work for her employer. He not only overburdened her with typing but sent her out for sandwiches, coffee and dessert every day. She felt a slave, as she had often felt a slave to her parents when they gave orders, ignoring her feelings.

One morning she decided this would be the day she would tell her employer how unfair he was—the worst he could do was fire her. After she brought his lunch, she said in a reasonably calm voice, "This is the last time I do this unless you pay me extra or add to my lunch hour the half hour I spend getting your food. Serving you a meal is not part of the job for which I am paid."

He looked stunned, told her he did not realize how unfair he had been, apologized. He thanked her for bringing his past meals, gave her a raise. She felt a new self-esteem for conquering her fear, anger and guilt, all based on unreal causes. She had wanted to please her employer at the cost of being exploited as, in childhood, she had wanted to please her parents. She was now ready to give up her role of masochistic victim.

She had been not only victim of a thoughtless employer but, more importantly, of her childhood guilt. She realized she could always leave a selfish employer but would never leave behind her unreal guilt unless she knew its causes and became aware she was entitled to resentment when placed in a servile state. She felt a new triumph—instead of acting like a child afraid of a parent, she felt an equal to her boss. She could finally tell herself, "Even though he is my employer, we are essentially two adults."

242

As our founding fathers expressed it, "All men are created equal." They were talking of political, economic and social rights. We would add another important right—emotional. We are "more human than otherwise," as Harry Stack Sullivan, a noted psychiatrist, once remarked. Which also means we suffer from accepting unreal guilts as real.

On the guilt trip, as we discover the unreal causes of our guilt, we break the power of our punitive conscience. Just because we hate someone who hurts our feelings does not mean we have murdered him. We are entitled to the *feeling* of hate but not to express it in violent behavior unless the hate is aroused by a direct attack on our lives. If we can distinguish the guilt that is valid from the ghost-guilt of childhood, we find the unreal guilt vanishes.

GUILT OVER SUCCESS

We have mentioned the causes of many unrealistic guilts—our sexual feelings, our dependency, our violent urges. But one cause not stressed so far leads to an unrealistic guilt many of us bear—guilt over success. Paradoxical though it may seem, as we achieve success or anticipate it, we may feel very guilty rather than proud of ourselves. Why should success—which brings admiration, praise, recognition and achievement of a goal we may have desperately wanted all our lives—disturb so many of us so deeply?

The reason you cannot enjoy success, or perhaps dare not even aspire to it, is that you feel guilty over hidden hostile fantasies. Instead of quietly exulting in success, you hate yourself for attaining it because of your unreal guilt. You may feel irritable, snap at those you love, lose your appetite, be unable to sleep at night. You act as though success were undeserved, as if you feared success more than you feared failure.

Many of us shudder at the idea of success as ominous. One exception is Norman Podhoretz, who wrote in *Making It* of his drive for success, honest enough not to deny his wish. In con-

---

trast to Podhoretz, an actor, after his success in a Broadway play, occasionally dreamed he was in prison. He had buried his feelings of guilt at success, but in his mind sentenced himself for them to a life behind bars. Acclaim was more threatening to him than failure.

As a boy, he knew he was his mother's favorite of three sons. He knew also he often tried and was successful at getting her attention away from his two younger brothers, then felt guilty. What was the crime that caused him in dreams to sentence himself to prison whenever he achieved the spotlight, literally, in his case)? Becoming a Cain to his brothers Abel, whom as a child he wanted to destroy. Success in his adult life, which meant he destroyed all rivals, awakened in memory his burning need for success as a boy in besting his brothers.

Millions of us could seek and be more comfortable with success and its resultant pleasures were we not so overburdened with guilt. Such pleasures include making more money, being more creative, enjoying the company of others more and, last but not least, using our sexual capacity more freely.

Many would rather consider themselves unattractive, unappealing, sexless, than face the guilt which keeps them from seeking successful relationships that include love, sex, friendship and respect. Guilt holds back countless of us from enjoying vacations. Many feel guilty when they even think of taking time off from work, much less making plans to relax away from work. Some who reluctantly embark on vacations cannot wait to return home, stricken with guilt at the idea of pleasure. Others feel guilty at separating from familiar surroundings, as they once felt leaving their childhood houses. Many do not take or enjoy vacations, feeling either too self-indulgent, too irresponsible or too uncomfortable in a new locale—all because of guilt.

Many others never achieve this highest potential in their chosen work, never find satisfaction in what they do or enjoy the moderate acclaim they receive, because of their guilt over possible success. The extreme in guilt is shown by some who achieve riches and fame only to commit suicide. Thomas Heggen, who wrote *Mr. Roberts*, drowned himself in the bathtub at the peak of his success. Ross Lockridge, author of *Raintree County*, killed himself as his book became a best-seller when he fell into a severe depression.

Alcoholics and drug addicts make sure they will not be successful as they function with less than full control of their senses. Or, if they are successful, they then throw away their careers, as did Richard Burton, John Barrymore and W.C. Fields, unable to handle the guilt at their great achievements.

Why does the thought of success cause such terror and guilt? Because success, on the deepest level of our mind, is to us what the death of his victim is to the hit man—a "killing." We are all hit men at heart, if not in deed. The very phrase "to make a killing" is used in the stock market, in the business world, in seducing a sexual partner, to indicate triumph over competitors. In football there is the "War of the Roses." Lawyers refer to each other as adversaries. As long as we equate "success" with "killing," we will feel guilty at the murderous wish implied by our use of the word and be unable to feel real pleasure at success.

Success bears the implication of vanquishing a foe and doing away with him. The foe? The gods of our childhood who gave us life, fed and clothed us, and the siblings who were our rivals. How dare we dream of killing off our parents, brothers and sisters? Or of surpassing a father's income and status or a mother's achievements? In this day of women's liberation many women feel guilty earning money because their mothers were never allowed to, or because their brothers and sisters earn less. Heaven help the woman who earns more than her father. To kill off in fantasy the rival mother is one thing but to kill off the loved father, the passion of the woman's dreams in childhood, brings unbearable guilt.

It is not the act of surpassing parents or siblings in wealth or fame that causes guilt. It is the *fantasy* that your success destroys their self-esteem, brings psychological annihilation, as you feel when someone surpasses you. Even as a child you want to feel victorious ever enemies, gratify your wishes of vengeance. Who, as a child has not gritted his teeth and muttered, "some day I'll get even."

A writer received a national award and at first was elated. Then he felt depressed and guilty. He feared his fellow writers, among them good friends, would now hate him because they wanted the honor. When his wife asked if he felt he deserved it, he replied that was an odd question. Whereupon she said, "It's the only question that matters."

After thinking this through, he understood what she meant—the opinion of others should not depress him. Even though he believed some other writers, better qualified than he, had been overlooked for the award, he could take heart in the knowledge he did the best he could and be proud of what he wrote, happy to receive an accolade from his peers.

To accept success without guilt is to achieve without wishing childish revenge. Perhaps a formidable task, but possible if you are aware you have had the fantasy to kill your parents and rival siblings and that this is natural to all children. You did not act on it and no longer have to fear the fantasy as though you were still four years old.

We wish others to envy us because we spent so many years, the years we were the most vulnerable and impressionable, envying our parents. Now we want to be the powerful one, the one in control. Children think, "When I'm big, I'll make my mother and father as jealous of me as I have been of them. I'll show them what it feels like to be inferior, stepped on, overruled." When we unconsciously want others to suffer because we achieve, we feel guilty and then demean or deny our success.

Thus one way to enjoy success is to accept you really *do* want others to envy you and there is no need to feel guilty for this natural wish. Though you envied your parents and their power over you as you grew up, the power you now possess does not mean you have destroyed them. A child who plays house frequently believes he *is* the mother or father and feels guilty about his wish to usurp the parental role. This is only child's play but the wish to take over our parents' roles never disappears since they are so strongly our models.

It is helpful in reducing guilt over success to remind yourself you may be angry and vengeful toward parents who had it rougher than you. If you realize your parents endured the slings and arrows of their outrageous parents, you see them as more human and no longer need to hate them. How rare it is to hear anyone say, "My mother and father never had a fair chance at happiness." Rather, it is common to hear, "My parents were monsters!" Or in denial of any childhood anger, some unrealistically insist, "My parents were ideal, they never did anything to hurt me." If you think of your parents as children, facing the same fears and terrors as you did (perhaps even more), they no longer terrify you.

When you are aware of the difference between childhood wishes to destroy and realistic wishes to achieve, you free yourself of the guilt of possessing more than your parents—in the material sense, the sense of achievement and the sense of enjoying life more. If you do not make the distinction between your realistic right to achieve and your unrealistic fantasies of destroying those you believe have hurt you, you continue to live under the cruel edict, "I may not feel happier or live longer than those who gave me life."

We all wish to retain our emotional attachment to parents. If there is not enough love to bind us, hate will keep us attached. This attachment goes back to the umbilical cord that bound us to our mothers. Some even say as adults, "I cannot cut the cord," unable to break away from their mothers in an emotional sense. "Cutting the cord," in our child-mind (which takes the word "cut" literally), means a stabbing and death—the end of life for both parent and the child murderer who has "cut" her.

In the same sense you live with the fantasy that achieving success is equivalent to "cutting" your parents and siblings, demolishing them, if you feel unworthy of success. This unreal fantasy has to be faced, accepted as appropriate for childhood but relinquished as unreal in adulthood, before you will enjoy success.

THE PURSUIT OF FAILURE

Another unrealistic guilt leads to the pursuit of the opposite of success—failure. Roy Schafer, psychoanalyst, points this out in his article, "The Pursuit of Failure and the Idealization of Unhappiness." He maintains many men and women feel "the self must always fall short." They have a severe conscience "with respect to which every pleasure must be paid for with painful guilt and self-destructiveness."

Schafer believes the pursuit of failure is more conspicuous in men while the idealization of unhappiness is more conspicuous in women. He mentions the widespread victimization of women in our society, the discrimination against and the brutalization of women, "not to speak of the many subtle forms of seduction of women into debased roles," as all playing a large part in women having "taken in, developed and rigidified the unhappiness they subsequently have come to idealize."

He gives an example of a woman's idealization of unhappiness in describing one woman's slip of the tongue. Intending to say, confronted by a threatening experience, that she felt "cold chills" going down her spine, her words were, "Cold thrills went down my spine." Schafer explained this woman had always tried to relieve others of their unhappiness by absorbing their unhappiness. "Unconsciously, as many women in our culture seem to do, she incorporated their unhappiness, and she suffered for others," Schafer says. "In so doing, she felt that she was being a good girl, that is, kind, compassionate, supportive, undemanding, even self-sacrificing. From a young age, she had been doing this to an extreme degree with all members of her family."

As a result of psychologically taking in the unhappiness of her mother and father, she could more easily idealize them as kind, compassionate and supportive to her as a girl, and later as a woman. In a sense she gained love and importance by being unhappy and added "worth to the idea of herself," Schafer said.

He quotes Freud's phrase, "those wrecked by success," and adds that some fear success so intensely they make sure they are failures. The pursuit of failure may, for one thing, ward off envy. For another, it may show an inability to dare recognize and assert achievement or the special talent implied by success.

Schafer believes both success and failure stem from the stresses and strains related to the concepts of success and failure which hold a "devastating force because they are feared in terms of childhood experiences in attachment to parents, losses, defeats and other dangers." The fear leads to anger and the anger to never-ending guilt.

Many who enter therapy show how they unconsciously seek failure. A woman patient who had just become engaged told her therapist, "I know I'm going to fail at this marriage. I feel if I succeed, I will be taking something from my mother." That night she dreamed she gave her engagement ring to her mother. In the next analytic session she spoke of her dream, then confessed that all her life she had wanted to steal things from her mother—jewelry, furs, dresses. When she informed the analyst she was going to fail at marriage, she was pursuing failure because of her guilt.

If you pursue failure, rather than success, you are beset by fears and fantasies natural to you as a child but no longer appropriate. If you seek to be a failure you have not given up the guilt over childish wishes. You still expect punishment for hostile wishes that are but nightmares of the past.

LITTLE HAPPENS BY CHANCE

Other signs of unreal guilt can be found in ways we act self-destructively, to punish ourselves for guilt. While accidents beyond our control do occasionally occur, when it comes to those we feel guilty about, most of the time we are in the driver's seat even though unaware we sit behind the wheel. One way to make contact with the fantasy and the guilt it produces is to become a detective of the mind and pick up clues that lead to the irrational guilt so you can be free of it.

To help stop the guilt trip keep in mind a psychological axiom: *rarely does anything that causes you to feel unreal guilt happen by chance.* In a broader sense, rarely does anything that troubles you happen by chance.

Any of your acts that puzzle, threaten or frighten you hold a specific meaning in your life though you may not wish to know that meaning—it holds danger to your self-esteem. So you keep your true feelings partially hidden from yourself. But the clues slip out in certain actions: a slip of the tongue; the forgetting of an appointment; an accidental fall or injury. When your narcissism is hurt, your omnipotent fantasies punctured, your dependency yearnings threatened, you may inflict punishment on yourself or others.

One man hid from himself his deep rage at a friend named Jack. He wrote Jack what he thought a routine letter to ask how he was and relay news of his own family. A few days later he received a phone call from Jack. In an angry tone, Jack demanded, "Why did you address me as 'Dear Jerk'? Were you trying to be funny?"

The man felt very embarrassed, explained he thought he had written "Dear Jack." The friend retorted indignantly, "I'm holding the letter in my hand and the salutation reads, 'Dear Jerk'." The man apologized, said he must have been thinking of something else as he wrote.

After he hung up he was shocked at the slip of his pen, felt acute guilt. He wondered why he had substituted "Jerk" for "Jack." Suddenly he realized he had felt furious at Jack, who had owed him $1,000 for two years without paying a cent or explaining the delay. Rather than embarrass Jack, this man, who had not even asked a token payment, had let his anger fester until it finally erupted. He wrote what he felt, without being aware of his error. His unconscious wrath had broken through to the surface. Part of him wanted Jack to know what he thought of him in one obvious word.

This man felt guilty because he had insulted a supposed friend. Granted, he was justified in his fury at Jack's not repaying the loan or apologizing for the delay. But he did not admire himself for the way he handled a delicate matter. Unintentionally calling his friend a "jerk" was not the wise or the courteous way to reprimand him. He should simply have stated he thought it time Jack pay part of the loan.

Slips of the tongue often reveal our hostility. Parents will wound a child's pride as they call the child by the name of another sibling. Children always feel angry when this slip occurs for they sense the parent, at that moment, prefers the other child. Why else would the other's name be substituted? One mother often called her son by his older sister's name, felt guilty each time at her error. She finally realized she had not wanted a son but another daughter—as the saying goes, "Girls are easier to bring up." Her slip revealed her forbidden wish her son had been a girl. He was angry each time she called him by his sister's name, sensing she favored her daughter. A mother with three daughters often called the eldest by the names of the two younger ones. The eldest, older by four years than her first sister and ten years than the youngest, realized her mother had difficulty with grown-up girls with minds of their own, preferred the younger, more pliable child who accepted domination without complaint.

You can learn far more about your unreal guilt if you examine why you are careless at times and, as a result, hurt others. A woman who worked in a large office building each morning as she rushed into the elevator, stepped on the toes of those in her way. She apologized profusely, then felt guilty, wondered why she could not be more careful. She was especially guilty when she came down hard on the shoes of a man who worked in the office next to hers, who asked her angrily to please keep her feet to herself.

She thought about the reasons why she could not control her feet in that elevator. She was always in a hurry to reach her desk because she was late and raced into the elevator, not looking where she was heading. She awoke in plenty of time but always left home at the last minute, reluctant to head for work. Suddenly she became aware she did not like her employer, a tyrannical man who treated her and the rest of his employees as though they were stupid. He reminded her of her father, a dictatorial man who had made her life difficult. She did not want to leave the employer because he paid high salaries and she liked her work as office manager, as well as enjoying her co-workers—except, she thought, the arrogant young man in the office next to hers. She often felt, when he or her employer walked into the room and gave her orders, she would like to kick them in the shins. She remembered as a little girl she had wanted to kick her father in the shins when he was mean, but never dared.

 She started to connect the wish to hurt her father with stepping on the toes of the innocent people in the elevator. She had acted out in the very place of employment what she wanted to do to her employer, and had actually landed a painful step on the toes of the young man she disliked so intensely. She believed her attack was based on the wish to kick the father who "knew it all" and would never listen to her point of view.

To her surprise she found she was now reaching the office with time to spare in the mornings. She walked slowly into the elevator and kept a space between herself and the nearest passengers, avoided stepping on anyone's toes. From then on she was no longer a menace. She had gained awareness of the hostile feelings that had caused her to be careless and physically hurt others.

A fifty-one year old man threw lit cigarettes into waste baskets in his office, starting a fire every few weeks. He felt embarrassed and guilty at creating such a hazard. The baskets were metal but even so he knew there was the chance a flame might spread elsewhere.

It was not until he burned an important paper by mistake, one he had inadvertently discarded, that he started to ask why he tossed lit cigarettes into the waste basket while a large ashtray lay on his desk. Most of the time he did put out cigarettes in the ashtray.

He thought about the times he resorted to the basket. He discovered each fire occurred after he had interviewed some attractive woman who had come to seek information about an insurance policy for herself or her husband. He realized he became sexually stimulated by the women and felt guilty, since he was married and had always been faithful to his wife.

In his mind, to be sexually attracted to a woman, especially at work, was a heinous offense against his wife and his work. He even had the thought, "I should be burned at the stake for being aroused by this woman."

When he accepted it was no crime to find a pretty woman sexually desirable, the fires ended. He could allow the fantasies into conscious awareness and no longer had to light threatening fires.

You can avoid embarrassment and guilt if you recognize the feelings that cause you to have accidents involving the innocent or yourself, or both. At a lavish cocktail party, a man spilled his martini all over the dress of a woman who he heard telling another woman, had paid $700 for it. He apologized profusely, felt ashamed, asked her to send him the cleaner's bill.

Later, in the quiet of his bedroom, he thought about the accident and his feeling of shame. He suddenly remembered at the age of eight he had been spanked by his father for spilling a glass of milk on his mother's sparkling evening dress as she was about to leave for a party. His father had called him "stupid" and "a little stinker." He recalled also how lonely he felt at the thought of his mother leaving him for the evening.

He now realized he had wanted his mother to stay with him that evening and the accident was his unconscious way of trying to keep her home—force her to take off her fancy dress—as well as expressing anger at her for leaving him alone. He became aware the woman at the cocktail party had reminded him of his mother, her blue eyes and slightly tipped blond head caused the image of his mother to come to mind just before he spilled the martini. He had thought the woman alluring, had obviously wanted *her* to stay by his side all evening. The accident was his way of telling her so—a compliment she would never know. But at least now that he was an adult he escaped his father's scorn and derision, he thought wryly—though his conscience was administering them instead.

As you face the conflicts that constitute the buried causes of your slip of the hand or foot, tongue or pen, you give up the guilt that lies behind your acts. Instead of feeling ashamed of such slips, try to examine possible causes related to your fear, anger and guilt.

If you are able to explore more freely what you feel, instead of feeling ashamed, you will be more in possession of yourself. You will have come a long way in rectifying that wrong turn on your guilt trip.

14

LIBERATION FROM GUILT

THE GOAL OF THE GUILT TRIP

We have taken a journey into the human mind and explored the way it tries to meet threats to your psychic survival and your self-esteem. We have called the journey the "guilt trip."

We described guilt in its many forms. Guilt in childhood. Guilt in adolescence. Guilt in love. Guilt in marriage. Guilt over-success. Guilt on the job. Guilt as a parent. Guilt in friendship. Guilt toward strangers. Guilt at the death of a parent. Guilt at the suffering that exists because of the poor and starving throughout the world.

We tried to portray the many faces of guilt and the various ways we all express guilt day after day. We showed how fantasies of revenge, sexual desire, dependency, greed and the wish to be perfect cause needless guilt. We described how too heavy a burden of guilt may lead to psychopathic or criminal behavior.

Every trip has a goal, a destination. This exploration of guilt was made in the belief that should you suffer undue guilt you can help ease your guilt and turn the released psychic energy into an asset. You will find communication with others more pleasurable, sex more enjoyable. You will also feel at home with a wider range of emotions within yourself and within others.

Perhaps most importantly, you will no longer feel angry at unknown irritants. The anger you have stored up over a lifetime ebbs away as you expose its irrational causes. As your anger disappears so does the guilt that has never, for a moment, left its side.

You feel a freeing of psychic energy formerly used to repress forbidden wishes, anger and guilt. Your energy was tied up in repressing anger and guilt because you were too terrified to face the cause of both the anger and the guilt. This freeing will bring new pleasures. Your energy can now be used for love, for creativity, for work, for joyous activities.

It has been estimated you use at least fifty to sixty percent of your mental energy to lock inside the wishes and emotions you feel dangerous. Freud discovered that repression was our greatest weapon in the battle against feelings and thoughts that brought pain. Repression requires mental energy to hold back the feared explosion of wishes that lead to acts of hate and lust. Because repression consumes so much energy, you feel fatigued and debilitated. As you free yourself from repression, guilt eases.

A large reservoir of new energy will become available when you face your guilt. Energy no longer needed to imprison the pain of the past, felt as rejection and hurt. It is this unexpected energy that is your hidden asset. You discover an increased ability to concentrate, to focus on many aspects of life you previously believed inaccessible. You are no longer the victim of tunnel vision caused by preoccupation with guilt. Even someone who opposes psychological explanations of human behavior will find it difficult to argue against this point of view unless too bound by guilt.

A young woman secretly yearned to be an actress but worked as a fashion model because she felt too shy to speak confidently onstage or before the camera. She asked an assistant film director, with whom she lived, how she could over-come her shyness and be an effective actress. He told her she would need to understand why she was afraid to speak up, what held her back, prevented her from using her voice fully. He said he found her soft voice very alluring but if it kept her from achieving her goal she should find out why she could not speak up in front of the camera or before the footlights.

She thought of what he said, especially his description of her voice as "very alluring." She remembered the voice of her mother, who screamed constantly at her when she misbe-haved. She recalled how ashamed she felt at twelve when her closest friend announced she was no longer permitted to visit the house because this girl's mother shouted and set a bad example for youthful visitors. From then on, this woman had vowed she would "never, never, *never*" be like her screaming mother, no matter how angry she became. She had knowingly kept herself from raising her voice even when she felt angry. She realized that when she was angriest she would lose her voice completely, as though to block all talk. Even in mid-sum-mer, when no cold winds blew, she would fall ill with a sore throat.

There was another reason for her too-soft voice besides her embarrassment at her mother's screams (there are usually several reasons for a mannerism, symptom or inhibition). Her father evidently could not stand his wife's screaming either, sought and found a mistress. He told his daughter, when she was nine, he had fallen in love with another woman. He saw the mistress openly, invited his daughter to join them at sup-per and on weekend vacation trips.

At an early age this woman envied "the other woman." She wanted to be like her, to display the "soft voice" that captivated her father. She unconsciously caricatured the successful rival by adopting an even softer voice. A voice that sometimes could be barely heard by the person sitting next to her. But accom-panying her envy went a hatred of her rival: the woman who had stolen her father from her mother and herself. She felt all the rage of the outcast simmer within.

As she became aware of feelings of anger and guilt related to her mother, her father and his mistress, she no longer had to feel guilty over feelings natural to a hurt little girl. Her voice slowly gained power so she could study at a prominent acting school. She had become aware of what had caused the muted voice.

Thus do we combat early threats to self-esteem. We harm ourselves by covering the truth of what we feel, bury the truth deep with a swift act of repression, our automatic reaction against an emotional danger. As a girl, this woman had felt emotionally assaulted by the screams issuing from her mother's throat and by her father's betrayal of his family as he sought a "soft-voiced" woman. She copied the ways of the successful rival, not her loved-hated mother. She seized on what brought others pleasure (the soft voice), tried to avoid what she felt dangerous. Yet told of the danger through the physical symptom that was crippling her career.

We are all primarily pleasure-bent on this voyage we take through the vicissitudes of life. We cannot help but realize as we mature that we can not avoid some of the pain. We can try to profit from the pain, learn what to do so it will not be repeated, find ways to lessen it.

The woman who wanted to be an actress successfully discovered the causes of her guilt and accepted them. This allowed the psychic energy formerly devoted to holding back memories and wishes she thought dangerous, plus the feelings attached to them, to be available for pleasurable use. She could finally enjoy the achievement she longed for. She could speak from the stage with poise and confidence, her creative self no longer eroded by guilt.

NEW FREEDOM TO LOVE

Easing guilt will help you feel more loving, more able to love, more receptive to love. When guilt is freed, the hate that caused it evaporates, increasing your capacity to love. "Love makes us happy, hatred makes us unhappy," says Reuben Fine in *The Meaning of Love in Human Experience.*

By facing unreal guilt, you become far less punitive to yourself and others. You realize much of your anger at current crises does not stem from them but occurs because it awakened repressed anger at similar early crises with your parents. You tend to choose as your loves and closest friends those similar in behavior and thoughts to the parents who so angered you. You seek the familiar because it is familial. The new loves will infuriate you at times, acting in ways similar to the earlier loves. This is when you feel the old anger.

The easing of unreal guilt, in addition to making love more available for your current relationships, also permits you to know, as you face your anger, that you will always feel some hate as well as love toward those who are close. You accept the reality that no one is, nor can be, perfect, that perfection is the myth of myths.

As you face your wished-for but never acted-out crimes, you no longer have to try to "win" love but can accept it warmly when offered. You are also able to give and share love to a far greater extent. Sometimes an adult has to learn to love as a baby does—by experimenting with hugs, caresses, close embraces, and slowly coming to believe he has a right to enjoy them.

To get pleasure from sex within the ambiance of love, you must face your guilt over infantile wishes and accept that sensual child within. You also have to realize endearing words of love and the foreplay of sex echoes the closeness you felt with your mother as a baby and not be ashamed of this feeling as part of adult sex.

Many more of us could enjoy sex in far freer spirit if we could accept without guilt our desire to be cuddled, held close, even rocked at times. Or if we could face our natural guilt over fantasies at earlier times in life of wanting sexual contact with mothers, fathers, siblings. That this is a universal wish can be seen in the large numbers of those who commit incest in spite of its clear position as the Number One taboo all over the world since ancient times.

Your early sexual wishes may be difficult to accept, yet every one possesses them and acceptance will reduce your guilt. If Hamlet could have faced his fantasies about Queen Gertrude, and Oedipus, Queen Jocasta, these sons would not have suffered so disastrously.

You may be suffering from a form of guilt we often see in lovers, married couples, in the way parents relate to children and children to parents. It is called "clinging dependency." The guilt stands as defense against the buried fury at the other person for not fulfilling impossible wishes—to be perfect, to grant every demand, to give pure love (which does not exist, except perhaps from a pet). When a defense is breached it is like skin punctured. But until you are aware of the defense which hides primitive wishes, you do not realize the wishes are not deeds but mere fantasies, about which you need feel no guilt.

Clinging love is not liberated love but love loaded with guilt. It is unrewarding, unpleasurable and bound to create further anger in those who cling and those clung to. It signals a fear of maturing, of dealing with your sexual desire and your angry feelings.

When you cling to someone you love, you are like the child who says to his parent, "I will not hate you if you will love me and grant all my wishes, and even if you do make me hate you I will pretend the hate doesn't exist." Herein lies the earliest roots of guilt. The denial of anger that can only create waves of unending guilt coursing through your veins throughout life.

You may also have tried unsuccessfully to love out of a feeling of revenge against the parents of childhood who failed to love you. As though to say, "You didn't love me the way I needed to be loved so now I'll show you I can find others who will love me and then I won't need you any longer."

A young man of twenty-five knew his parents wanted him to be successful in business and marry a millionaire's daughter—these were their wishes for his happiness. He had attended a university where professors in political science and psychology had stressed other values such as helping to bring peace to the world and the need for statesmen in high places, men who understood humane issues, not merely munitions. This man felt contempt for his parents and their superficial values. Rather than face his anger or allow his parents to live by their values, granting them the right to be different, he took secret revenge.

He compromised with his parents by starting on his way to success in business. He became vice-president of a large scrap-metal concern. But then he married a girl from the opposite side of the tracks. Though lovely in appearance, she had grown up in near-poverty and was unsophisticated and ill at ease during parties at his parents' lavish home. They could hardly conceal their scorn in her presence.

This young man took pleasure in flaunting his wife in front of his parents as though to say, "Your values stink. This woman loves me for who I am, not because I am rich. The way I wanted you to love and as I love her, though she hasn't a nickel."

The marriage lasted only a year because he had wed primarily to spite his parents. Too much of his energy was tied up in repressing guilt over his anger at his parents. You cannot be at war with parents and love someone else in a mature way. The war keeps you immature. Like the nation whose primary concern is munitions, so will you have little capacity to consider peaceful ways to solve conflicts.

For you to achieve freedom in love also means awareness of your forbidden sexual fantasies. Unless you are at home with your fantasies, you will not feel at ease in sexual intimacy with someone you love. Love without fulfilling sex is frustrating, just as sex without love leaves you emotionally starved and rarely endures. With a lessening of guilt over sexual fantasies you can love warmly in an emotional sense and, at the same time, enjoy the erotic aspects of love. If you expect sex to provide the ability to love you live in fantasy.

It also helps to realize that cooperation with a loved one is not subjugation and a certain amount of dependency is not a regression to childhood. You will always in this complex world be dependent on others for many necessities—love, companionship, friendship, respect, admiration, not to mention the mundane necessities of food, clothing and shelter. It is the intensity of your dependency and the spirit in which it is asked for and received that determines whether it is normal or excessive.

Also, to face your guilt you have to acknowledge your secret wishes to debase the one you love. If you still wish in fantasy to verbally assault or physically attack your mother or father, you may take out this anger on those who later are close. You still live with exaggerated expectations of what others should do for you, expecting them to be perfect and not accepting your and their imperfections as part of the human condition.

Until you accept your own anger you are caught in the swirl of impossible dreams. To dream is admirable, for it is the dreams of men and women over the centuries that have made the world more just, less savage, that have brought more reason to this planet. But these are dreams of hope and helpfulness, of caring and sharing not of anger and violence.

If love makes us happy and guilt makes us unhappy then we should try to remove the major obstacle to love—guilt. In *Shame and Guilt*, Gerhart Piers and Milton B. Singer maintain that of all the more organized forms of "intrapsychic tension," those shown in the feelings of guilt and shame are possibly the most important. Not only in our emotional development, they add, but in how our character forms and how we relate to others we need and love.

Guilt constricts your emotions, particularly the ability to love. You hide from love when you feel guilty. Facing guilt helps you express love more honestly and eloquently. If you are tongue-tied, afraid to reveal your feelings even in conversation, suffer a creative block, cannot sing, laugh, joke or enjoy the full range of pleasures life offers, you hide unreal guilts. You would do well to face and accept them so they can be banished. Facing them means admitting them to yourself or verbalizing them to a loved one, friend or therapist. In this way the unconscious becomes conscious and the fears and fantasies lose their power.

THE ABILITY TO FEEL CONCERN

When you are able to face guilt you can then develop a true concern for yourself and others. A concern that enriches and stimulates both yourself and those for whom you show the concern.

This conclusion was persuasively pointed out by D.W. Winnicott in his article, "The Development of the Capacity for Concern," appearing in the *Bulletin of the Menninger Clinic* (1963). Winnicott describes concern as "a word used to cover in a positive way a phenomenon covered in a negative way by the word 'guilt'." He adds, "A sense of guilt is anxiety linked with ambivalent feelings and implies a degree of integration in the individual ego that allows for retention of love along with hate."

Concern, he says, implies growth and a positive sense of responsibility. The person "cares," he feels and accepts responsibility. He is able to set pleasure aside for the moment in his ability to think about others.

A capacity for concern lies behind all constructive play and work and belongs to "normal, healthy living." If a mother shows concern, "so does a child," for concern is contagious. It is also part of "that inner stabilizing that belongs to the development of independence."

When you face guilt squarely you are not only able to love more and allow yourself greater pleasures but you start to treat others in a more caring, stimulating and warm manner. Instead of thinking, "What am I doing to cause you to hate me?", then feeling guilty, you think, "What can I do to make your life easier?" You consider the suffering of others, rather than expect them to relieve your suffering. You have learned unhappy people do not have the psychic energy to invest in the consideration of and compassion for others.

One mother was aware she felt guilty about her angry feelings towards her sixteen-year old son, an only child. She worried about him when he stayed out late on dates or whenever he was out of her sight for a few hours. She was repeating, she knew, the pattern of her mother, who always kept a strict eye on her as a girl when she started to go out with boys.

One night she decided to go to bed early, not stay up until her son returned. She slept soundly and the next morning he expressed surprise she was not awake to kiss him goodnight when he arrived home. She explained she had decided he should lead his own life, remembering how much she hated it when her mother insisted on waiting up for her. He thanked her, said this made him feel like a man. He seemed far more at ease with her after that. She sensed greater acceptance by him.

As a parent, it is unwise for you to police a child until the moment he leaves for college or the world of work. Unless you allow the child freedom while at home to become independent, he is likely to carry with him his deep dependency on you. He will find it difficult to get a sense of his own identity.

One adolescent girl whose mother watched over her with the eagle-eye went off to college, 800 miles from home, feeling confused. She wanted to break free of her mother's domination yet wondered how she would survive without her over-possessive mother to tell her what to do, when to come home, who to see. Her mother had made her feel, as she grew up, that her life was not her own. She had been forced to report her every move. She seethed within, always felt guilty because of her rage at such domination.

After several months at college she realized she was completely on her own—no one checking her whereabouts, her plans for the day or evening. She thought, "It's as though my mother doesn't care what I do. And it's a strange, lonely feeling."

She felt abandoned, without a friend in the world, until she met a young man in her class, became involved with him and her studies, learned the taste of independence. She found she enjoyed it, it had been late in arriving but she was happy to know and feel it. Her mother showed not concern but overconcern. Overconcern will cripple you emotionally, whereas concern, for yourself and others, sets you free. Overconcern defends against anger felt as a child against your parents. The overconcerned mother unconsciously wants to destroy the child, thinks of him as an unwanted burden, as her mother thought of her.

If you have been unable to marry, a new ability to feel concern for yourself and others may lead to that "lasting, meaningful, intimate relationship" with a partner who will feel concern for you. Seek and ye shall find—find what you are able to give in return. You will draw to you and be drawn by what you emanate. As one aware young woman put it, "We choose as lovers and friends who we are."

If you feel guilty, you attract the guilty. We might say that psychological birds of a feather flock together. Also, as the eminent philosopher Pogo put it, "We have met the enemy and they are us." If you show capacity for concern you will be a magnet for those who realize what a vital quality this is.

The development of your ability to be concerned makes you a better marital partner, better parent, better friend, better lover, better employee or employer, as well as a better member of the human race. Your childhood wish to be a tyrant diminishes. Instead you wish to think of the welfare of others.

If you feel guilty, you want others to suffer as you suffer. But if you feel concern, you want others to have the chance to be happy, to live in comfort as you now live in comfort with feelings that once may have brought guilt but, now that you have faced them, no longer cause torment. As you increase your pleasure in living, you want others to do so.

CHOICE, NOT COMPULSION

Your ability to feel concern is part of a deeper feeling that pervades your life as guilt eases. You find you now possess the ability, when beset by decisions or hard tasks, to be more thoughtful, more concerned about your choices.

You now "choose" freely rather than being driven compulsively by anxiety. Your capacity to make a wise choice is a direct result of confronting your guilt—perhaps its most important result. Your horizons widen, you take more factors into account when you make a choice. You act less from anxiety and anger, less from a hidden script and more from contemplation and reflection.

Most beneficial, if you make a mistake you learn from it rather than repeat it. It is the repetition of mistakes that have made you feel so defeated as you endlessly wander in confusion through the maze of your errors.

A young Wall Street broker, when he wanted to invest a client's money, would consult his older colleagues as to the stocks expected to rise. He dared not trust his own judgment. Sometimes his colleagues advised wisely, sometimes, as a result of their choices, his clients lost money.

One night his wife asked, after he complained of a colleague's choice of stock, why he listened to others, why he did not trust his own judgment. He told her he thought his older colleagues knew more since they had been studying the market for years. She pointed out that over the years many of their choices had been wrong and suggested perhaps there were other reasons he needed to consult them.

Feeling attacked, he asked what she meant. She said she had observed him around his mother and father. He always deferred to them even when they were wrong. He then asked her, defensively, what good it would do to argue and offend them. She replied that if he did not want to hurt them out of concern for them, that was admirable. But if he were afraid to know how he felt, afraid to speak up because he thought them

266

the last word in authority who would punish him if he dared differ, that was destructive to him.

He carefully considered what she said, realized he did not know his feelings well enough. She had been right—he was afraid to speak up in front of his mother and father, whom he believed as forbidding in the present as in the past. He decided, on the basis of what he had learned about the market over the years, he now had the right to advise stocks for his clients. Right or wrong, at least it would be his choice.

In the next few months he discovered he did better for his clients than his colleagues did for theirs. Confidence in his own ability to stand up for what he believed, as he had never dared in childhood or adulthood, increased his thoughtfulness in choosing stocks. He paid more attention to their ups and downs and the reasons for variations. He no longer had to be subservient to anyone's authority, especially the older colleagues he once thought knew more than he. He did not verbally disagree with his parents or colleagues. It was enough he knew he differed—had the right to differ.

He also realized he now avoided many of his past mistakes made because he was uncertain and took the advice of others. The disappearance of guilt at his anger for dependence on his older colleagues allowed him not only to make wiser choices but increased the pleasure and pride in his work. It was his choice alone that brought him the admiration and gratitude of clients.

The easing of guilt greatly affects your choice of those you love. A woman of thirty-two, who had indulged in a number of affairs but never married, one day asked her closest friend, who had been married to the same man for sixteen years, how she had selected him as husband. The friend replied he was the man with whom she felt the least guilty.

The woman was surprised, she had never heard love described in those terms. The friend further explained she had felt at home with this man the first night she met him. She did not have to play a role as she did with other men, hoping they would like her but feeling discomfort at not being herself. Whereupon the woman still searching for a husband admitted she knew the feeling well. Then she asked her friend why her husband had this ability to put her at such ease. The friend explained she thought it was because he did not feel guilty, he considered himself human, entitled to mistakes, and did not ask her to be perfect. She referred to the night she spilled a drink over his new tweed suit and he looked at her more in sympathy than reproof.

The woman then asked where she could find a similar man. Her friend advised that if she could feel less guilty, she would not unconsciously look for a man to punish her for her guilt but seek a man with whom she could feel at ease.

As you lessen the grip of guilt that has plagued your child-conscience, you are able to be more thoughtful not only about choices in love but all aspects of living. You cease punishing yourself for the imaginary crimes of the past and face head-on the unreal causes of your anguish. You no longer are terrorized by the fear of losing control over the primitive, natural wish to murder when you feel hurt, or the fear of acting out wild sexual dreams.

Your forbidden desires no longer have the power to haunt you. Their revelation to the light of reason nourishes your emotional strengths. You find new courage to accept yourself as you are, accept others as they are. You no longer need the camouflage of useless defenses that have maimed your ability to accept truth and act thoughtfully.

Theodor Reik, in *The Need to Be Loved* comments, "When the candle is down to a nub we recognize—too late—that we have led a kind of half existence. Is this life, or is it mere vegetating?" Our unreal guilt has stifled the other "half" of existence.

Reik also says: "To injure others is certainly wrong, but it is equally wrong to sabotage and injure oneself. It is not only more realistic but also more dignified to acknowledge our violent and sexual needs."

"Dignity" is a word we rarely hear or use these days, we

tend to think of it as rather old-fashioned. But it is a word that conjures up pleasurable associations: worthiness, nobility, self-possession, self-respect. Qualities that bespeak a lack of unreal guilt.

A FINAL WORD

Throughout this book we have emphasized the following prescriptions for understanding and easing guilt:

1. Stop denying your guilt
2. Admit your forbidden wishes
3. Face the child within, who may still control many of your thoughts and acts
4. Know your anger of the past
5. Be aware of your sexual fantasies
6. Stop projecting your guilt on others
7. Do not allow your own guilt to be manipulated
8. Accept and mourn your many losses
9. Give up trying to be perfect and omnipotent
10. Face how dependent you feel at times
11. Know when guilt is real, when it is unreal
12. Accept the difference between righteous rage and unjustified fury
13. Become aware that fear of success hides hostile wishes
14. Realize accidents seldom happen by chance, they tell what troubles you
15. Know laughter often hides hostility, as does sarcasm
16. Learn to feel concern for yourself and others
17. Make wise choices rather than acting compulsively
18. Face the fact that addictions, overwork and overeating stem from guilt

19. Understand the destructive ways you have copied parents

As the final point, we might say, "Realize you have nothing to lose by facing your guilt except guilt itself." You have everything to gain, including the conviction you alone are in charge of your life and the choices that lead to greater happiness.

Phil Niekro, now with the Cleveland Indians, put it: "I've always realized that I can't always control what happens to me but I can control how I react to what happens to me." This is not only the answer to becoming a great pitcher, still on the mound at forty-six (considered an old man in the world of baseball), but also to a life of minimum guilt.

You can become more in control of how you react to life's ups and downs as you shed the unreal guilt that has weighed on your heart like a tombstone. As you understand and ease guilt you free yourself of the torment of the past, no longer by guilt possessed. You will find new joy in life from the experience of "letting go."